LAWYERS AS
MANAGERS

LAWYERS AS
MANAGERS
How to Be a Champion for Your Firm and Employees

Andrew Elowitt and Marcia Watson Wasserman

ABALAW
PRACTICE
DIVISION
The Business of Practicing Law

Cover design by Lachina

Printed in the United States of America.

21 20 19 18 17   5 4 3 2 1

Library of Congress Cataloging-in-Publication Data
Names: Elowitt, Andrew, author. | Wasserman, Marcia Watson, author.
Title: Lawyers as managers : how to be a champion for your firm and employees
  / by Andrew Elowitt and Marcia Watson Wasserman.
Description: First edition. | Chicago : American Bar Association, [2017]
Identifiers: LCCN 2017026983 | ISBN 9781634259682 (print)
Subjects: LCSH: Law offices—United States—Management. | Practice of
  law—United States—Management. | Law offices—Employees—Selection and
  appointment—United States. | Lawyers—United States—Recruiting. |
  Lawyers—Training of—United States. | Mentoring in the
  professions—United States.
Classification: LCC KF318 .E46 2017 | DDC 340.068/4—dc23
LC record available at https://lccn.loc.gov/2017026983

Discounts are available for books ordered in bulk. Special consideration is given to state bars, CLE programs, and other bar-related organizations. Inquire at Book Publishing, ABA Publishing, American Bar Association, 321 N. Clark Street, Chicago, Illinois 60654-7598.

www.ShopABA.org

TABLE OF CONTENTS

ABOUT THE AUTHORS

Andrew Elowitt

Andrew Elowitt, JD, MBA, PCC, worked for over 20 years both in law firms and as the head of a corporate legal department before becoming a practice management consultant and professional certified coach. He is the Managing Director of New Actions LLC, a firm that specializes in talent, strategy, and leadership development for law firms, businesses, and government agencies.

His work focuses on the people side of legal practice: how lawyers manage, lead, thrive, change, and find satisfaction. He is regarded as an expert on the use of coaching and emotional, social, and conversational intelligences in leading and managing legal organizations of all sizes.

Andrew is a Fellow in the College of Law Practice Management, an International Coach Federation Professional Certified Coach, Vice Chair of the ABA Law Practice Division Publications Board, and founding member of its Lawyer Leadership and Management Board.

Andrew is regularly invited to conduct workshops and retreats for his clients and present programs to bar associations. He is the author of numerous books and articles on various law practice management topics, including *The Lawyer's Guide to Professional Coaching: Leadership, Mentoring & Effectiveness* (American Bar Association, 2012).

Marcia Watson Wasserman

A seasoned legal management professional of more than 25 years, Marcia Watson Wasserman, Founder and President of Comprehensive Management Solutions, Inc., provides "C.O.O. To Go"™ services to boutique and mid-sized law firms. Her expertise includes operational management reviews, management development and training, succession planning, strategic planning, retreat facilitation, cash flow projections and financial management reports, recruitment, compensation and benefits administration, development of employee handbooks and job descriptions, business formations, and relocations.

As a thought leader, Marcia leads multiple monthly Managing Partners' Roundtables focused on elevating the legal management discussion and sharing best practices. She serves as an Associate Editor and on the editorial board of *Law Practice* magazine and is also a member of the Law Practice Division's Publications Board. Marcia frequently presents on law practice management topics at local, regional, and national conferences, and her writings can be found in leading legal publications. Marcia's efforts have garnered the recognition of her peers as she is a Fellow in the College of Law Practice Management.

Prior to consulting, Marcia served as Chief Operating Officer and Executive Director at several law firms—both local and national—including an AmLaw 200 firm

ACKNOWLEDGMENTS

From Andrew Elowitt

I am very grateful for the assistance and support I have received in the writing of this book. Many people have generously shared their time, knowledge, and expertise with me. This book is all the better for their contributions. First and foremost among them is my coauthor, Marcia Watson Wasserman. Her extensive experience in law firm management and consulting ensured that our ideas and advice were not only sound but also practical. Her diligence and tenacity made our collaboration a pleasure. I'd like to also thank our colleagues on the ABA Law Practice Division's Publications Board (Wendy Werner and Tom Mighell) and our editors at Lachina (Jenni Claydon and Molly Montanaro) for their always helpful feedback and support.

I'd be remiss if I didn't acknowledge the people I have managed throughout my career and the people who have managed me. Whether I was your boss or your report, you helped me understand what works in people management and what doesn't. From you, I learned the necessity of managing the individual not the title or job description. I have also learned much from my mentors, friends, and colleagues in the fields of management consulting, executive coaching, and leadership development. Our conversations and collaborations have helped me immeasurably in bringing the best practices of leadership and management to the legal community and the writing of this book.

A special thank you to my clients who have trusted me with their firms, businesses, and careers. Our work together has validated and refined the skills, tools, and models contained in this book. It has been a joy to see your growth and success.

On a personal note, I'd like to thank my wife Gisele for her care and support, and for reminding me from time to time that writer's block is temporary and should not be confused with existential angst. And to my daughter Claire, a Millennial who has begun managing, for our conversations about the best ways to organize, motivate, and hold people accountable . . . even when they don't want to be.

I dedicate this book to the memory of my parents, Norman and Ruth Elowitt, who in their quiet and unpretentious way personified basic human decency. From them, I learned that if your head and heart are in the right place, it's really not all that difficult to treat people with dignity and respect regardless of their race, class, religion, ethnicity, gender, or sexual orientation. My father, a child of poor immigrants, became a very successful entrepreneur and executive. He taught me that the best managers are thoughtful, big-hearted, and remember to read the footnotes on financial statements. My mother (quoting Eleanor Roosevelt) often reminded me that it's better to light a candle than to curse the darkness. I hope this book sheds a great deal of light.

From Marcia Watson Wasserman

I dedicate this writing effort to my husband Charles Wasserman, Ph.D., for his constant nurturing support, encouragement, and love. Thanks to our Australian Shepherds Blossom and Coco, who sat beside me through hours of writing, editing, and proofing and herded me away for play time when they felt I needed a break. A very special thank you to Andrew Elowitt, who suggested we go on the journey of writing this book together, for his friendship and invaluable contributions to the book, and to his wife Gisele for her patience and support for the many hours Andrew spent working on it. Without the following people this book could not be in your hands: Wendy Werner, for her patience in reading our drafts and challenging us to take the book farther; Tom Mighell, for his feedback; Jenni Claydon and Molly Montanaro of Lachina, who have made working on the book a pleasure; Mark Goulston, M.D.; Grover Cleveland; Karen Gabler; Jonathan Fitzgarrald; and Jennifer Guirl and Kelli Dunaway, for their contributions to this book. Finally, I acknowledge all the lawyers who have challenged, motivated, and inspired me over my career. This book is for all of you.

FOREWORD

by Mark Goulston

My good friend, the late leadership guru and best-selling author Warren Bennis, was fond of saying that managing people is like herding cats. To the best of my knowledge, Warren never considered how much more challenging that would be if a lot of those cats had law degrees.

I enjoy frequent opportunities to speak with groups of lawyers, and I often begin those talks by saying, "I know a single word that causes you more problems than nearly any other word in your practice, in your career, and possibly in your life. Do you want to know what it is?" Priding themselves on being discerning, and skeptical about such a seemingly audacious but foolhardy challenge, they say, "Yes," but are no doubt thinking to themselves, "Okay, Dr. Mark, this had better be good or else you're starting with one big strike against you."

I then reply, "That word is 'p-e-o-p-l-e.'" At that point nearly everyone in the audience laughs or groans. I then go on to explain that the word "people" often reminds them of those 20 percent of their colleagues and employees who make up 80 percent of the headaches (it's actually more like 10 percent and 90 percent). And the sad thing is that too often thinking about and dealing with those few high-maintenance people will cause them to overlook and underappreciate the vast majority of great people who work for and with them.

At times, even managing great colleagues and employees can be a challenge for lawyers. Although lawyers are excellent problem solvers, too often that talent doesn't extend to dealing with management problems and problem people. Even with loads of intelligence and determination, lawyers often struggle when it comes to motivating, developing, and holding their people accountable. Which leads me to this much-needed and wonderful book written by two nationally recognized practice management consultants and business coaches, Andrew Elowitt and Marcia Watson Wasserman. Given Andrew's prior career as a lawyer and his current practice that focuses on developing people in law firms, and Marcia's prior experience managing law firms and her current consulting practice devoted to legal management best practices, they are uniquely qualified to write and speak about how lawyers can become champion managers.

I'm sure most of you have heard the old proverb, "Where there's a will, there's a way." In reality and practice, this proverb has it slightly backwards. As important as resolve and perseverance can be in finding a way to solve problems, it's frequently more a matter of: "Where there's a way, you will find the will to do it." Or, in other words, once you know how to approach and solve a problem, it's much easier to find the motivation and backbone to tackle it. You need look no further than *Lawyers as Managers* to find that way, and once you understand its approach to people management in law firms, your motivation and backbone will surely follow.

Information on the way to manage people in law firms has been sorely lacking. That is—up until now. *Lawyers as Managers* fills the gap and gives lawyers everything they want and need to know about managing people that they never learned in law school. It is not just a book to help you deal with the challenging people in your law firm – it is a primer, guide, and road map all in one on how to empower, motivate, inspire, and bring out the best of everyone in your law firm . . . including you!

And therein lies a great opportunity. How well or poorly you manage the people in your law firm will determine how successful, effective, and well respected you are. Manage well and people will feel it's an honor and privilege to work at your firm under your supervision. Do it poorly and they'll be sending out their resumes to go elsewhere.

Mark Goulston, M.D., Co-Founder, Heartfelt Leadership and author of *"Just Listen": Discover the Secret to Getting Through to Absolutely Anyone, Talking to Crazy: How to Deal with the Irrational and Impossible People in Your Life,* and *Get Out of Your Own Way at Work . . . and Help Others Do the Same: Conquering Self-Defeating Behavior on the Job.*

LAWYERS AS
MANAGERS

PART I

An Introduction to People Management

The first part of this book will introduce you to the importance of managing and motivating people in your law firm. It explains why and how your ability to do so contributes to the overall success of your firm and employees. Your fellow firm members—attorneys and staff alike—are your firm's most significant asset and the magic ingredient that will go far in distinguishing your firm from others and ensuring its success.

As a manager, it is your responsibility to hire, train, develop, coordinate, and motivate the people in your firm. This part will introduce you to the "champion manager"—a man or woman who is extraordinarily skillful and effective in the performance of his or her managerial duties. It will give you the foundation you need to not just become more effective but to also think and act like a champion for your firm and employees.

1

Why People Management Matters

If you're like most lawyers, you graduated from law school with relatively little, if any, management experience. Perhaps you're one of the few who held a management position before entering law school. Or you may lack hands-on experience, but know something about management theory from undergraduate courses. Or you may have graduated with neither knowledge nor experience, but tried to learn management by trial and error or by reading a management bestseller. Or maybe you haven't cared much about management until now, as you find yourself responsible for and challenged by the supervision of other people. Whichever group you fit into and whatever your level of managerial experience, this book will accelerate your growth as a manager of lawyers and legal professionals.

One of the catalysts for writing this book came from working with a recently promoted partner in a boutique law firm. She had no real training on how to delegate, supervise, and give constructive feedback yet show appreciation.

Her aggressive personal style made her an excellent litiga-
tor, but got in the way of her ability to successfully delegate to and train the associates who now reported to her.
We searched for a management course or existing book for
lawyers that would teach her how to develop, supervise,
and motivate the people in her firm. Finding nothing current or relevant, we took on the challenge ourselves.

The need for this book became even more apparent soon
thereafter when we facilitated a series of Managing Partners'
Roundtable meetings for small to mid-sized law firms. When
asked to identify their single most significant management
challenge, the partners responded it was managing the people in their firms—not receivables, not expenses, not risk,
not technology—but people. Finding good talent, mentoring young lawyers, getting their writing ability to "excellent," and developing them for potential partnership were
common themes. Many of the managing partners wanted
to improve their own mentoring, delegation, and feedback
skills. Also mentioned were people issues of transition, succession planning, and passing the torch to the next generation of leaders and potential rainmakers.

THE IMPORTANCE OF PEOPLE MANAGEMENT

The managing partners' focus on people is not surprising: a
firm's most significant asset is its people. Although managing partners and firm owners have traditionally dedicated
most of their time to marketing and providing their firms'
services, an increasing number are understanding the critical importance of developing the "product" that the firm
is trying to persuade its clients to buy: the knowledge and

skill of its members (Maister, 1993). To develop a firm's human and intellectual capital—and by this we mean the collective judgment, knowledge, experience, and ability of its members—there must be an *ongoing, continual* effort at all levels (Maister, 1993, p. 155). Absent this effort, firms will have little to sell and limited means to deliver it.

This became especially clear to us in the aftermath of the 2008 economic crisis when law firm clients cut their legal spending, pushed back on attorney billing rates, and engaged in fewer transactions. Many firms that had been doing well began questioning whether they could survive, let alone remain profitable. Under these new and increased financial pressures, some imploded or dissolved, while others merged into healthier firms. Some firms survived but became less profitable as partners and practice areas left them to start or join new firms. In the midst of this instability, we saw startling differences between how well-managed and poorly managed firms dealt with what would soon be called the "new normal."

Firms with weak management fared worse than their better and more actively managed counterparts. We found that prior to the downturn most partners in both kinds of firms overlooked some important problems because they were generally satisfied with their compensation and career development. More importantly, they believed in their firm's future. But once the effects of the recession were felt and dollars became scarce, many once-latent problems became heated points of contention. Disagreements about compensation, allocation of resources (both human and financial), governance, strategy, and direction were more frequent in both kinds of firms.

Well-managed and led firms had an easier time dealing with these complex and difficult issues. Because communication was better in these firms, managing partners had a deeper and quicker understanding of their firm members' concerns. As a result, they could act sooner, people felt heard, and morale remained reasonably high. The relationships that formed the core of these healthy firms were certainly tested, but they, for the most part, survived and, in some cases, were strengthened by the members' shared predicament. Firms that had already paid attention to training and development had an easier time of retraining and reallocating their people to practice areas like insolvency that were active during the recession.

Poorly managed firms, on the other hand, had to play catch-up ball. It is sad and ironic that some firms that did an excellent job of preparing for the worst and hoping for the best when working with clients had so neglected their own management needs. In many cases, poor communication and passive management left them ill prepared to promptly address issues and respond to their members' fears. One managing partner we worked with described it as trying to finish building the car after the race had already begun. Levels of stress and distrust were higher in these firms, which only made necessary decisions and conversations between firm stakeholders that much harder. For the most part, they were slower to adapt to changing economic conditions, and they showed higher levels of turnover—both planned and unwanted. In some of these firms, attorneys and staff were treated poorly and "discarded" in shortsighted efforts to quickly reduce expenses. Many of these firms now have gaps at certain levels of partners and associates as a result of those hasty layoffs, while firms that treated their employees well have seen employees stay more loyal as the economy has improved.

Today, more than ever, in this 24-hour-a-day business world, all members of a firm (whether they are partners, associates, of counsel, paralegals, legal secretaries, managers, or other staff) must work together as a team for the benefit of their clients. Each person makes his or her own unique contribution to the team based on what the law firm's culture values as important. Coordinating and getting the most out of everyone's contributions is the responsibility of the firm's management, and treating employees well is a good strategy for winning the war for talent.

PEOPLE MANAGEMENT IS THIS BOOK'S MAIN FOCUS

This book focuses on people management and, more specifically, on the conversations, interactions, and relationships that are essential for engaging the people in your firm, developing them, coordinating them, holding them accountable, and fostering their morale and retention. Simply put: your people are the key to getting things done in your firm. How well you manage them will have a significant impact on your firm's profitability, culture, and sustainability.

There are other aspects of people management that we have chosen to exclude from the scope of this book, such as human resources administration, employment law compliance, compensation, perks and benefits, staffing strategies, personnel policies, and employee handbooks, just to mention a few. By omitting them, we are not suggesting they are of secondary importance. We've simply found that lawyers are often more comfortable and adept in these more technical and tangible aspects of people management. Some very good resources are already in print (see the Resources list at the end of this chapter).

It's helpful to look at people management in terms of "what" and "how." Attorneys are usually better at figuring out *what* needs to be done when it comes to managing their people than *how* to go about doing it. Articulating policies and setting procedures aren't terribly difficult for them, but *how* these policies and procedures are communicated, implemented, monitored, and enforced is often a greater challenge. They may have a clear idea of what their reports need to do better, but not know how to help them to make those improvements. They may also avoid difficult management conversations or struggle to sustain the good working relationships that are the glue of a high-functioning firm. Some attorneys confound their employees by making frequent exceptions to stated policies, giving the appearance that management decisions are being made on an ad hoc basis (Maister, 2006).[1]

People management is an undervalued and overlooked way to promote productivity, performance, and profitability. Why is this the case? Although it seldom requires an investment of money, it does require an investment of time. Even those lawyers who acknowledge the importance of management often complain they can seldom spend the time they need for it. There's no question that time is of

---

1. Maister likens this tendency to the common law tradition of making distinctions between the facts in a prior case and holding from those in a current one. He suggests that because of this, lawyers become adept and comfortable at making frequent exceptions to established firm policies and practices.

paramount importance to attorneys—wasted and lost time can result in lower realization rates, revenues, and profits. Many attorneys we work with initially feel that time spent on management matters can better be spent on billable matters, especially urgent ones.

We encourage them to see management time as an *investment*, not an *expense*! Like any investment, there may not be an immediate payback. It may take several billing cycles before the time spent developing an associate or resolving a conflict is reflected in higher productivity, revenue, morale, and retention. But the benefits of good people management are likely to be long lasting, a sort of human capital annuity over the long run.

INTRODUCING THE "CHAMPION MANAGER"

There are many adjectives that can be used to describe the best law firm managers. These men and women are more than competent and effective. Referring to them as exemplary, consummate, or complete managers is better, but it still leaves the focus solely on the individual manager. We have chosen to call them "champion managers" for three reasons:

- First, they are champions in demonstrating the highest levels of people management skills.
- Second, and of more importance, they are dedicated to championing the members of their firms, by developing them to their full potential, and fostering relationships among them so they can work together smoothly and efficiently for the benefit of their firm and its clients.

- And third, through their development efforts, they end up managing their own team of champions.

THIS BOOK'S ORGANIZATION

This book is divided into four parts that build upon one another.

- **Part I: An Introduction to People Management** explains the vital importance of people management, describes the key attributes and responsibilities of champion managers, and explains the relationship between people management and leadership. It also explains why it's necessary to think like a champion manager before you can act like one.
- **Part II: The Champion Manager Toolkit** identifies the three things you will need to become a champion manager of people: the right mindset, the right skills and tools, and the right resources and support from others. Chapters 4 through 13 provide practical and detailed guidance on how to hone and expand your communication skills; hire and onboard new employees; delegate and assign work; give and receive feedback; train, supervise, develop, and mentor your employees; engage, motivate, and retain them; promote collaboration and teamwork; manage conflicts; and create high morale and a positive firm culture.
- **Part III: Managing Specific Individuals and Situations** looks at some of the common personalities and people management challenges that lawyers

encounter in running their firms. It also discusses various facets of what we call "ethical management," such as promoting diversity, responding to harassment and bullying, and dealing with substance abuse and addictive behaviors.

- **Part IV: Becoming the Complete Champion Manager** helps readers reflect on their management abilities; discover whether they are doing a good job; and find the management styles that work best for them, their firm, and their reports.

HOW TO USE THIS BOOK

This book is designed to make it easier and less time consuming for attorneys to effectively manage the people in their firms. Whether you are a new partner, a new managing partner, or a new lawyer, it is a resource you can turn to when challenges arise—be they interpersonal conflicts, how to build a team mentality, or simply how to delegate work. Even though it has been written with the management needs of small and mid-sized firms in mind, managers in corporate and government legal departments will also find our advice relevant and valuable.

We recommend that lawyers with limited management experience use this book as a primer or training manual, and start at the beginning and read chapter by chapter in sequential fashion. Each chapter and part builds on earlier ones that provide helpful context for those that follow.

More experienced managers may be tempted to skip directly to the skills and tools discussed in Part II or the specific management challenges addressed in Part III. This is understandable—you want to get to the tangible take-aways and techniques that this book offers. But before doing so, we ask you to at least skim and familiarize your-self with the chapters "The Champion Manager Mindset" in Part I and "Building a Champion Management Support System" in Part II. There are two good reasons we make this request. First, it will be a lot easier for you to learn and employ champion management skills and techniques if you first understand the concepts that underlie them. Some traditional assumptions and beliefs we all share can get in the way when we're trying to manage. Second, people management isn't a solo act. It's important that you have support and buy-in from the members of your firm and that you know how and when to ask for their commitment and other necessary resources.

After you're familiar with the first two parts, you can continue on to the following two at your own pace and use this book as a reference. When learning to use and master the skills and techniques explained in Chapters 4 through 25, make sure to allocate time (and patience) to practice them. Mastery comes from repetitive mindful practice and from making (and correcting) mistakes. Like any good reference, you can always check back on the skills and the specific challenges discussed in Parts II and III when the need arises.

Finally, don't be so focused on managing others that you forget to manage yourself. Reread Part IV of this book at least once a year to reflect on your own progress and effectiveness as a manager. There is always room for all of us to improve.

We hope you will share this book and what you learn from it with others. You don't have to have the title "managing partner" or "practice group head" to use this book and become a champion manager. We've found that superb management skills cascade down to all levels of a firm and improve everyone's performance and satisfaction. When this occurs, firms are not just a pleasant place to work, they are also profitable and resilient.

REFERENCES

Maister, D. (1993). *Managing the professional service firm*. New York: Simon & Schuster.

Maister, D. (2006, April). Are law firms manageable? *The American Lawyer*. Retrieved from: http://davidmaister.com/articles/are-law-firms-manageable/

RESOURCES

Cotterman, J. D. (2015). *Compensation plans for law firms* (6th ed.). Chicago, IL: ABA Law Practice Division.

Greene, A. G., & Boyer, S. J. (2015). *The survival guide to implementing effective law firm management strategies*. Chicago, IL: ABA Law Practice Division.

rose, j. j. (Ed.). (2009). *Effectively staffing your law firm*. Chicago, IL: ABA Solo, Small Firm and General Practice Division.

Shannon, M. P., & Manch, S. (2015). *Recruiting lawyers: How to hire the best talent* (2nd ed.). Chicago, IL: ABA Law Practice Division.

2

What Does It Mean To Be a Champion Manager?

Lawyers manage people. They don't make widgets; they build lawyers and they hire, supervise, train, review and hopefully promote them. A widget machine will produce more widgets if it is properly maintained, oiled and adjusted. Lawyers will be more productive and profitable if they are well-trained and supervised, and if they get sufficient feedback as they develop their craft to learn how to improve their skills.

(Werner, 2013)

The challenge of effectively managing people in a law firm can seem overwhelming at first, especially when added to existing client and administrative responsibilities. It's difficult for many lawyers to understand what exactly constitutes people management and what their priorities should be. To simplify matters, we've identified seven key people management responsibilities:

1. Hire and onboard
2. Train, supervise, and develop
3. Ensure productivity and efficiency
4. Foster collaboration and teamwork
5. Engage, motivate, and retain
6. Manage conflicts
7. Maintain positive morale and culture

If you feel the divisions between these seven responsibilities are a bit arbitrary or fuzzy, you're right. They are. These facets of people management are interrelated, overlapping, and mutually reinforcing: success in one supports positive results in another. For example, doing a good job of engaging and motivating members of your firm will contribute to the maintenance of high morale and a positive culture. Conversely, fostering a healthy culture and high morale will make it easier to motivate and retain your employees. Consider this too: doing a good job of training, supervising, and developing the members of your firm will help you understand who is a good hire and what you need to know and do to quickly and effectively onboard them; when you do a better job of hiring and onboarding people, it is much easier to train and develop them.

Skillful conversations and interactions are necessary for effectiveness in each of these seven areas of people management, but they must also be supported by strategic analysis, clear policies and procedures, and administrative support.

1. HIRE AND ONBOARD

People management begins by selecting and hiring the best candidates for a position. Interviews of prospective attorneys and staff are potentially the beginning of mutually beneficial working relationships. When pre-employment conversations are conducted with a spirit of curiosity and learning, it is easier to assess a prospective member's capabilities, personality, and cultural fit.

Onboarding is a new hire's first substantial introduction to the culture of a firm, and it's an opportunity for a firm to create a good first or second impression. As the pleasantries of recruiting fade, new hires get a better feel for how things are really done and how people really act. Considering its importance, it's a shame that the onboarding of new firm members is often approached in a haphazard or unsystematic manner. Valuable time and energy can be wasted, and new hires can be left wondering just how much they (and their career development) truly matter to the firm.

2. TRAIN, SUPERVISE, AND DEVELOP

People management continues with the training and supervision of firm members. Developing the people in your firm means helping them not only increase their knowledge but also improve their skills. Attorney training in the past emphasized the mastery of substantive law and procedure; it is now important to help them to also develop expertise in areas as diverse as marketing and the use of technology. Enhancing the skill and knowledge of all members benefits the firm as a whole.

Knowledge can often be gained from a wide variety of continuing legal education sources. Skill development on the other hand requires sustained practice with guidance from those more knowledgeable and skilled. Senior firm members can offer that guidance through both day-to-day, in-the-moment feedback as well as through formal mentoring programs. Vendors and trainers are helpful in learning and developing technology-related skills; while coaches are particularly useful when needed skills are interpersonal, nuanced, and complex.

3. ENSURE PRODUCTIVITY AND EFFICIENCY

Law firm managers can improve their firm's overall productivity, efficiency, and profitability through skillful people management. This begins with curiosity and concern about the productivity and efficiency of individual firm members. When a firm member's performance slips, it may be attributable to a struggle with time management, attentiveness, resilience, stress, energy management, personal problems, or some combination of these factors. Managers can help them discover the cause of their performance problems, coach them, and offer needed resources.

If the performance of several firm members is declining, managers should be even more curious. It may signal that there are larger-scale problems with infrastructure (e.g., a cumbersome and user-unfriendly document handling system), conflicts (e.g., monopolization of resources by one practice group), or a culture that doesn't encourage cooperation and collaboration.

4. FOSTER COLLABORATION AND TEAMWORK

Collaboration and teamwork are the hallmarks of a high-functioning firm. When they are present, there are fewer problems with disconnects, dropped balls, and redundant or unnecessary work. Interpersonal and group conflicts are also minimized because skillful people managers are clear about tasks and overall objectives, and they connect individual contributions to team efforts and firm goals. With larger and more complex legal matters, this is even more critical because they typically involve the contributions of more people.

Managers may find that coordinating the activities of attorneys can be a challenge at times, since their work allows for more autonomy that that of many other professionals. But the benefits of fostering teamwork and collaboration certainly outweigh the difficulties. When firm members know their actions are aligned with what's important, they feel a greater sense of belonging and engagement. With everyone rowing in the same direction, firms can move faster and are more agile.

5. ENGAGE, MOTIVATE, AND RETAIN

Lack of employee engagement is costly in all businesses and organizations, including law firms. Gallup's 2017 *State of the American Workplace* report estimated that actively disengaged employees cost the U.S. $483 billion to $605 billion each year in lost productivity and are almost twice as likely as engaged employees to seek new jobs. They are also more likely to steal from their companies, negatively influence their coworkers, miss workdays, and drive clients and customers away. Poor management is one of the leading causes of disengagement, and more recent studies have shown that managers too often experience feelings of disengagement.

Disengagement can lead to higher staff and attorney turnover, which can be extraordinarily costly to law firms. In 2007, the UC Hastings College of the Law Project for Attorney Retention estimated that it costs a firm $200,000–$500,000 to replace a second-year associate, once "soft costs" such as interviewing time spent by partners and associates, lost training costs for the departed attorney, and additional costs of training the new hire are combined with hard compensation costs such as salary and signing incentives.

Law firm managers need to monitor the engagement of firm members by scrutinizing, among other factors, unwanted turnover. Rather than waiting for problems to arise and then reacting to them, they need to proactively take steps to keep morale and engagement high. People management is indispensable in this regard. Managers need to know the members of their firms well enough to understand what motivates them, because not everyone's motivators are the same or stay the same over time. While Millennial employees, for example, may still be influenced by the motivators traditionally used in law firms, such as higher compensation and equity partnership, they are also interested in better work-life integration and more flexible working arrangements.

6. MANAGE CONFLICTS

The mindsets and skills that enable lawyers to win in their negotiations and trials often work poorly in the fishbowls that firms tend to be. Lawyers swim together in their bowls and need to keep the water clear. If they are to do that, they can't leave toxic deposits behind—they have to operate with a true partnership mentality, knowing that their fishbowl is shared and that they all win when they can see clearly and work effectively. This is much easier said than done, and it's incumbent upon managers to keep the water as clear as possible.

Conflicts are a normal part of everyone's work and personal lives, yet people often ignore, defer, and avoid them. Managing partners and other law firm managers are often called upon to resolve conflicts, whether they arise between lawyers, staff, lawyers and staff, practice areas, or within executive committees. Developing "conflict competence" helps managers reduce the harmful effects of conflicts while improving interpersonal communication and building stronger relationships throughout a firm (Runde, 2010).

7. MAINTAIN POSITIVE MORALE AND CULTURE

Many people misunderstand the terms "morale" and "culture." Morale isn't the same thing as happiness, and though firm-wide happiness can be a manifestation of good morale, it's rarely the cause of it. Morale is the confidence, enthusiasm, and discipline of an individual or group at a particular time. It comes from a sense of shared purpose, mission, opportunity, or predicament. Even in dire situations—perhaps especially in dire situations—morale can be extraordinarily high if everyone sees him- or herself in the same proverbial boat.

Every firm has a culture, regardless of whether or not its managers and members are aware of it. For most people, their business or firm's culture is pretty much invisible—it's just the way things are. David Foster Wallace (2008) gave a great example of culture in his 2005 commencement address at Kenyon College:

> There are these two young fish swimming along, and they happen to meet an older fish swimming the other way, who nods at them and says, "Morning, boys, how's the water?" And the two young fish swim on for a bit, and then eventually one of them looks over at the other and goes, "What the hell is water?"

Culture is the water that lawyers and staff swim in in the fishbowls that are firms. It's what people at a firm actually do every day, rather than any platitudes they may place on their websites or reception area walls. It starts with the mindsets of a firm's members and manifests itself in their conversations, interactions, and relationships (see Figure 2.1).

Whether a firm's culture is articulated or even recognized, it has a significant impact on productivity, retention, and morale. Positive cultures can facilitate growth and change, while negative ones can be hidden obstacles. Keeping the waters healthy and clean should be a managerial priority.

Figure 2.1

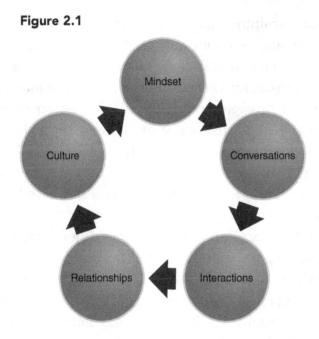

LEADERS OR MANAGERS?

Astute readers may feel that the seven people management responsibilities described above sound a lot like leadership, and may be wondering whether they need to be *managers* of their firms or *leaders*.

Both are needed for law firms to function well and adapt to ever-changing environments. Firms with weak leadership lack direction, cohesiveness, and purpose; firms with weak management struggle to get things done and are often inefficient and unprofitable. Leadership skills and management skills aren't the same, and they're not mutually exclusive.

Leadership is sometimes likened to setting the course for a ship, while management is steering that proverbial ship and keeping it running on course. In that metaphor, people management would include making sure the crew knows their jobs (training and development), does them well (evaluation and accountability), is well fed and clothed (given adequate resources), and is rowing or sailing together in the same direction (teamwork and morale). The leader of the voyage would articulate a vision or goal for the crew (perhaps discovery or riches), set a destination (the New World, Singapore, or 16.5004° S, 151.7415° W), determine how best to sail there (around the Cape or through the Canal), and keep the crew's spirits high even in times of adversity.

Warren Bennis (1999) explains this difference: "Management is getting people *to do* what needs to be done. Leadership is getting people *to want to do* what needs to be done. Managers push—leaders pull. Managers command—leaders communicate." People management skills encompass the pushing and pulling that Bennis references. They are essential for both firm management and leadership.

Management encompasses activities that are primarily people oriented and many that are not. Those that are more technically oriented have been customarily thought of as using the metaphorical left side of the brain, relying on rational, analytical, data-based skills to solve problems. Their emphasis is typically on the tactical, logistical, and shorter term. They are usually concerned with execution and establishing and achieving clear goals. The key functions of management are usually planning, organizing, budgeting, controlling, and coordinating; managers focus on obtaining, allocating, and using resources such as money, materials, time, office space, equipment, personnel, and information.

Leadership, by comparison, relies more on right-brained, emotional, non-linear, inspirational, and people-oriented approaches for critical tasks such as gaining buy-in and commitment. Leaders emphasize direction, strategy, and relationships. They address interpersonal concerns, such as motivating, influencing, and inspiring people through a compelling vision, a personal example, or strong relationships. Their focus is typically more on the long-term and the big picture.

A law firm's need for leadership and management depends on many factors, principally the complexity of its organization and operation and the degree of predictability or certainty in its external environment. As a law firm's "complexity" grows, so does its need for management. As a firm's "uncertainty" grows (i.e., existing in a rapidly changing and often unpredictable environment), so does its need for leadership. The table summarizes these needs.

Law Firms	Stable Environment	Rapidly Changing Environment
Simple Organization	Low need for both management and leadership	Leadership needed more than management
Complex Organization	Management needed more than leadership	High need for both management and leadership

LEADERSHIP AND THE PEOPLE SIDE OF MANAGEMENT

Although leadership and management differ, distinctions between leadership and *the people side of management* (as opposed to the technical aspects of management) are few and negligible when it comes to getting things done in the real world of law firms. The various skills needed for leadership and the technical side of management are better thought of as lying on a continuum, with cognitive and analytical undertakings at the left end of the continuum and emotional and social ones at the right (see Figure 2.2). Technical management skills such as budgeting and planning lie towards the left side of the continuum; leadership skills like inspiring and motivating lie towards the right. People management skills—necessary for both managing and leading—are found throughout the middle of the continuum.

Figure 2.2

Technical Aspects of Management	People Management	Leadership

Cognitive Analytical		Emotional Social
Tactical and logistical		Strategic and big picture
Shorter term		Longer term
Creating firm policies, procedures, and action plans		Creating firm vision, values, culture, and strategy
Obtaining, allocating, and utilizing resources		Identifying resources needed for firm vision and strategy
Rational and data-based approaches to problem solving		People-oriented and non-linear approaches to problem solving
Achieving results by planning, budgeting, setting goals, and monitoring progress		Achieving results by inspiring motivating, gaining buy-in, and commitment

The similarities and interconnectedness between people management and leadership become clearer when we consider a list of critical tasks for law firm leaders (Salacuse, 2006).

1. Articulate a strategic *Direction* for their firm and persuade their lawyers to accept it.
2. *Integrate* the lawyers in their firm into a cohesive team.
3. *Mediate* the diverse interests of their firm's lawyers and resolve conflicts.
4. *Educate* the lawyers in their firm by providing them with the necessary coaching, advice, and support to do their jobs and achieve the firm's goals.
5. Inspire, *Motivate*, and encourage the lawyers in their firm.
6. Earn and maintain the *Trust* of the firm's lawyers.
7. *Represent* their firm to the outside world.

It's readily apparent that a firm leader's effectiveness in each of the first six of these areas largely depends on the quality of the conversations, interactions, and relationships he or she has with the members of his or her firm. For the seventh, it is conversations, interactions, and relationships with clients (past, present, and prospective), community members, lenders, bankers, and other external stakeholders.

IQ VS. EMOTIONAL, SOCIAL, AND CONVERSATIONAL INTELLIGENCES

Intelligence and academic achievement alone are weak indicators of management success and effectiveness. Managers not only need cognitive intelligence (IQ) to be effective in each of the seven critical tasks, but also emotional intelligence (EI or EQ or, colloquially, "people smarts") and social intelligence (SQ or "people skills"). Because the implementation and execution of management decisions require the coordination of the contributions and efforts of many individuals, people smarts and people skills are indispensable. Conversational intelligence—our ability to connect with people through language, learn from them, and influence them—also plays a major role in the application of these skills (Glaser, 2014). Research has shown that pure intellectual firepower is not enough for long-term career success. Cognitive intelligence has been found to be a valid predictor of success in the first few jobs a person may have, but as people rise to higher management and leadership positions, emotional and social intelligence show a much higher correlation with career success and achievement (Goleman, 1998).

CHAPTER SUMMARY

There are seven key interrelated and overlapping people management responsibilities that we have identified. How to master them yourself and champion them in your law firm will be explained in greater detail in later chapters in this book.

1. **Hire and Onboard.** Taking the time necessary to recruit and hire the best candidates for positions will increase the likelihood that your new hires will become productive and happy members of your firm. Once they arrive, thoughtful and systematic onboarding will enable new employees to embrace the firm's culture and quickly become valuable team members.

2. **Train, Supervise, and Develop.** People management continues with training, supervising, and developing the people in your firm. Development of necessary skills for success can be obtained through mentoring by more senior firm members, consultants, trainers, and coaches.

3. **Ensure Productivity and Efficiency.** Productivity, efficiency, and profitability can be improved through savvy people management. If performance problems surface in a firm member, work with the individual to discover the cause, coach him or her, and provide needed resources to help him or her do better.

4. **Foster Collaboration and Teamwork.** Encourage collaboration and teamwork through clarity about tasks and objectives. Remember to connect individual contributions to team efforts and firm goals to enhance attorneys' and staff members' sense of belonging and engagement.

5. **Engage, Motivate, and Retain.** Lack of employee engagement can lead to higher staff and attorney turnover, which can be extraordinarily costly to the firm. Managers need to understand what motivates each of their direct reports, taking into account generational differences that impact employee motivation.

6. **Manage Conflicts.** Conflicts often arise among lawyers, staff, lawyers and staff, practice groups, or within executive or management committees. Managers need to develop "conflict competence" to eliminate or reduce the toxic deposits that otherwise will cloud the firm fishbowl.

7. **Foster and Maintain Positive Morale and Culture.** Culture begins with the mindsets of a firm's members and manifests itself in their conversations, interactions, relationships, and behaviors. Firm culture can impact morale, positively or negatively. Good morale comes from a sense of shared purpose, mission, opportunity, or response to a predicament.

Both leadership and management skills are needed for law firms to function well and adapt to change. Leadership sets the course for the ship, and management steers it and keeps it on course. Most management activities rely on the left side of the brain to solve shorter-term tactical, logistical, and data-based problems. Management's key functions encompass planning, organizing, budgeting, controlling, and coordinating. Many management responsibilities also encompass training and development, evaluation and accountability, and teamwork and morale. Leadership, on the other hand, relies more on the right-brained, emotional, non-linear, inspirational, and people-oriented approaches for critical tasks. A leader is generally focused on the long term and the big picture.

The need for leadership and management depends on many factors. As a firm's "complexity" grows, so does its need for management. As a firm's "uncertainty" grows, so does its need for leadership.

People management skills are essential for leadership. A leader's effectiveness depends on the quality of conversations, interactions, and relationships he or she has with firm members, clients, vendors, consultants, and other external stakeholders.

In order to be effective, managers need cognitive intelligence as well as emotional and social intelligence for seven critical management and leadership tasks. People skills, people smarts, and conversational intelligence are prerequisites for successful managers. Cognitive intelligence is a necessary trait, but as people rise to higher management and leadership positions, success is also the result of emotional and social intelligence (Deutschendorf, 2015).

REFERENCES

Bennis, W. (1999). *Managing people is like herding cats*. Provo, UT: Executive Excellence.

Deutschendorf, H. (2015, June 22). Why emotionally intelligent people are more successful. *Fast Company*. Retrieved from https://www.fastcompany.com/3047455/hit-the-ground-running/why-emotionally-intelligent-people-are-more-successful

Gallup. (2017). *State of the American workplace*. Retrieved from http://www.gallup.com/reports/199961/state-american-workplace-report-2017.aspx

Glaser, J. E. (2014). *Conversational intelligence: How great leaders build trust and get extraordinary results*. Brookline, MA: Bibliomotion.

Goleman, D. (1998, November–December). What makes a leader? *Harvard Business Review, 76*(6): 93–102.

Runde, C. E., & Flanagan, T. A. (2010). *Developing your conflict competence: A hands-on guide for leaders, managers, facilitators and teams*. San Francisco, CA: Jossey-Bass; Center for Creative Leadership.

Salacuse, J. W. (2006). *Leading leaders: How to manage smart, talented, rich, and powerful people*. New York, NY: American Management Association.

UC Hastings College of Law—Project for Attorney Retention. (2007). The business case for a balanced hours program for attorneys. Retrieved from http://apps.americanbar.org/labor/lel-aba-annual/2008/pdf/Williams2.pdf

Wallace, D. F. (2008, September 19). Plain old untrendy troubles and emotions. Retrieved from https://www.theguardian.com/books /2008/sep/20/fiction

Werner, W. L. (2013, January–February). Management skills for lawyers. *Law Practice*, *39*(1).

3

The Champion
Manager Mindset

LEARN TO THINK LIKE A CHAMPION MANAGER—
BEFORE ACTING LIKE A CHAMPION MANAGER

While prior experience and knowledge of management theory can certainly be advantageous, at times they can also become hindrances. Extraordinarily little of what has been written and taught about management specifically deals with professional service firms. Most is based on research into the operations and dynamics of large, complex businesses. Even when content and advice are excellent, a fair portion of it is of limited value and relevance to law firms. Translating general advice on management to the specifics of law firm administration can be tricky and at times counterproductive. Only in the last few years has more attention been paid to the unique characteristics and challenges of professional service firm management, and although there are still very few books, some excellent ones are listed at the end of the final chapter of this book.

Why is this the case? Law firms are not like other kinds of businesses (Elowitt, 2012). They tend to be less pyramidal, with power and authority more evenly distributed than in other business organizations. Law firms often look like flat collections of individual professionals who work in parallel with a fair degree of autonomy. A key characteristic of that autonomy is their ability to take their clients with them should they choose to leave their firm. Lawyers also tend to be more skeptical, cynical, judgmental, impatient, analytical, introverted, ambitious, defensive, pessimistic, and controlling than the general public and presumably workers in other kinds of businesses (Richard, n.d., 1993, 2002). Managing a law firm is often like managing a sports team of individual players: the challenge is getting them to work together for the benefit of the team or firm.

Because of these unique characteristics, law firm leaders and managers face challenges that aren't prevalent in other kinds of businesses. To be effective, they must develop a somewhat different set of management skills; although prior non-law firm management experience can be a sound foundation, it is rarely a complete substitute for these additional skills.

PREPARING TO LEARN LAW FIRM MANAGEMENT SKILLS

The good news is that the skills required for championship-level law firm management can be learned. They are not the product of certain innate personal qualities, nor are they esoteric or difficult to understand. But like any other set of skills, you will need to practice them before you become comfortable and adept at their use. Although they may at first feel awkward or even counterintuitive, sustained practice will bring effectiveness, mastery, and a sense of great satisfaction.

As tempting as it may be to jump immediately to learning those skills, some preparation is necessary before you start on your path to becoming a champion law firm manager. Like any other journey, you will need an accurate roadmap (which the following chapters will provide) and a good "packing list" (which the rest of this chapter will supply). Your packing list isn't just the skills you may already possess—it's just as important that you have the right mindset before starting!

Your mindset is the collection of assumptions and beliefs you already have about management, leadership, law firms, the legal profession, your firm, and yourself. Some of your assumptions and beliefs are no doubt valid and helpful; others are misconceptions that may get in your way. While you can probably articulate some of your assumptions and beliefs, you undoubtedly have others that you might not be aware of that are nevertheless in play and shaping the way you approach management. These tacit beliefs and assumptions can be potent obstacles to becoming a champion manager, so it's worth considering some of the most common ones.

YOUR RECOMMENDED PACKING LIST

Before beginning this journey, it's helpful to know what to bring with you and what to leave behind. As any seasoned traveler will tell you, packing too much or the wrong things can slow you down and ruin your trip. So let's start with three of the most common beliefs and assumptions you can leave behind.

What to Leave Behind

1. **The idea of "born" leaders and managers.** At one time people believed that leadership and management skills were innate personal qualities that only a few were fortunate enough to be born with—if you lacked those traits, your chances of being an effective manager or leader were slim. Autocratic leadership was in style and "natural born leaders" ran the show. Fortunately, research into the question of whether leaders are born or made has shown the answer to be more complex and nuanced. Today we recognize it's not a matter of nature vs. nurture, but rather a combination of both (Center for Creative Leadership, 2012; Locke, 2014).

   While some traits may make it easier for a person to learn management and leadership skills, they are just one piece of the entire picture. Without the right mindset and sustained practice, the advantage they provide is negligible. It's like expecting a person with perfect pitch to automatically become an excellent musician.

   Management and leadership skills such as effective delegation, feedback, and teambuilding can be mastered through learning, self-reflection, practice, and experience. Though a few people find this incredibly easy, managers who have had to work the hardest to develop their championship-level management skills often end up being the most polished and effective.

People also used to believe that there was an ideal manager or leader personality. Conventional wisdom and a few behavioral studies had it that charismatic, action-oriented, loquacious extraverts were the best leaders. There was little basis for this belief: the correlation between extraversion and leadership skill in these older studies was modest and the studies focused on followers' perceptions of who was a good leader, rather than the delivery of actual results (Cain, 2012).

Recent and more rigorous studies have shown that a quieter, more introverted, and less dynamic style of leadership is often the better choice in certain organizations or contexts. For example, when followers are passive, extroverted leaders enhance group performance; but when employees are more proactive, introverted leaders are more effective. Lawyers may be called many things, but they are seldom described as passive employees. So introverted leaders may do well in legal environments, and while extraverts are often perceived as the best leaders, their performance is not significantly superior to that of introverts or ambiverts (Cain, 2012).

2. **Your "lawyer mindset."** It's understandable that many of us approach people management the same way we approach the practice of law. When handling legal matters, we've found that being a smart, analytical, dispassionate problem solver works really well. Too often we assume that this same approach is all we need to also be an effective manager. This may be true for technical aspects of practice management such as budgeting and financial analysis, but when

managing people, being smart and fast is often less important than the quality of the conversations and relationships we have with the people who work with us.

Having "all the answers" is an important (though at times tacit) aspect of our lawyer mindset. Our clients expect us to have the answers to their questions and the solutions to their problems. After all, that is why they are retaining and paying us. But in managing people, lawyers and staff alike, there are frequent situations when collaborating to come up with a shared solution or answer is the better approach. Rather than dictate the solution to them, discuss the issue and ask them for their input. Whether it's trial preparation or getting ready for an important client meeting, when employees participate in decision making and feel heard and understood, they are more likely to take ownership of a decision and do a better job of implementing and following it.

A few lawyers unconsciously take an adversarial approach to people management and get stuck in some of the least useful aspects of the lawyer mindset. They see interactions with employees as a series of negotiations or win-lose competitions where they can demonstrate their superiority or authority. They also tend to assess blame and culpability rather than trying to understand their employees' point of view. In discussions with employees, they have difficulty stepping out of their role as an advocate: their questions are typically close-ended and designed to support their point of view rather than seen as opportunities to learn and understand the larger picture. The key is not to completely abandon the lawyer mindset—it is far too valuable—but to learn how to use it selectively and add a complementary set of people skills.

3. **The "Golden Rule."** You may be one of many people who believe the Golden Rule—*do unto others as you would have them do unto you*—is a great life principle that works equally well when it comes to managing the people in your firm. You try to manage other people as you would like to be managed. Even though your intentions may be virtuous, you're overlooking a fundamental fact—not everyone wants to *nor should be* managed in the same way you wish to be managed.

   We all have different strengths, weakness, temperaments, and blind spots. What works to motivate and hold you accountable may not work for the next person. When you assume that everyone is like you, you're unintentionally taking a "cookie cutter" or "one size fits all" approach to people management that ignores individual differences. It's far better to treat everyone fairly and equitably but not necessarily identically. Beware, too, of playing favorites by intentionally or unintentionally working more closely with or giving the best assignments to attorneys who are most like you. Look at each person you supervise as an individual and take the time to learn what motivates them.

What to Bring

The following four mindsets are important tools to support your efforts to learn and practice champion management:

1. **A belief that management is a necessary, high priority, daily activity.** You may feel that with all your client responsibilities you simply don't have enough time to be an active manager. If that's the case, you are being penny-wise and pound-foolish. Managers who avoid or defer decisions usually end up spending a lot more time and energy resolving problems that over time have grown in severity, complexity, or urgency because of their neglect. Prompt, proactive responses save time over the long run.

   Many lawyers make client work and business development much higher priorities than practice management responsibilities. This is perfectly under-standable. It's not very difficult to connect the dots between client lists, billable hours, and dollars in the bank. It takes a bit more imagination and experience to realize that sound practice management is neces-sary to not only control expenses, but to also maxi-mize revenue. Consider the plight of firms that spend too little management time on hiring, developing, and supervising their people: they typically underperform and write off considerable attorney and staff time; and while they may still be profitable, they usually leave a lot of money on the table. Business develop-ment and client work generate revenue; management generates profit.

   This is not to suggest that lawyers have an end-less supply of time for management activities. Most

> Business development and client work generate revenue; management generates profit.

lawyers face very real dilemmas about where to devote their time and energy. Champion managers have two ways of resolving the problem of not enough time for managing. First, they become so skilled at managing people that it takes them less and less time to get results. Second, they make people management and leadership part of their everyday interactions. For them, management isn't a separate, time-consuming calendar item, but rather an integral part of the way they work with partners, peers, associates, staff, and clients on an everyday moment-to-moment basis.

2. **A desire to be a proactive people manager.** You may be one of the many lawyers who are reluctant to be a proactive people manager. You may simply be more comfortable with the analytical and quantitative aspects of practice management, and would rather establish metrics and evaluate monthly reports than closely supervise and develop the people in your firm. You may feel—rightly or wrongly—that this is where your strengths lie, and that people management will be a bit of a stretch for you.

   If you feel this reluctance, you are not alone. Lawyers are generally risk-averse high achievers who hate to fail. Some realize they have little knowledge or training in the area of people management, and don't want to risk doing a poor job. As a result, they become passive and inconsistent managers who fear that taking an active role may do more harm than good to their working relationships. They tend to take a reactive approach, addressing problems only after they have occurred or perhaps worsened. In doing so, they generally make managing (and being managed) more difficult than it needs to be. If you have absolutely no interest in managing, then don't. Either work for someone else or find someone to whom you can hand over management responsibility and authority.

3. **The right side of your brain . . . metaphorically speaking, of course.** Numerous studies have shown that effectiveness in management and leadership depends more on emotional and social intelligence (your EI) than cognitive intelligence (your IQ) (Goleman, 1998). As people reach higher levels in their organizations, the correlation between leadership success and EI grows even stronger. Leadership and management are not about personality or intellect; they're about behavior— observable sets of skills and abilities that can be learned and developed through practice. Self-awareness and self-management are the keys to developing the people smarts (social awareness) and people skills (relationship management skills) that are needed to connect with people and successfully lead and manage them.

4. **Curiosity and a willingness to try new ways of managing.** Most of us are self-taught managers. We start by imitating—either deliberately or unconsciously— our past bosses (including parents and teachers), and we generally don't stray very far from that style unless it no longer works for us or we are exposed to a different style that works better. Lawyers, being conservative and risk averse, are often comfortable making only small incremental changes from their initial

management style. When a situation requires larger changes, a "growth mindset" is needed to develop a champion management style.

People with growth mindsets believe they can develop their talents through hard work, smart goals, dedication, and input from others (Dweck, 2016). They challenge themselves, persevere when they are stuck, and learn from their failures. They tend to achieve more than those people with a "fixed mindset," who believe their innate intelligence and talents are all they have to work with and that they're either good at something or they're not. Growth mindsets can be contagious: when people work for a manager with a growth mindset, it rubs off on them and they begin to believe there are fewer limits on what they can learn and achieve.

The first part of a champion manager's growth mindset is a willingness to admit and accept his or her ignorance about management. Some lawyers struggle with this. They view their ignorance as a lack of intelligence, preparation, or strength; they are hesitant and sometimes embarrassed to ask for help. As a result, they make learning management skills unnecessarily difficult. Acknowledging what we don't know is, of course, the first step in learning something new. You can make time to attend management seminars and webinars and participate in a managing partners' roundtable of law firm peers to expand your management vocabulary and toolkit. It's okay to say, "I don't know how to manage." Faking it creates far more serious problems in the workplace.

The second part of the champion manager's growth mindset is a willingness to explore, try new and different approaches to management, and (please take a breath here) occasionally fail (you may exhale now). Yes, failing is part of the process when learning communication and relationship skills. Trial and error can be awfully good teachers. Not everything you do is going to work; what works with one employee may not work with another; what works in one situation may not work in the next. Over time you will learn what works and which managerial style is the best fit for a specific employee, issue, or moment. (Please see Chapters 26 and 27 for discussions of how to assess your successes and failures as a manager and how to use and refine different management styles.) And you can learn from the small failures how to avoid the big ones.

As lawyers, failure is somewhat of an anathema, but as novice managers, it's somewhat of a necessity. If you're not having some failures, you're probably not being bold enough. Stepping outside of your comfort zone is needed if you are going to make and sustain significant changes in how you manage people.

CHAPTER SUMMARY

Being a champion manager is as much about developing a managerial mindset as it is about mastering a set of skills and techniques. One of the common mistakes many people make when beginning to learn management skills is skipping any consideration of their managerial mindset and springing immediately into learning and action.

One of the main problems with this approach is that, like your colleagues outside the legal community, you may have bought into popular myths and misconceptions about management and leadership. These can be obstacles to your learning and development. In fact, without the right mindset, your management efforts may be ineffectual and come across as insincere or mechanical. Plus, the right mindset will make it much easier for you to learn and use the skills and approaches described in the following sections.

The right mindset means leaving three beliefs and attitudes behind:

1. Leaders and managers are born not made.
2. Your lawyer mindset and education are all you need.
3. The Golden Rule works in managing people.

Four beliefs and attitudes should be adopted or retained:

1. Management is a necessary, high priority, daily activity.
2. Foster a desire to be a proactive people manager.
3. Utilize the right (emotional, creative, etc.) side of your brain.
4. Be curious and develop a willingness to try new ways of managing.

REFERENCES

Cain, S. (2012). Quiet: The power of introverts in a world that can't stop talking. New York: Crown.

Center for Creative Leadership. (2012, March). Are leaders born or made? Retrieved from https://www.ccl.org/wp-content/uploads/2015/02/AreLeadersBornOrMade.pdf

Dweck, C. (2016, January 13). What having a growth mindset actually means. *Harvard Business Review*. Retrieved from https://hbr.org/2016/01/what-having-a-growth-mindset-actually-means

Elowitt, A. (2012). The lawyer's guide to professional coaching: Leadership, mentoring, and effectiveness. Chicago: American Bar Association, Law Practice Management Section.

Goleman, D. (1998). *Working with emotional intelligence*. New York: Bantam Books. (See Chapter 2: Competencies of the Stars.)

Locke, C. C. (2014, March 14). Asking whether leaders are born or made is the wrong question. Retrieved from https://hbr.org/2014/03/asking-whether-leaders-are-born-or-made-is-the-wrong-question

Richard, L. (n.d.). Herding cats: The lawyer personality revealed. Retrieved from http://www.lawyerbrain.com/sites/default/files/caliper_herding_cats.pdf

Richard, L. (1993, July). The lawyer personality. *ABA Journal*. Retrieved from http://lawyerbrain.com/sites/default/files/the_lawyer_types_mbti.pdf

Richard, L. (2002). Herding cats: The lawyer personality revealed. *Altman Weil Report to Legal Management, 29*(11), 1–12. Retrieved from http://www.managingpartnerforum.org/tasks/sites/mpf/assets/image/MPF%20-%20WEBSITE%20-%20ARTICLE%20-%20Herding%20Cats%20-%20Richards1.pdf

PART II

The Champion Manager Toolkit: What Every Champion Manager Needs to Know and Do

---

Now that you have a champion manager mindset, you are ready to learn a set of skills that you can keep in your management toolbox. These tools are essential for creating the conversations, interactions, and relationships that are the foundation for a thriving legal organization.

Like most tools, they can be used wisely or poorly; and, like most tools, they take time and practice to become comfortable with and finally master. Please avoid being that person who, when holding a hammer, sees the entire world as a nail. Knowing when and where to use (and not use) the tools explained in this part of the book is a sure sign of wisdom and mastery.

4

Communication Basics

As an educated and articulate attorney, you may feel there is little need or room for improvement in your communication skills. Your legal writing is clear and your presentation skills are sound. You are easily understood. You are an effective advocate for your clients, and you have mastered the arts of argument and persuasion. So what more do you need?

As a championship-level lawyer manager, you need to raise your game by broadening your repertoire of skills. The communication skills you've relied on as a lawyer are not the same you will need as a manager. While there are certainly overlaps, there are also differences. Sometimes, as you may already know, it's a good idea to *not* think and talk like a lawyer. And though it may sound somewhat paradoxical, this holds true even when the people you are managing are also lawyers and legal professionals.

One of your top priorities as a champion manager is to create and sustain high levels of engagement and trust. The quality of your managerial conversations and working relationships will largely depend on your ability to create rapport and understand others' values, perspectives, and goals. Your firm members need to feel listened to and understood, regardless of whether you agree with them or not. The skills and tools explained in this section will make it much easier for you to do all this. They will complement— not replace—your legal communication skills and make you an even more effective lawyer.

Before diving into the skills, take a moment to answer the questions in the quick diagnostic (found here and in Appendix A) for identifying communications problems in your firm.

A Quick Diagnostic For Identifying Communications Problems In Your Firm

Check all of the following that apply:

- ❑ Meetings are too long, frequent and unproductive
- ❑ Disagreements are not resolved
- ❑ Decisions are not made in a timely manner
- ❑ Teamwork is poor
- ❑ Shared understandings and assumptions are lacking
- ❑ Requests are unclear
- ❑ Promises are not kept
- ❑ Feedback is missing, ineffective or not helpful

If you checked four or more of the above signs, chances are you and the members of your firm are locked into some very common but seldom useful patterns of communication and action. Take a moment to reflect, and then check any of the following boxes that describe how you and the members of your firm behave from time to time.

- ❑ We advocate our views.
- ❑ We minimize others' concerns.

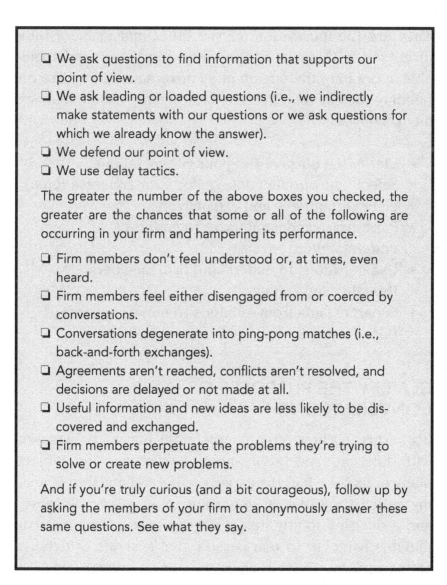

❏ We ask questions to find information that supports our point of view.
❏ We ask leading or loaded questions (i.e., we indirectly make statements with our questions or we ask questions for which we already know the answer).
❏ We defend our point of view.
❏ We use delay tactics.

The greater the number of the above boxes you checked, the greater are the chances that some or all of the following are occurring in your firm and hampering its performance.

❏ Firm members don't feel understood or, at times, even heard.
❏ Firm members feel either disengaged from or coerced by conversations.
❏ Conversations degenerate into ping-pong matches (i.e., back-and-forth exchanges).
❏ Agreements aren't reached, conflicts aren't resolved, and decisions are delayed or not made at all.
❏ Useful information and new ideas are less likely to be discovered and exchanged.
❏ Firm members perpetuate the problems they're trying to solve or create new problems.

And if you're truly curious (and a bit courageous), follow up by asking the members of your firm to anonymously answer these same questions. See what they say.

If the quick diagnostic revealed some problems in your firm, don't feel bad. These problems are common in all kinds of organizations, not just law firms. To address and mitigate these sorts of problems, you will need to learn and practice just a handful of conversational skills.

They are the foundation for the other management tools discussed in this part of the book, and they're indispensable in creating the one-on-one conversations that are the building blocks of effective relationship-based management. They are:

- Clarify the purposes of your conversations.
- Select appropriate contexts for your conversations.
- Listen attentively and expansively.
- Paraphrase and summarize to confirm understanding.
- Use questions to understand firm members' thoughts and feelings.
- Separate facts from opinions to move conversations forward.

CLARIFY THE PURPOSES OF YOUR CONVERSATIONS

It's surprising how often people enter into a conversation with different expectations about its purpose and subject. Many of us have had the experience of walking into a meeting anticipating that an important topic will be discussed and a decision jointly made, only to spend the next sixty minutes listening to one person give a series of detailed status updates. Or the experience of an annual review in which an employee wanted to talk about compensation and his or her manager only about performance.

Conversations at cross purposes waste time and at their worst can contribute to mistrust, cynicism, and disengagement. As a champion manager, you can specify a conversation's purpose, or you can simply check in with the other person or persons and ask, "What do we want [or what are we trying] to accomplish in this conversation?" Your management conversations will likely fall into one or more of the following categories:

- Action Conversations: decision-making and discussions of next steps and action items
- Possibilities Conversations: focus on brainstorming and visioning
- Information-Gathering Conversations: comprised of updates, status reports, data exchange
- Relationship-Building Conversations: include greetings, small talk, and rapport building
- Conversations about Future Conversations: plans to talk later

No one of these conversation categories is inherently better or more helpful than the others. You will need to use all of them in the course of your management duties, and it's likely that a conversation may have multiple purposes. Your goal is not to limit your conversations to a single purpose, but rather to make sure you and your firm members have a shared understanding of a conversation's purpose or purposes.

SELECT APPROPRIATE CONTEXTS FOR YOUR CONVERSATIONS

Another secret to having productive conversations is selecting the right time and place for them. Managers should determine whether it is better for a conversation to take place in a public or private setting. Distractions and interruptions can make it difficult to have a serious, thoughtful conversation in a public setting. People may also be more candid and less defensive when they can speak privately rather than in a group setting. On the other hand, public conversations can be useful in demonstrating transparency or ensuring that all members of a group have a shared understanding of a particular matter.

Attention should also be paid to when a conversation takes place. People may be fresher and better listeners during certain hours of the day, and adequate time should be allocated for a conversation depending on its complexity and importance. Starting an involved conversation when you have only ten minutes to spare is a bad idea that often results in rushing, misunderstanding, and frustration. It's better to reschedule to a time when the conversation can be completed. One partner we worked with would habitually forget about important conversations during the day and then grab people at the elevator when they were rushing to catch public transportation home. She was upset when she learned that her firm members resented her poor timing, and even more surprised to learn that many of them were using the stairs and service elevator to avoid her at day's end.

LISTEN ATTENTIVELY AND EXPANSIVELY

Listening—true attentive and effective listening—is the foundation for all communication skills and, for that matter, all management and leadership skills. It is more than merely hearing what the other person has said. It is taking in what has been said, showing that you are listening and engaged, and letting the other person know they have been heard and understood.

Remaining attentive and engaged while listening may be easier said than done because we generally think about three or four times faster than we speak. Research shows that we speak an average of 150 to 200 words per minute, yet we can understand up to 800 words per minute (Wolvin & Coakley, 1996). During this listening gap, which is the time difference between our mental ability to interpret words and the speed at which they arrive to our brains, we often tend to drift off or think about what we will say next in response. Closing this listening gap and remaining focused requires practice.

Most lawyers are already very adept at listening, since their success depends in part on their ability to listen attentively and critically to clients, opposing counsel, judges, witnesses, and colleagues. While they are generally quite skilled at listening to *what* is being said (i.e., words, facts, and ideas) and *how* it is being said (i.e., tone, volume, inflection, and tempo), many ignore or underestimate the importance of non-verbal content.

Non-verbal communication or "body language" is expressed through a person's posture, movements, expressions, and gestures. Experienced attorneys and effective managers expand their awareness to include these subtle but critical elements. A person's true underlying emotions are often more clearly revealed through their body language than their words. Managers should be aware of any mismatches between a firm member's verbal and non-verbal content. It may be a tip-off that there is a lack of clarity or trust in the conversation. And managers should also be cognizant of any mismatches between *their own* verbal and non-verbal content—they may be giving off mixed messages without intending to.

PARAPHRASE AND SUMMARIZE TO CONFIRM UNDERSTANDING

Paraphrasing and summarizing are the most powerful tools a manager can use to let people know they've been heard and understood. After a person has spoken, a champion manager can say something like:

- *I want to make sure I've fully understood what you've been saying. I believe you said . . . Did I get that right or did I miss anything?*
- *So what you're saying is . . . Did I leave anything out?*
- *I heard you say . . . Did I get that right?*

This gives the speaker a chance to correct any misunderstandings. They can confirm that the manager has indeed understood what they've said, or they may offer clarification or elaboration. The champion manager can then paraphrase and summarize as many times as is necessary until it's clear that both parties fully understand one another. When conversations are confusing, stuck, or emotionally charged, this technique is especially useful.

As useful as this technique is, some people hesitate to use it because they feel it is too time consuming and can come across as unnatural and insincere. This is certainly the case when a person dryly and mechanically repeats what they've just heard another person say. The goal is not to slavishly imitate a tape or digital voice recorder. A champion manager should instead distill and summarize what a person has said, using the speaker's key words and language whenever possible, so as to capture not only information but also the emotional valence of a conversation.

This takes practice—a manager's first efforts may sound and feel awkward, but over time a sense of authenticity and tact will emerge. This is not just a tool for champion managers: they should encourage others to paraphrase and summarize what they've said to make sure understanding is mutual.

USE QUESTIONS TO UNDERSTAND FIRM MEMBERS' THOUGHTS AND FEELINGS

Because people management depends on the quality of relationships, champion managers use questions to understand how the members of their firms are thinking, feeling, and acting. Asking the right question of the right person at the right time and in the right way can save time, build consensus, and resolve problems.

The most simple and familiar reason for asking questions is of course to gather and clarify information. Lawyers are generally quite good at asking these sorts of questions, particularly close-ended ones that call for concise answers and specific information.

- *On what day was the deed signed?*
- *Was the car registered in your name when the accident occurred?*
- *Is it wrong for us to assume that you knew the gun was loaded? Yes or no?*

Close-ended questions are useful, but there are drawbacks to using them too frequently. At times they can have the effect of directing and narrowing management conversations, and whether asked deliberately or unconsciously, they can end up limiting learning. For example:

Close-Ended	Open-Ended
Q: Will you be able to coordinate better with co-counsel in Atlanta? A: I think so.	Q: What, if anything, will you need in order to better coordinate with co-counsel in Atlanta? A: From Atlanta, we just need them to realize that there's a three-hour time difference. The much larger problem we're facing is with our electronic discovery vendor in Chicago.
Q: Did the judge moving up the date for the mandatory settlement conference prevent you from updating your research? A: Yes, we didn't have enough time.	Q: What factors contributed to your research not being updated? A: There were several: the judge moved up the date for the MSC; we had just learned about an ex parte motion in another, larger case; and our research portal was offline for two days.
Q: How many new offices do you think we will need for IP litigation personnel? A: Three spots for attorneys and three more for support personnel.	Q: How do you see the growth in our IP litigation practice affecting our space needs? A: It depends more on the size and complexity of our cases than the number of them. I can see us hiring two to five new attorneys over the next two years. One thing to keep in mind is that some of our support staff don't need to be collocated with the attorneys.

Questions should not be limited to facts and what is being said. They can also clarify what is being felt, what is being assumed, and what is most important to a speaker. They are very useful in uncovering or clarifying the emotional aspects of a conversation. For example, a manager can gain deeper understanding by saying or asking:

- *What are your thoughts (or feelings) about what I just said?*
- *I'm not sure I understand the significance of what you're saying about . . .*
- *Of all the things you've said, what is your primary concern?*
- *Please tell me more about that.*

SEPARATE FACTS FROM OPINIONS TO MOVE CONVERSATIONS FORWARD

Conversations often get stuck. People repeat and re-repeat their position, conclusion, or point of view. At times conversations resemble table tennis matches with the ball batted back and forth and back and forth *ad nauseam*. Seldom are agreements reached or anything learned from these kinds of conversations.

If we confuse our assumptions, inferences, and opinions with observable and verifiable facts, conversations can be ineffective or locked in conflict. This is a very human thing to do. We are constantly bombarded with more sensory input and data than we can perceive and process. To deal with this overload, our minds focus on some things and ignore others. This unconscious selective filtering process shapes the assessments we make and the conclusions we draw. We do this so automatically that we often confuse inferences with facts. And as a result, we blindly assume that others share our views without checking with them.

This process of moving from information to decisions and conclusions can be likened to scaling a ladder of inferences (Senge, Kleiner, Roberts, Ross, & Smith, 1999). We start with a pool of available data that we then (moving up a rung on the ladder) either consciously or tacitly filter and select. We then (moving up another rung) interpret the data by making assumptions and adding meaning. This allows us to draw conclusions (another rung) and make decisions (the top rung). (See Figure 4.1.)

The ladder of inference is a tool for reflecting on how we frame situations. It helps us retrace the steps we take from what we see and hear to our conclusions and decisions. When people disagree, they often hurl conclusions at each other from the tops of their respective ladders of inference. Playing table tennis on top of ladders makes it hard to resolve differences and learn from one another.

Figure 4.1

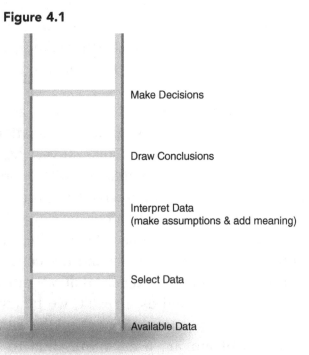

Make Decisions

Draw Conclusions

Interpret Data
(make assumptions & add meaning)

Select Data

Available Data

The goal is *not* to stop drawing inferences. If we consciously thought about each and every inference we made, we'd be virtually paralyzed, incapable of acting or deciding in a timely manner. Inferences and reasoning are indispensable processes. However, they subtly contribute to communications, teamwork, and management problems. People can and will reach different conclusions, but when they view their conclusions as obvious, they see no need to explain how they reached them.

When conversations are stuck, ineffective, or locked in conflict, the goal is to make inferences explicit and go up and down the ladder of inference *together*. As a champion manager, go through the following steps and help your firm members do the same.

- Take a moment to reflect on the inferences you're making.
- Don't underestimate the tremendous impact your emotions have on the process of selecting data and drawing inferences.
- Recount the data you selected and say how you got to your conclusions (i.e., how you went up the ladder).
- Ask others to describe how they got from the data to their conclusions (i.e., how they went up the ladder).
- Paraphrase what they have said to test your understanding.
- Ask others whether they are using different data or whether they have other ways of interpreting the data you're using.

- Work with others to ground assessments and inferences by offering and asking for specific observable examples. Ask questions like, "What did you observe that leads you to that conclusion?" "Tell me what is behind your thinking," or "What are some examples of your concern?"

In the process of going down and up the ladder of inference, try to avoid asking questions that start with "why" and instead ask questions that start with "what." "Why" questions often lead to answers about causality and conclusions, while "what" questions are more likely to lead to answers about observable facts. For example, a "why" question would lead to the following exchange:

Q: *Why don't we just try what I'm suggesting?*
A: *I doubt it will help.*

Asking a "what" question, on the other hand, would lead to the following exchange:

Q: *What about what I'm suggesting raises doubts?*
A: *I don't think last year's figures support your conclusions.*

Above all, approach this with an open mind. Assume you may be missing things others see, and seeing things others miss. Even if you don't agree with them, try to understand how others are thinking and acting. Actively seek different views and data that might change your thinking and actions. Ask questions such as:

- *What might we miss by looking at it this way?*
- *Does anyone have other thoughts or other data?*

Encourage others to challenge your views and actions and to identify possible gaps in your thinking. Ask questions like:

- *What about my view raises doubts in your mind?*
- *Do you have a different view? Tell me about it.*
- *What are your thoughts or feelings about what I'm saying?*

Some managers feel that inviting challenges and seeking different views conveys a sense of tentativeness and a lack of confidence in one's decisions. They fear asking questions like these will subtly undermine their authority. This is rarely the case and usually more a result of the manager's tone of voice and body language. Try asking each of the above five questions first with a voice and attitude of timidity and insecurity, and then with a voice and attitude of confidence and curiosity. You will see how the nonverbal communication makes a difference in how your message will be perceived.

CHAPTER SUMMARY

Legal communication skills are different than management communication skills. As a championship-level lawyer manager, you need to acquire other skills to complement your legal communication skills.

Take the diagnostic on page 50 to determine whether communication problems exist in your firm. If they do, to address and reduce them you need to learn and practice the following conversational skills:

- Clarify the purpose of your conversation depending on what you are trying to accomplish. This may include active conversations, possibilities conversations, information-gathering conversations, relationship-building conversations, and conversations about future conversations.
- Select appropriate contexts for your conversations. Choose the right time and place to have a conversation depending on the subject matter, complexity, and importance of the message.
- Listen attentively and expansively. Listen carefully to what others are saying and pay attention to "body language."
- Paraphrase and summarize to confirm understanding. Use the speaker's language and key words and be authentic.
- Use questions to understand firm members' thoughts and feelings. Use close-ended questions for fact gathering and open-ended questions that uncover feelings to probe deeper.
- Separate facts from opinions to move conversations forward. Our selective filtering process shapes assessments we make and conclusions we draw. Remember the ladder of inference in decision making. Use it to ask "what" questions rather than "why" questions.

REFERENCES

Senge, P., Kleiner, A., Roberts, C., Ross, R., & Smith, B. (1999). *The fifth discipline fieldbook*. London: Nicholas Brealey.

Wolvin, A. D., & Coakley, C. G. (1996). *Listening* (5th ed.). Boston, MA: McGraw Hill.

5

Hiring and Onboarding

HIRING

Championship-level management starts with hiring the right people and not "rushing to hire" to fill an open position. Often the perceived urgent need to find a replacement for a departing employee can result in superficial recruiting efforts and a too-quick hire. The best approach is for you to slow down the process and assess the situation with fresh eyes.

Whenever an opening arises, you should create an accurate updated job description for the position. If, for example, you need to replace a long-time legal secretary, start with a review of the essential job duties he or she performs.

- Can other employees assume any of those duties?
- Are there job duties you would like the position to take on instead?

- Should you perhaps consider hiring a hybrid para-legal/legal secretary who can better support the needs of your clients?

Reach out for recruiting to the right people and places. Decide whether you are going to advertise in your local legal newspaper, through a professional or industry association, on LinkedIn, with other online job boards, and/or use a recruiter.

Take adequate time to review resumes and look for red flags such as gaps in employment or frequent job changes that are not due to career advancement. Supplement the resume that is submitted by having the applicants complete an employment application. When you compare the information contained on the resume and employment application, discrepancies between the two often surface. Pre-screen candidates by telephone and only bring in those candidates for face-to-face interviews that best meet the qualifications for the position. Your firm culture and size will dictate who participates in the interview process.

One boutique law firm with a strong team culture invites every employee to interview potential new hires. Prospective attorneys are interviewed not only by the firm's attorneys but also by the receptionist, legal secretaries, office manager, and all other support staff. The same people participate in the interview process when support staff is being hired. The firm has low turnover and a strong esprit de corps because there is buy-in from the outset and everyone has a vested interest in seeing that new employees are successful at the firm.

Large law firms have recruiting and development professionals to shepherd the hiring and onboarding process.

The same hiring best practices they use can be incorporated into smaller law firms as well. For example, many large firms now incorporate some format of structured panel behavioral questioning for their in-house interviews as it helps eliminate unconscious bias and is a better predictor of future job performance than simply interviewing off the resume and/or interviewing for "fit."

The large Midwest office of international business firm Bryan Cave has moved to a hybrid in-house interview process that utilizes a 45-minute structured behavioral panel session along with several typical 30-minute interviews. According to Jennifer Guirl, Legal Recruiting Senior Manager, the panel consists of four interviewers, including at least one partner, a combination of associates and counsel from the recruiting committee, and a recruiting administrator. Each interviewer is assigned a series of behavioral questions and follow-up questions that focus on identifying four competencies the firm has identified as consistent among successful attorneys—work ethic, resiliency, team work, and positive attitude. Each candidate is asked the same series of questions, including such questions as:

- Describe a significant project idea you initiated. How did you know it was needed? Was it used? How did it work?
- Give us an example of a time when you made an error or mistake. What happened? What was the outcome? What did you learn from the situation?
- When in a team/group committee setting, how often are you asked to be the leader? Why? Were your outcomes successful? If not, why and what did you learn from it?

- What are the three top factors you would attribute to your success?

However, follow-up questions can vary based on candidate responses, leading to a more conversational platform. Interviewers score candidates on each competency, resulting in an overall composite score. The firm found that this format provided candidates with equal opportunity to demonstrate and be evaluated on the same qualifications, resulting in increased objectivity. Interviewers at the firm also felt the format yielded more authentic answers from respondents.

Any firm that is interested in using behavioral interviews should ensure that people get training on utilizing the format and that all candidates are informed in advance that the firm uses them. For more information about how to develop your own behavioral interviews, there are consulting firms such as Lawyer Metrics that specialize in creating evidence-based systems for selecting, recruiting, developing, retaining, and promoting top talent and have relevant articles posted on their website.

During the in-person interview, always ask relevant, probing, open-ended questions. A boutique employment lawyer, Karen Gabler of LightGabler in Camarillo, California, suggests these as examples of general questions to ask:

1. What is your preferred style of leadership/ supervision?
2. Tell me about your most difficult client. How do you handle him or her?
3. What was your best hire? Worst hire? Why?
4. What is your proudest achievement on a personal level? Professional level?

5. How would your boss get your very best effort out of you?
6. Tell me about the worst business decision you ever made.

Ask questions that seek responses that indicate whether the candidate will fit into your culture, such as these (adapted from Bouton, 2015):

1. In what kind of culture do you thrive?
2. What values are you drawn to and how would they be expressed in your ideal workplace?
3. Based on what you have seen so far, how would you describe our firm culture?
4. What best practices would you bring with you from your previous employment? How would you attempt to implement these best practices in our environment?
5. Tell me about a time when you worked with or for a law firm or other company where you felt you were not a strong fit for the culture. Why was it a bad fit?

Millennials currently represent a large percentage of today's work force. In order to understand what motivates them in the workplace, consider asking a few of these questions (adapted from Rooy, 2015) when you interview them:

1. If you are in a meeting with a senior firm leader that is running long and you receive an important phone call that you have been expecting, what would you do? Would you handle it differently if it were a personal call rather than a business call? If so, why?
2. Tell me about a time you failed and why you consider it a failure.

3. Give me an example of a situation in which you worked in a diverse group with different opinions.
4. Give me an example of a time you were passed up for an award or promotion you felt you deserved and why you felt you deserved it.

When conducting an interview, remember to give the applicant ample time to talk and spend the majority of your time during the interview listening. (See Chapter 4 for tips on how to listen.) Avoid the tendency to "sell" the firm by monopolizing the interview with what you are looking for and why your firm is a great place to work. The purpose of the interview is to learn what you can about the applicant, particularly whether that person is likely to meet the qualifications for the position and fit into your firm culture. A reasonable ratio is to speak 25 percent of the time and allow the candidate to speak 75 percent of the time.

Law firm attorneys often ask candidates for associate positions to provide a writing sample. The problem with writing samples is that you never really know how much of the document was written by the candidate and how much of it was edited or written by someone else. A better way to ascertain suitability for the position is to create a test for the position that gauges interest in the position as well as skills. For example, give a candidate for an associate attorney position a homework research assignment that is relevant to your practice. You will quickly learn who is truly interested by the amount of effort that goes into the assignment (or whether the candidate even bothers to complete it). In some jurisdictions, depending on local wage and hour laws, you may need to pay candidates for the time devoted to preparing the assignment. Firms can and should also test an applicant's skill and sophistication in using technology.

At Schiff Hardin, which has over 300 attorneys, their summer associate candidates are asked to complete a writing exercise during callback interviews. They are given a short document that sets out a legal issue and are asked to summarize it in a few paragraphs for a specific audience. Their exercises are based on real-world cases. Their website (Schiff Hardin, LLP, n.d.) describes the process: "We may give you a court order and ask you to summarize it for a potential client affected by the ruling. We provide an hour to complete the exercise. What are we looking for? Organized thoughts, clear and accurate writing, and a responsive tone appropriate for the identified audience. We are not—we promise—testing your knowledge of any particular area of the law, or your familiarity with Bluebook form."

Candidates for support staff positions should be given skills tests as part of the interview process. If you are hiring a legal secretary, test the applicant's proficiency in keyboarding and using relevant software applications such as Word, Excel, PowerPoint, and document management systems. Ask candidates questions specific to their practice areas. If your opening is for a litigation legal secretary, ask candidates about filing procedures in the local courts in which your firm practices. Just because someone has worked in another law firm does not mean that she or he possesses the necessary skills to succeed in your law firm. Make sure that your skill tests are job specific and consider testing technological competence for law clerks and attorneys as part of their hiring process.

When narrowing down candidates to finalists, completing a background check and conducting other due diligence are crucial. Where you are located will determine the type of background information you can legally obtain. People are not always who they seem to be. Reference checks provide helpful information if you contact the right people, ask the right questions, listen, and learn to interpret pregnant pauses and deflections. If your candidate for office manager provides the names of associates and staff who worked with him or her at a prior employer as references, but does not provide the name of the managing partner or other partners to whom he or she reported, consider that a red flag. In all likelihood, your candidate is trying to hide something and that something could be as significant as being terminated for embezzlement.

ONBOARDING

When people management and leadership are ignored or avoided, turnover is often the result. Assuming the perfect, smart, highly motivated first year associate is hired by your firm to fill an opening (let's call her "Nancy"), how is the orientation and training of Nancy handled by the firm? Consider the following questions.

- Is a senior associate or junior partner assigned in advance as a mentor for Nancy with a clear understanding of what that role entails?
- Is there a welcome lunch on her first or second day at the firm?
- Is she introduced to her secretary with an explanation of the responsibilities her secretary will and will NOT assume for her?

- Is there a one-firm mentality where all employees are on the same team?
- Does the firm administrator or other manager walk her through how to enter her time into the billing system, how to use document management software, and other relevant firm procedures?
- Is her first legal assignment given to her in person by her supervisor with an explanation of the task required and the deadline?
- Are follow-up status meetings held between Nancy and her supervisor to see how she is coming along with the assignment?
- Are substantive training and opportunities for her to obtain MCLE credit provided?
- Is she encouraged to reach out to her mentor and are regular meetings with her mentor scheduled to assist in Nancy's orientation?
- Or is she shown to her office and left there to figure it all out on her own with all communications sent to her by email?

If the latter resembles what happens to new attorneys in your firm, you should not be surprised if Nancy does not succeed, and either voluntarily leaves or is asked to find another job after a year or so with your firm. Very few newly hired employees thrive in a sink-or-swim environment, even bright young attorneys. Six months or a year later, you do not want to discover that most of Nancy's time is being written off and senior attorneys will not delegate work to her, so she is sitting in her office with nothing substantive to do without understanding why.

Thoughtful onboarding is just as important for newly hired support staff. Because someone has prior relevant experience as a paralegal or legal secretary does not mean that he or she will immediately understand how things are done at your firm. Orientation and training are as necessary for support staff as they are for attorneys regardless of the size of the firm. The following steps are very helpful:

- You should assign a mentor to every new employee to assist them in learning the rules, regulations, and procedures of your firm.
- Prior to becoming a mentor to others, the mentor should be trained on how to be a mentor and understand their role in the onboarding process.
- A welcome breakfast or lunch will make the new employee feel like a member of the firm and ease the transition.
- Document procedures and provide orientation training on docket/calendar control, how to perform conflict checks, use of checklists, telephone procedures, email procedures, document creation, records management, use of specific firm software, client relations, and the like.
- Provide each new employee with an up-to-date job description against which his or her performance will be measured.
- In addition, distribute and go over the firm's Employee Handbook during orientation and provide detailed information about the firm's employee benefits and its rules and regulations. You may want to divide the discussion of the

Employee Handbook into two meetings—the first during orientation to go over benefits and legalities and the second during week two after the new employee has had a chance to settle in to discuss firm culture and other aspects of the firm mentioned in the Employee Handbook.

If you take adequate time to recruit, hire, orient, and train your new employees, you will have a better chance of retaining them and reducing expensive turnover costs. The cost of turnover can easily reach 150 percent of the individual's compensation or more when you factor in such costs as:

- Lost productivity
- Lost investment in training
- The cost of a temporary or contract employee to cover the position until a replacement is hired
- Overtime if work is distributed to existing staff employees
- Severance and benefits
- Lost knowledge and skills
- Cost of position postings
- Recruiting agency fees that could equal 15 percent to 25 percent of annual base compensation
- Interview expenses
- Background checks
- Relocation expenses
- Cost of orientation and training

Additionally, we should not overlook the impact on firm morale, which is harder to quantify.

CHAPTER SUMMARY

Hiring is a process that should not be rushed. When an opening occurs:

- Update the job description, taking into consideration the current essential job duties for the position.
- Use it to match a candidate's skills with the job's requirements.
- Review both resumes and job applications carefully and watch out for red flags.
- Involve relevant people in interviewing candidates and strive to be inclusionary in the process.
- Tailor interview questions for the position and applicant pool.
- Include open-ended probing questions as well as those that indicate whether a candidate will fit into your culture.
- Be an active listener during the interview.
- Use skills tests for lawyers and staff positions.
- Conduct both background and reference checks.

Thoughtful onboarding is equally as important as taking enough time for the hiring process. The first impression a new employee gets on his or her first day at your firm forms the foundation for whether the employee will fit into the culture and be successful at your firm. Orientations for attorneys and staff should include the following:

- Assign a mentor with a clear understanding of the mentor's role.
- Have a welcome lunch with relevant members of the team with whom the new employee will be working.

- Provide adequate one-on-one training on software and firm procedures.
- Provide work assignments that are clear about the scope and timing of the project.

Have status meetings to check in on how the new employee is progressing. Onboarding is a process and will not be complete the first week of employment; integrating into a new firm and becoming part of its culture may take up to six months.

REFERENCES

Bouton, K. (2015, July 20). Recruiting for cultural fit. *Harvard Business Review*. Retrieved from www.hbr.org

Rooy, D. V. (2015, May 20). 12 interview questions you should always ask Millennials. *Inc*. Retrieved from www.inc.com

Schiff Hardin, LLP. (n.d.). Retrieved from http://www.schiffhardin.com/

RESOURCE

rose, j. j. (Ed.). (2009). *Effectively staffing your law firm*. Chicago, IL: ABA Solo, Small Firm and General Practice Division.

6

Delegating and Assigning Work

MANAGERS BENEFIT WHEN THEY DELEGATE

Almost every day, lawyers ask themselves, "How much time can I spend on billable client-related work, and how much time do I have left to devote to non-billable activities like client development and administration?" When lawyers become managers, this problem becomes more frequent, complicated, and difficult. When lawyer managers delegate, everyone benefits—their firms, the people they delegate to, their clients, and, of course, themselves. Delegation offers managers the opportunity to better use their available time and energy by focusing on their most important and profitable tasks. Having others take care of mundane tasks frees a manager to take care of more challenging and fulfilling matters. When done skillfully, it also reduces managers' feelings of stress, overwhelm, and burnout.

In spite of its many benefits, some lawyer managers struggle with delegation because it goes against the grain of their personalities and training. Studies have shown that when compared to the general population, lawyers have a tendency to be more autonomous, introverted, defensive, controlling, skeptical, cynical, judgmental, analytical, risk averse, impatient, and pessimistic (Richard, 2002, 2013). While many of these personality traits can be useful in protecting clients' interests, some of them may inhibit a lawyer's ability to fully and effectively delegate.

A lawyer manager who is risk averse, impatient, controlling, and autonomous will, for example, be more likely to hold onto work and do it him- or herself. When faced with an opportunity to delegate a task, these managers may say to themselves, "It will take too long to give it to someone else," "I can do if faster myself," or "This is so important only I should do it." Even when these assumptions are accurate, there may still be compelling reasons for them to delegate to others. A recent study of thousands of law firms found that median partners earned 20 percent more when they delegated to associates, and top lawyers could earn at least 50 percent more. The study also showed that these returns have increased substantially over time as new technologies such as email, word processing software, and online legal research have made delegation easier and less time-consuming (Hubbard, 2016).

HOW TO BECOME AN EFFECTIVE DELEGATOR

To overcome a limiting, non-delegation mindset, a manager needs to learn what to delegate, to whom it should be delegated, and how it should be delegated. Effective delegation is a learnable skill, and, as is true of all skills, mastering it takes some practice. There are four steps managers should take in delegating work. Each step can be summarized in a simple question that managers should ask themselves as they go through the process of delegating.

1. What work can and should be delegated?
2. To whom should the work be delegated?
3. How should the work be initially delegated?
4. How should the work be managed after the initial delegation?

1. What Work Can and Should Be Delegated?

The first step in effective delegation is knowing what work *can* be delegated and what work *should* be delegated. These are not always the same thing. For example, a manager may want to handle a highly sensitive and confidential firm matter rather than assigning it to another person, or an important client may insist that a firm manager do their work even though another lawyer is just as qualified and capable. These circumstances are exceptions to the general rule that managers should *not* spend time performing tasks that more junior lawyers, paralegals, or staff could perform just as well and at significantly lower costs. In most law practices, these situations infrequently occur and should not be used by managers or lawyers as a pretense for indulging and perpetuating their habit of not delegating.

Confidentiality concerns and billing rate differentials should not be the sole criteria for delegating work. It is still necessary for managers to determine whether it is safe and appropriate to delegate a specific task. A useful way to assess each item of work is to look at it terms of its complexity and importance.

IMPORTANCE		
	LOW	HIGH
COMPLEXITY **HIGH**	Break down into simple components and delegate to others. *A development and mentoring opportunity.*	Do it yourself. But if there are components that are simple and/or less important, delegate those.
LOW	Delegate it. If it is very simple and routine, see if you can automate or eliminate it.	Delegate and closely supervise. *A development and mentoring opportunity.*

- Low importance and low complexity. Since someone else can usually handle these items, they
  should definitely be delegated. They are rarely the
  best or highest use of a manager's time. Routine
  legal and administrative matters such as the preparation of IOLTA or receivables aging reports fall
  into this category. If a capable person cannot be
  found within a firm to handle these kinds of items,
  it may make sense to use an outside vendor (such
  as a COO for hire, bookkeeper, human resources
  administrator, or law librarian) to handle them.
- Low importance but high complexity. Many managers are understandably hesitant to delegate matters
  that are complex even when they are of low importance. They often procrastinate until these matters
  become urgent. As a result, they often end up doing
  the work themselves with the added pressure of
  much tighter time constraints. A better short-term
  approach is to see if some aspects of these matters
  can be broken down into simple tasks that can be

delegated to others. That leaves the manager with the few remaining items that no one else is capable of handling. A wise long-term approach is to mentor and develop others in the firm so that they can handle more complex tasks.

- High importance but low complexity. The high importance of some matters deters managers from delegating even when the work is relatively simple. This is unfortunate because these are the sorts of matters that are perfect for delegation if adequate supervision and mentoring is given. The delegation of these sorts of tasks is critical to the long-term professional development of both attorneys and staff, and consequently to the long-term viability of a firm.

- High importance and high complexity. When stakes are high and issues complicated, it is often a wise decision not to delegate. At the same time, there may be opportunities for delegation that are not readily apparent. A task of high importance and complexity may have components that are relatively simple, less important, and capable of being safely delegated to attorneys and staff if adequate supervision and mentoring are provided.

This method of assessing work and deciding to delegate is not a foolproof tool. It can be misused, especially when managers are not cognizant of their own issues relating to delegation. A highly stressed, perfectionist lawyer manager may, for example, consider almost all matters to be highly important and complex, thus justifying their refusal to delegate.

2. To Whom Should Work Be Delegated?

It is hard to answer the question of what work should be delegated without also considering to whom the delegation should be made. As a general guideline, managers and lawyers should delegate work to the available associate, paralegal, or staff member with the lowest billing rate who is competent to do the work. In practice, applying this broad rule can be tricky. Discerning a delegatee's competence can be challenging, and it is seldom a simple black and white matter. At times there will be Catch-22 moments when a manager recognizes a delegatee's lack of abilities only after work has been given to him or her. To minimize these situations, managers should ideally be familiar with the level of skill and experience of each person in their office. They should hire qualified people and provide them with adequate training and resources. The delegation of work to them should be seen as an integral part of their continuing professional development and an investment in the firm's future.

Managers should also consider other factors when deciding to whom work will be delegated. For example, they may assign work to a certain lawyer or staff member to stretch their capabilities or build their management or leadership skill set. In these situations, managers should be prepared to invest extra time offering guidance and resources to the delegatee. In other circumstances, they may decide that a particular firm member is the best person to gain expertise and experience in a given area, even though another, less expensive, professional in the firm could also do the work.

3. How Should the Work Be Initially Delegated?

The old adage "well begun is half done" is especially appropriate when it comes to delegation. When care is taken at the initial stages of delegation, confusion is minimized and most problems avoided. Extra time and attention spent when first delegating assure higher quality work product, as well as smoother coordination. The following guidelines for delegation save everyone time, energy, and angst.

- Delegate as early as possible. Procrastination reduces the amount of time available for the completion of a task and puts unnecessary pressure on both the manager and delegatee.
- Instructions to a delegatee should be clear, concise, and complete. Written instructions can be useful in tracking a project and providing a delegatee with a record of expectations, timelines, and milestones.
- Be as specific as possible with regard to due dates and timelines. "Friday at 10:00 am" is a much clearer and more workable deadline than "sometime towards the end of the week."
- If work is lengthy or complicated, then break it down into phases and create a timeline for each phase of the project. For example: "Your research should be completed by the 20th; provide an initial draft memo of your recommendations by the 23rd; we'll review it together on the 24th; the final draft should be given to me on or before the 28th; we'll review it on the 30th; and we'll jointly present it at the partners' meeting on the 1st."

- Avoid unnecessary work by being clear about expectations regarding the desired end product. Should the delegatee prepare an email, a memo, a rough draft, or a finished product? Is a written report necessary or will a conversation suffice? Doing superfluous tasks delays the completion of projects, and often leads to writing off a portion of the delegatee's billable time.
- If the delegatee's time is billable, provide them with a sense of how many hours it should take them to complete the project. This not only reinforces deadlines but also motivates them to work more efficiently.
- Provide delegatees with some context: let them know how their contribution fits into the larger picture. This will focus and expedite their work and is an important teaching tool. It is also an excellent way to motivate and develop firm members.
- Delegatees work more efficiently when they are provided with the resources they will need. Unless it has developmental value, there's no point in having delegatees reinvent the wheel. Pertinent information, references, and examples of similar work should be shared.
- For complex projects, be clear about what decisions delegatees can make on their own, which they need to get approval for, and which they can communicate after decisions have been made.
- Help delegatees understand whom they may contact for further information and assistance. This is particularly important for tasks involving contact with clients and people outside of a law office.

- Check to make sure that delegatees understand instructions and expectations. Encourage them to ask questions even if everything seems clear. Have them paraphrase and summarize what you've said. Ask them to describe how they will proceed and where they think they may need further guidance.

The above guidelines are summarized in Appendix B.

4. How Should the Work Be Managed after the Initial Delegation?

A manager's responsibilities seldom end with the initial delegation. Only the simplest of matters require a hand-off with no further communication between manager and delegatee. There are several ways managers should collaborate with their delegatees.

- Establish a written or electronic system for tracking and reviewing tasks and projects that have been delegated. Indicate to whom the work has been delegated and what the timeline is for its completion. This minimizes the chances of work being late, overlooked, or delegated twice to different people.
- During the initial delegation of a project, set check-in dates to monitor a delegatee's progress. Check-ins keep work on schedule and on budget, and also give delegatees an opportunity to ask questions.
- Provide delegatees with timely feedback throughout the course of a project. Feedback early in the process will help delegatees focus their efforts and avoid tangents and false starts. (A detailed discussion of how to give feedback appears in the following chapter.)

- As part of their feedback, let delegatees see the final work product (or the work due at the end of the phase of a project) so they can see how their efforts contributed to the overall results. This allows them to see, for example, how their research memorandum contributed to the adoption of a new office technology platform or selection of a new professional liability carrier.
- At the end of a project, thank delegatees and provide them with meaningful feedback. Let them know what they did well and how they can do even better in the future. Ask them what they have learned from doing the project and what they still have questions about. Be curious about their perspective and find out if anything in the delegation process could be changed to help them do a better or faster job. For larger and more complex projects, it's often useful to conduct a group debrief to discuss lessons learned and best practices discovered or refined.

The above guidelines are summarized in Appendix C.

When lawyers do work a more junior person in their office could do, they reduce their office's profitability. Delegation helps lawyers focus on higher-value work, which in turn makes them more valuable to their firm and their clients. Delegating to competent firm members with lower billing rates reduces legal bills, which of course pleases clients.

Effective delegation is the key to creating a profitable, high-performance law firm. When delegation is done consistently and well, a culture of teamwork emerges where everyone appreciates that they must collaborate with one another to deliver the highest possible client service. Mistakes are minimized when work is delegated—either down, up, or sideways—to the right person, and it is a relief for lawyers to know that they have capable people around to cover for them when they are sick, on vacation, or otherwise unavailable.

BE A CHAMPION MANAGER— NOT A MICROMANAGER

For effective delegation, the most important thing is not something managers and lawyers should do, but rather something they should *avoid* doing. Managers need to resist the urge to routinely micromanage or take work back once it has been delegated. Doing so inhibits a delegatee's professional growth and damages their morale. The line between micromanaging and helping a delegatee work through difficulties can be a fuzzy one, and it is particularly fuzzy for those lawyer managers who are fearful, perfectionist, or controlling.

Many lawyers and managers struggle with the delegation of tasks, preferring to do them themselves. They believe that no one can do the task as well or as quickly as they can. Some also see only one right way to do the task—their way. When they're compelled to assign work and delegate tasks, rather than giving their delegatees clear instructions and then focusing on end results, they stay overly involved—monitoring, assessing, and directing every step their delegatees take. They closely observe or control the details of their delegatees' work, often dictating that a job must be done in a certain manner, regardless of whether it's the best way to get it done. They may also discourage delegatees from making their own decisions, preferring instead that decisions be run by them or made by them. This management style wastes time and energy, frustrates employees, and contributes to an atmosphere of stress and mistrust.

Reluctance to delegate and let subordinates make decisions are just two forms of micromanagement. Many micromanagers also pay an excessive amount of attention to the most minute and trivial details of a project. They often drive their subordinates crazy by focusing on tiny and relatively insignificant details, constantly suggesting corrections or "improvements." When they do find a mistake, they may take back the work rather than helping their subordinates learn from it. Their hyper-attention to detail and need for control often leads them to insist upon unnecessary and overly detailed reports, as well as an excessive number of check-ins, progress reports, and status meetings.

Signs of Micromanagement

Are you a micromanager? Check any of the following boxes if they describe your behaviors or attitudes.

❑ Refusal or reluctance to delegate
❑ Constant monitoring and directing of a subordinate's work
❑ Excessive attention to minute details
❑ Insistence upon too-detailed reports and too-frequent check-ins
❑ Reluctance to allow subordinates to make decisions
❑ Taking back work once it has been delegated

If you're curious whether other people see you as a micromanager, ask them to anonymously assess you using the same six boxes.

WHY DO SOME LAWYER MANAGERS MICROMANAGE?

Many of the concerns that micromanagers have—such as getting things done right, paying attention to details, and providing direction and guidance—are necessary and beneficial parts of management. But in a micromanager's hands, these concerns grow to unwieldy and dysfunctional proportions. Micromanagers lose sight of the big picture and the long term as their guidance and direction degenerate into complete control. Their concerns take on such extreme importance that other considerations, such as employee development and cost-effectiveness, are neglected.

What causes people in general, and lawyers in particular, to become micromanagers? There are usually several reasons contributing to their micromanaging behavior. Some of these reasons may be internal and emotional, while others may be external or environmental. Often both are at play when lawyers micromanage. Regardless of the source, lawyer managers often remain unaware of their micromanaging, let alone its underlying causes.

As mentioned previously, when compared to the general population, lawyers demonstrate a greater tendency to be autonomous, introverted, defensive, controlling, skeptical, cynical, judgmental, analytical, risk averse, impatient, and pessimistic (Richard, n.d., 1993, 2002). Although no studies have been conducted that definitively show that lawyers micromanage more than others, the prevalence of several of these personality traits suggests that lawyers are more prone to do so. Fear, anxiety, and emotional insecurity can exacerbate these personality traits and micromanaging behaviors; unresolved family of origin issues such as dysfunctional parent-child relationships have been cited as psychological causes for micromanaging in all people. In some cases, perfectionism (discussed later in this chapter) may drive a lawyer to micromanage; in rare cases, more serious psychological problems such as obsessive-compulsive disorder may play a role.

Micromanaging is not always the result of deep-seated emotional issues. For many lawyers, micromanaging simply seems normal and familiar. It was the way they were managed, and they in turn imitate and perpetuate it without giving much thought as to whether there are better ways of delegating, collaborating, and supervising. In some firms where micromanaging is the commonly accepted style of working with others, lawyers may find themselves adapting to and copying that style without even realizing it.

Micromanaging is a matter of degree, and there are certain circumstances that will exacerbate a manager's otherwise slight propensities to micromanage. The fear and anxiety that occurs when a lawyer knows their position in a firm or relationship with a client is threatened may trigger an increased impulse to micromanage. Extremely stressful, unstable, and volatile situations may also boost a lawyer's need to micromanage and feel in control of the few things that appear to remain within their influence. Even relatively commonplace experiences such as time, performance, and financial pressures can heighten the urge to micromanage.

Micromanagement does not always occur outside of a person's awareness; some people micromanage selectively and consciously. A manager may, for example, feel the need to tightly manage a firm member who is relatively inexperienced or has performed poorly in the past. Frequent check-ins and intense scrutiny may be needed to help him or her develop to acceptable levels. At some point, however, a more healthy and productive style of delegation should emerge and the manager should be able to step back and be less involved in every aspect of the subordinate's work. Managing becomes micromanaging when the manager remains overly involved well after the point where a subordinate should either be working independently or dismissed.

Not all micromanaging is well-intentioned. A few managers will micromanage simply to bully and assert their power over subordinates. Others may set overly detailed and unreachable standards for their subordinates as a way of showing their technical superiority or as a pretense for terminating them. And still others may rely on micromanaging as a way to keep subordinates dependent and prevent them from developing into peers and competitors.

THE EFFECTS OF MICROMANAGING ON EMPLOYEES AND THE WORKPLACE

Even when lawyers are well-intentioned, their micromanaging behaviors have negative effects on productivity and morale. Micromanagement slows down workflow; it is not the best use of a manager's time, or for that matter, anybody's time. Projects are frequently delayed by a micromanager's excessive attention to trivial details, insistence upon too frequent check-ins and reports, and reluctance to allow subordinates to make decisions.

Micromanagers can become "choke points," and the delays they cause often result in late nights and last minute "fire drills" to get work completed before a critical deadline. Even when projects are completed on time, they are far more likely to be over budget. The superfluous work and meetings that micromanagers demand add hours to legal bills that are often written off because clients feel they are excessive.

Micromanaging limits subordinates' opportunities to learn, develop, and make decisions. This extends to both substantive legal expertise as well as interpersonal and practice management skills. With fewer opportunities to develop, subordinates are conditioned to rely more on their (micro)managers. Though this may satisfy micromanagers' emotional needs, it can also become a steady drain on their time and energy, creating a vicious cycle that hurts everyone's productivity.

Micromanaging also has a pernicious effect on individual and firm morale. Micromanaged employees almost always assume that their managers don't trust their abilities. Some of these employees begin to doubt their own abilities and become timid and passive. Their self-esteem and productivity falter as they become increasingly tentative and unable to think independently and make decisions. Other employees grow resentful and disaffected when working for micromanagers. They may be openly hostile, referring to their bosses as "control freaks," or they may passively resist their efforts to micromanage by avoiding contact and begrudgingly doing the bare minimum required of them. Either way, their performance is likely to be poor and they are at greater risk for leaving. With these dynamics in play, it is extraordinarily difficult for managers to build high-performing teams.

HOW TO STOP MICROMANAGING

Relatively few micromanagers readily accept that description of their management style—they prefer to think of themselves as aggressive, highly organized, rigorous, or detail-oriented managers. The above discussion provides ample information to help lawyers decide whether those more positive sounding labels are hiding the fact that they are actually micromanaging. If they acknowledge that they are and want to change, then their next question undoubtedly is, "How can I stop micromanaging?"

Micromanagement is a habit, and like all habits it can be changed with a combination of awareness, support, and practice. Self-reflection is often the best way to begin making this change. Though not necessarily easy, it is very helpful for lawyers to get curious and better understand why, how, and when they micromanage. When they learn what situations and emotions trigger their need to micromanage, they usually become better at handling them. They also begin to develop a sense of when they're micromanaging and when they're not.

That distinction—good management versus micromanagement—can be a very difficult one for all managers to make. Rather than going it alone and relying solely on self-assessment, champion managers can invite feedback from their superiors, peers, subordinates, and, when applicable, human resources managers or directors. Many managers hesitate to do this, feeling it is admitting a weakness or flaw. They worry that they will lose control over their subordinates if they appear vulnerable and ask for feedback. In reality, most employees are already painfully aware of their boss's micromanaging and are only too happy and relieved to help them work on changing it.

Simply asking, "Are there things I do that you would characterize as micromanaging?" can open the door to productive conversations about how to improve delegation, collaboration, and accountability. The delegation steps described earlier in this chapter can be used as an initial framework for such discussions. These conversations can be the starting point for rebuilding trust in firms and improving morale: employees will feel heard and become more engaged and productive, while bosses will devote their time to larger and more important matters once they feel less harried and overwhelmed.

It is unrealistic to expect that lawyers can change their micromanaging habits overnight. To cease micromanaging, they must learn how to effectively delegate and consistently practice those skills. Even with sustained practice, it is predictable that these lawyers will have a tendency to revert back to old micromanaging habits when they are experiencing greater stress. Support from peers, superiors, and subordinates can be very helpful; coaches can be of great benefit to managers and lawyers in making and sustaining these kinds of changes. When managers and lawyers find it impossible to let go of micromanaging and sense that there are deep psychological roots to this issue, they should not hesitate to seek the services of a qualified therapist or counselor. (This topic is covered in greater detail in Chapter 25, "Managing for Wellness.")

From Your Employees' Perspective— How to Work with a Micromanaging Boss

You may be a manager who currently has a micromanaging boss or has had one in the past. In either case, you may all too well know that working for a micromanager can be a very challenging and frustrating experience. As your confidence and motivation wanes, you may get to the point where you feel you have no other option but to either resist your bosses' micromanaging or confront them to get them to stop it. A word of advice: neither approach is usually productive.

Telling a superior that he or she is overly controlling is a poor approach unless they are one of the few that is receptive to such feedback. Most micromanagers discount such feedback as the mistaken point of view of a defensive and ill-informed subordinate. Micromanagers often see an employee's independence, resistance, or defiance as proof that they need to be managed even more closely. With either approach, micromanagement problems end up being exacerbated rather than ameliorated.

The better strategy is for subordinates to become more skilled at managing up. There are several things they can do to help their bosses become less controlling when delegating and managing. Subordinates should be familiar with the four steps of effective delegation mentioned in this chapter. When a manager skips one of the steps—for example, stating a clear deadline or providing necessary context, information, and resources—the subordinate should be proactive and make sure that step is covered and the delegation is clear, concise, and complete. Paraphrasing and summarizing to a manager what has just been delegated often goes far in building the level of confidence and trust that is needed to minimize the controlling and micromanaging behaviors.

When check-ins and milestones are established at the beginning of a project, managers may be less likely to constantly look over a subordinate's shoulder. Even when check-ins haven't been established, subordinates should be proactive and provide regular and detailed updates so their managers will be aware that progress is being made. This goes far in reducing managers' fears that work is not on schedule.

Anything a subordinate can do to increase a micromanaging boss's trust and confidence is helpful. Excellent performance is of course the best way of achieving this. Subordinates should also get to know their bosses' unique fears and motivations. If, for example, a boss is especially anxious about missing filing deadlines, a subordinate can make sure that work is done early and repeatedly assure him or her that the filing deadline is in sight. Or if a particular client has a reputation for closely reading all documents, a subordinate can comment on this to the manager and make sure that all work product going to that client is grammatically correct and error free.

WHEN MICROMANAGERS ARE PERFECTIONISTS

Many micromanagers are also perfectionists who believe that anything less than flawless work product is unacceptable. They can be the most exacting and difficult of micromanagers. They set high and sometimes unrealistic standards for themselves and often insist on the same level of performance from those with whom they work. They are also often reluctant to delegate for fear that others will not meet and maintain their own high standards.

When perfectionists do delegate, they can be extremely difficult to work with. Their fear of flaws can cause them to review and re-review reports' work, creating unnecessary delays and frustration. Reports often feel even their best efforts will never be appreciated and considered good enough. As a result, morale and employee retention suffer.

Perfectionism should not be confused with a healthy desire for excellence both in oneself and in others. Those who strive for excellence rather than perfection maintain a sense of proportion and regard mistakes (both theirs and others) as valuable opportunities for learning and improvement. Perfectionists, on the other hand, believe that working hard, paying scrupulous attention to detail, and being flawless are the only ways they can be safe, beyond reproach, and approved of by others. For them, the desire to excel is the same as the desire to be perfect, and a lack of perfection is something to be condemned and concealed.

As difficult as it can be for your subordinates and clients if you're a perfectionist manager, you may be suffering even more. The emotional drives and dilemmas perfectionists experience create a tremendous amount of stress and inner conflict. Many perfectionist managers are workaholics, whose longer hours and higher levels of stress end up causing them exhaustion and burnout. Perfectionism can also be a risk factor for a host of psychological problems such as substance abuse, clinical depression, social anxieties and phobias, eating disorders, body dysmorphic disorder, and obsessive-compulsive personality disorder.

Am I a Perfectionist?

If you suspect you're a perfectionist or have been told you're one, consider how many items on the following list describe your behaviors and attitudes.

- ❏ I have very high standards.
- ❏ I obsess over trivial mistakes.
- ❏ I procrastinate or put off work until I can do it right.
- ❏ I feel anxious about potential errors and failures.
- ❏ I take criticism and feedback personally.
- ❏ I tend to think in all-or-nothing or black-and-white terms.
- ❏ I overestimate the importance and desirability of flawless work product.
- ❏ When I make mistakes—no matter how inconsequential—I can be unforgivingly self-critical.
- ❏ I see minor mistakes as a sign of personal failure and inadequacy, both in myself and in others.
- ❏ Once I take on a task or set a goal, I'm all in and will not stop until I accomplish it.
- ❏ I'm a people pleaser who avoids conflicts and can be overly deferential.

The more boxes you've checked, the more likely you're a perfectionist, especially if the frequency and degree of those behaviors is high. Becoming aware of your perfectionist tendencies is the first step in becoming less of a perfectionist and micromanager. Qualified professional coaches and therapists can be very helpful in the process of changing deeply held beliefs that lie beneath perfectionist behaviors and attitudes.

Psychologists generally agree that perfectionism stems from unresolved family of origin issues, such as being raised by a highly critical parent. Many psychologists consider all perfectionism dysfunctional, while others believe some forms can be adaptive. When perfectionism merely drives a person to improve their performance in athletics, science, the arts, or professional practice, it can be seen as adaptive and positive. But when perfectionists set wholly unrealistic expectations, believe they will be valued only if they are perfect, or consider any shortcoming (no matter how trivial) to be a complete failure, their attitudes are plainly dysfunctional and damaging—not only to themselves, but also to their reports and firms.

CHAPTER SUMMARY

Delegation is essential to the smooth and profitable functioning of law offices. It offers managers the opportunity to better use their available time and energy by focusing on their most important and profitable tasks. In spite of its many benefits, some lawyer managers struggle with delegation because it goes against the grain of their personalities and training. Managers should ask themselves four questions as they go through the process of delegating.

1. **What work can and should be delegated?** A useful way to assess each item of work is to look at it terms of its complexity and importance. The confidentiality and sensitivity of a matter should also be considered.

2. **To whom should the work be delegated?** Managers should generally delegate work to the available associate, paralegal, or staff member with the lowest billing rate who is competent to do the work; however, they may want to delegate to a particular person to improve their abilities or introduce them to a new skill or area of expertise.

3. **How should the work be initially delegated?** Managers should follow the 11 guidelines on pages 85–87.

4. **How should the work be managed after the initial delegation?** A manager's responsibilities seldom end with the initial delegation. Only the simplest of matters require a hand-off with no further communication between manager and delegatee.

Managers should resist the urge to micromanage or take work back once it has been delegated. Reluctance to delegate and let subordinates make decisions are just two forms of micromanagement. Many micromanagers also pay an excessive amount of attention to the most minute and trivial details of a project. Concerns such as getting things done right, paying attention to details, and providing direction and guidance are necessary and beneficial parts of management, but in a micromanager's hands, these concerns grow to unwieldy and dysfunctional proportions.

Micromanaging has several negative effects on employees and firms:

- Micromanagers can become "choke points," and the delays they cause often result in late nights and last minute "fire drills."

- Micromanaging limits subordinates' opportunities to learn, grow, and make decisions.
- Micromanaging hurts individual and firm morale.

Many micromanagers are also perfectionists who believe that anything less than flawless work product is unacceptable. They set high and unrealistic standards, and can be the most exacting and difficult of micromanagers. Perfectionism should not be confused with a healthy desire for excellence: those who strive for excellence rather than perfection maintain a sense of proportion and regard mistakes (both theirs and others) as valuable opportunities for learning and improvement.

Portions of this chapter appeared in *The California Guide to Growing and Managing a Law Office* (The State Bar of California, 2012).

REFERENCES

Hubbard, T. N. (2016, November 12). Research: Delegating more can increase your earnings. Retrieved from https://hbr.org/2016/08/research-delegating-more-can-increase-your-earnings

Richard, L. (n.d.). Herding cats: The lawyer personality revealed. Retrieved from http://www.lawyerbrain.com/sites/default/files/caliper_herding_cats.pdf

Richard, L. (1993, July). The lawyer personality. *ABA Journal.* Retrieved from http://lawyerbrain.com/sites/default/files/the_lawyer_types_mbti.pdf

Richard, L. (2002). Herding cats: The lawyer personality revealed. *Altman Weil Report to Legal Management, 29*(11), 1–12. Retrieved from http://www.managingpartnerforum.org/tasks/sites/mpf/assets/image/MPF%20-%20WEBSITE%20-%20ARTICLE%20-%20Herding%20Cats%20-%20Richards1.pdf

Richard, L. (2013, February 11). The lawyer personality: Why lawyers are skeptical [Web log post]. Retrieved from http://www.lawyer brainblog.com/2013/02/the-lawyer-personality-why-lawyers-are -skeptical/

State Bar of California. (2012). *The California guide to growing and managing a law office.* San Francisco, CA: Author.

7

Giving and Receiving Feedback

Skillfully delivered feedback is a powerful tool for improving the performance and morale of law firm employees. It gives them the opportunity to learn, improve, and stretch to their full potential. It solves problems, develops skills and careers, increases collaboration and teamwork, improves profitability, and gets better results for clients. It's also an opportunity for managers to build trust and learn from their employees. In spite of these many benefits, managers—in all kinds of organizations—routinely resist giving feedback. In fact, 63 percent of surveyed executives feel that their managers' lack of courage and ability to have difficult feedback conversations is the biggest challenge to company-wide effective performance management (World at Work and Sibson Consulting, 2010).

Why then, if feedback is so important and great, do one in four employees in the United States feel their performance reviews don't help improve their performance (Kong, 2015)? And why do only 47 percent of survey respondents feel their performance reviews were a fair and accurate representation of their performance (Kelton, 2013)? Employees' discomfort with performance reviews and receiving feedback is not difficult to understand. In a sense, we're wired to expect bad news. Studies have shown that people generally respond more strongly to negative events than positive ones (Gottman, 1994), and that employees react to negative interactions with their bosses six times more strongly than they react to positive interactions (Zenger & Folkman, 2013). When people hear they will be receiving feedback, they often automatically assume it will be negative and critical before considering that it might just as well be positive and laudatory. One of a lawyer manager's first challenges in delivering feedback is working with and through a firm member's resistance, defensiveness, skepticism, and, at times, hostility.

It may surprise many employees to learn that their managers also find feedback conversations to be stressful and difficult. Positive messages are, of course, easier for managers to deliver than negative ones, but even when managers see problems with an employee's performance that need addressing, many of them avoid or defer feedback conversations. They often find themselves in a dilemma in these sorts of situations.

Giving an employee critical feedback may end up hurting the employee's feelings, leaving the problem and working relationship in worse shape than before. The employee's performance may actually get worse in response to the feedback. In these situations, managers may ask themselves whether the problem is so bad that it's worth saying anything at all. At those times, it may be safer (and at times wiser) to simply avoid giving feedback and hope that the problem will take care of itself through benign neglect, an employee's growth or departure, or someone else's intervention.

Not giving an employee feedback can leave working relationships unharmed, but it runs the very real risk of perpetuating or exacerbating underlying problems. As these problems persist or worsen, they may become far more difficult to address and resolve. These managers may avoid immediate conflicts and strained relationships only to discover that they've traded them for worse ones in the future.

Faced with these unattractive alternatives, many managers don't know exactly what they should say and how they should say it. More often than not they try to resolve this dilemma by giving feedback in a manner that addresses problems, but minimizes the risks of defensiveness, hurt feelings, and heightened conflict.

NEGATIVE FEEDBACK DOESN'T HAVE TO BE DESTRUCTIVE FEEDBACK

Destructive feedback shouldn't be confused with negative feedback. There will always be times when a lawyer manager must give a firm member negative feedback about their performance; there may be mistakes to correct, improvements to be made, or problems to be solved. Because it may be more difficult for a firm member to receive negative feedback, his or her manager should exercise care and skill in its delivery. In those situations, it's important for managers to demonstrate an intention to help employees grow rather than to show they are mistaken or at fault. The feedback should increase, not drain, the employee's motivation and resources for change.

Feelings Are Triggered When Receiving Feedback

Champion managers know that their employees will undoubtedly have an emotional reaction to the feedback they are hearing, and that their reactions may prevent them from understanding the feedback and fully engaging in the conversation. Studies have shown that there are three kinds of triggers to these reactions:

- Truth triggers are set off by the content of the feedback itself. Employees feel it's inaccurate, unfair, unhelpful, outdated, or incomplete. Even though they may not express their reactions to their manager, they will tend to reject, defend, or dismiss the feedback.
- Relationship triggers are set off by something about the manager who is giving the feedback. How an employee reacts depends on how they feel treated by the manager and their assessment of the manager's intelligence, expertise, credibility, trustworthiness, and motives.
- Identity triggers are all about an employee's sense of who they are and what the future holds for them. Regardless of whether the content is accurate or their relationship with their manager is good, old feelings of inadequacy, despair, shame, or overwhelm resurface.

By knowing their employees and understanding what is likely to trigger them, champion managers can craft their feedback conversations so they remain productive in the presence of these very real and normal reactions (Stone & Heen, 2014).

Managers are human: at some point an employee's attitude or behavior will frustrate or anger them. While it's healthy for managers to experience those emotions, they must take care in how they express them. Feedback conversations are a poor place for managers to unload their anger and express their frustrations. Doing so decreases rather than increases the chances of a firm member understanding the feedback, learning anything, and changing their behavior. Instead they are likely to feel defensive, powerless, and angry as well.

Yelling, name-calling, and using profanity are some of the more easily recognized forms of abusive behavior and destructive feedback. Other, subtler forms, such as reprimanding, shaming, and scolding, should also be avoided. They engender fear and hostility, ruining both working relationships and performance.

If critical or negative feedback is to be given, it should be of the employee's work product or behavior, not of the person. Calling someone marginally literate is far more hurtful and counterproductive than telling him or her that the grammar in a memo they drafted is confusing and needs fixing, and calling someone lazy is not as helpful as exploring the reasons why they aren't as productive as their fellow firm members. Attributing an error or failure to someone's intelligence, personality, gender, ethnicity, or other innate quality is likewise indefensible and may give rise to hostile workplace or employment discrimination claims.

When champion managers get angry (you thought because they're champions they don't feel anger?), they know it is best to take a moment (or several) to calm down, connect with their anger, let it subside, refocus on the desired results of the conversation, and think about how to best deliver the negative feedback. It's also helpful if they remember what Aristotle (n.d.) once said:

> Anybody can become angry—that is easy—but to be angry with the right person, and to the right degree, and at the right time, and for the right

purpose, and in the right way—that is not within everybody's power and is not easy.

CONSTRUCTIVE FEEDBACK

Negative and critical feedback need not be destructive feedback. Even the toughest messages can be delivered in a constructive manner. In fact, those are the messages that are most in need of skillful delivery. Constructive approaches are:

- Timely,
- Specific,
- Supportive (Positive), and
- Future Oriented.

Timely. Feedback works best when given soon after a problem occurs or a task or project is completed. Frequent feedback conversations are a better alternative than waiting for annual or semi-annual performance reviews. Waiting too long can lead to unproductive conversations where there are differing recollections about what actually occurred. Waiting leaves problems unaddressed and is likely to cause the problem to recur when it could have been addressed the first time that it happened.

Feedback does not need to be instantaneous. It is important to find the right time and place to give an employee feedback. Pay attention to where you are delivering feedback. Giving employees critical feedback in a public space may embarrass them and increase their defensiveness. But praising them and giving them positive feedback in a public space can be an opportunity to show appreciation and recognition.

Specific. Lawyers, particularly employment lawyers, appreciate the importance of clearly documenting problems and describing an employee's behavior in specific terms. In addition to this, it's helpful for managers to explain the impact of those behaviors on other members of the firm. Blanket condemnations and vague generalizations about a firm member's performance—such as, "He chokes during negotiations," or, "She's too easily intimidated by opposing counsel"—provide little useful information and are certain to increase defensiveness. For example, telling an associate he's chronically late is an assessment he can choose to either acknowledge or dispute. It's far more powerful for a manager to provide him with a list of the days he was late, the amount of time he was late, and the consequences of his lateness for his fellow employees and the firm's clients.

Supportive. Firm members generally feel punished, angry, and defensive when their managers only provide negative feedback or attribute problems to innate qualities like a firm member's intelligence or personality. Champion managers recognize that feedback works best when firm members feel that their manager understands them and has a sincere interest in their improvement and well being. Champion managers also know how supportive they should be: though tact, empathy, and compassion are important in creating a supportive tone, managers must at the same time guard against diluting, bypassing, or sugarcoating a message to such a degree that firm members don't understand the importance of a situation or problem.

Future Oriented. Reviewing and acknowledging past problems is great for figuring out what's gone wrong, but stopping there results in incomplete and ineffective feedback. Champion managers focus on the future, work with their employees to develop positive solutions, and suggest ways for them to improve. When managers offer no hope for change or suggestions for improvements, employees typically feel demoralized and confused. This easily leads to feelings of disengagement and worse rather than better performance.

		DELIVERY	
		CONSTRUCTIVE	DESTRUCTIVE
CONTENT	POSITIVE	Recognizing Appreciating Praising Explaining positive impact	Minimizing Using sarcasm Left-handed complimenting Overpraising trivial efforts
	NEGATIVE	Focused on work product Focused on specific behavior Descriptive and fact-based Future oriented	Reprimanding Scolding Berating Shaming Abusing Yelling Name-calling

BEYOND THE CONSTRUCTIVE APPROACH

Champion managers learn to think outside the box—at least the above box (see table) of constructive and destructive feedback. They realize that other approaches to feedback exist. Like all managers, lawyers approach feedback conversations with certain assumptions—both explicit and tacit—about the purposes, logistics, roles, and "etiquette" of the conversation. By looking at and shifting those assumptions (especially the tacit ones), champion managers develop a more effective way of giving feedback.

Most feedback conversations—even when handled skillfully in a constructive manner—share the following three core assumptions:

1. The overall purpose of the conversation is to get the employee to see things accurately and do what the manager wants.
2. Managers feel they have most of the responsibility for the conversation. As a result, they believe they should do most of the speaking and directing, while the employee should do most of the listening, accepting, and receiving.
3. Managers feel their point of view is the most legitimate one for the situation, and by inference, the employee's is not.

A manager's belief that he or she has the sole "right" answer may hold true in simple situations, but a single correct answer seldom exists in complex situations where there are unknown facts and multiple tradeoffs, dilemmas, or legitimate interpretations of events. Champion managers move from assuming things are black and white to acknowledging that there are multiple perspectives and many shades of gray.

Even when a manager does see a problem correctly, unintended consequences can arise when they become overly attached to being right and having the sole legitimate viewpoint. When they "know" with absolute certainty that they have the right take on an employee's problem, they're less likely to inquire deeply and be open to changing their point of view. If a manager even asks questions, they're liable to be unconsciously framed to support the manager's existing point of view. When a manager participates with this attitude, employees often feel that they're not being heard and become defensive and cynical. And when an employee indicates (verbally or non-verbally) that he or she disagrees, the manager (not doubting his or her own point of view) may interpret these messages as evidence that the employee is resistant to changing, can't learn, is stupid, doesn't care, or is clueless. With these core beliefs working in the background, managers have limited chances of learning anything new, even when they're perfectly delivering constructive feedback.

A CHAMPION MANAGER'S COLLABORATIVE APPROACH TO FEEDBACK

The first step champion managers take in developing a truly collaborative approach is reflecting and becoming aware of their own general beliefs and assumptions about feedback. Some will be useful, others not. As their awareness grows, champion managers become less attached to and reliant upon their old mindset. They begin to see feedback conversations in a different light; new options for giving feedback (summarized in the table) become possible.

For example, rather than taking the customary manager role of omniscient authority or diplomatic teacher, champion managers will instead collaborate with an employee to explore the entire situation rather than focusing solely on the employee's perceived problems. To accomplish this, it's important for champion managers to move from *automatically* thinking that their employee is ignorant,

Assumptions & Attributes	Constructive Feedback	Collaborative Feedback
Timely and specific?	Yes	Yes
The "gap" between employer's expectations and employee's behavior is seen as:	A management or behavior modification problem in need of resolution.	An opportunity for individual and collective learning that can result in improved performance for all.
The manager's goal is to:	Get the employee to see his or her error and change.	Figure out how the problems arose in the first place and who and what contributed to them.
The truth lies with: (Who is "right"?)	Manager.	Could be the manager, employee, both of them, or neither of them.
The employee is seen as:	Someone who is ignorant, confused, misinformed, and/or in need of correction and improvement.	One person in an entire system, who may have a valid point of view, and may be acting correctly given their understanding.
Manager's approach is that of:	A tactful, supportive, and sensitive teacher.	A genuinely curious and interested collaborator.
Who will learn from the feedback?	Employee will learn what the manager thinks or wants.	Both manager and employee will learn what happened and how to prevent recurrences.
Solutions and understandings are:	Driven by manager.	Mutually developed.
Conversation and feedback are:	Largely directed by manager to employee.	Reciprocal and mutual.
Conflict and discomfort are:	Alleviated, by-passed, or sugar-coated.	Acknowledged and productively engaged.
Employee likely feels:	Receptive, a bit defensive, hopeful, and better informed about his or her weaknesses and how to improve.	Involved, energized, and better informed about how his or her behavior can improve the firm's overall performance.

misinformed, or in need of correction to a mindset where they hold their point of view lightly, staying open to changing it when new information and points of view are encountered.

When champion managers drop the notion that they are holders of the single truth of the situation, they become less concerned about figuring out clever and kind ways to help their employee see it the "right" way. As champion managers practice a collaborative approach, they learn to rely less on diplomacy and tact, and more on candor and curiosity. Differing opinions and accounts don't magically disappear, but they can be explored with less defensiveness and polarization. Conflicts and discomfort still arise, but they are more likely to be productively dealt with, rather than bypassed or sugar coated.

With a collaborative approach to feedback, employees become less defensive and more active. They feel less need for avoiding responsibility, protecting themselves, or justifying and excusing their actions. They become partners with their champion manager in solving a problem and learning how things can be done better in the future.

RETURNING TO THE BIG PICTURE

With this new collaborative mindset, champion managers are ready to look at the big picture and explore an entire situation—not just their employees' behaviors that they may initially see as a problem. Unburdened by sole responsibility for directing feedback conversations, they can more easily and attentively listen to their employees. With their employees' input, they can consider whether there are external factors (e.g., unclear instructions, inconsistent guidelines, or conflicting priorities) that are contributing to the problem. Because they are more directly impacted by such factors, a manager's employees often have an earlier and greater sense of office-wide problems. Collaborative feedback lets champion managers tap their employees' expertise and enlist them in addressing larger and emerging problems. What's more, their employees gain a keener sense of how improving their individual performance will contribute to the performance of the entire firm.

With its different set of core assumptions, collaborative feedback is a powerful tool for improving employee morale and retention. It is also a valuable, though often overlooked, way of demonstrating and reinforcing a firm's values. In an environment where there is increasing competition for finding and retaining quality employees, collaborative feedback provides firms with a tangible advantage. Like any new skill, learning a collaborative approach to feedback requires practice, but the time and energy invested lead to a more profitable and energized law office environment.

Annual Performance Reviews

Many employees cringe at the idea of performance reviews, and many managers—both inside and outside of law firms—see them as a necessary burden and occasional annoyance. At the same time, one of the most common complaints employees have about their managers is that they don't receive regular constructive feedback.

Employees perform better and have higher morale when they understand not only what is expected of them, but also whether they are meeting or surpassing those expectations. Waiting for yearly reviews can leave them uncertain and confused; without frequent feedback, they are left to assume they're doing okay if they don't hear complaints or get fired. This may be an acceptable policy if a firm's goal is to have employees with "good enough" performance, but it will undercut any efforts to encourage excellence. Worse still, it may send employees unintended messages that improvement is not necessary and their development is not a priority. It is much easier to help employees change or unlearn their behaviors when they haven't been "practicing" them for the twelve months between annual reviews.

Annual or semiannual performance reviews are not a substitute for timely feedback. It is not surprising that many large organizations have done away with them completely as a tool for talent development (Cappelli & Tavis, 2016).

CHAPTER SUMMARY

Feedback can be a potent tool for improving performance and morale if skillfully delivered. It creates an opportunity for managers to build trust and learn from their employees.

Critical feedback need not be destructive if delivered in a way that demonstrates an intention to help employees grow rather than just show they are mistaken or at fault. Feedback conversations should not be used for managers to express anger or frustration. Criticism should focus on the employee's work product or behavior, and not be about the person.

Critical feedback can be constructive by being:

- Timely—offer it soon after a problem occurs or a task or project is completed;

- Specific—provide concrete examples of problems;
- Supportive—use tact, empathy, and compassion but don't sugarcoat a message; and
- Future oriented—focus on positive solutions and ways to improve.

A champion manager uses a collaborative approach to feedback to explore the entire situation rather than focusing solely on the employee's perceived problems. Using a collaborative approach enables managers to rely less on diplomacy and tact and more on candor and curiosity. Employees become partners with their managers in solving problems and learning how things can be done better in the future.

The collaborative mindset enables champion managers to look at the big picture and not just see their employees' behaviors as a problem. They can more easily and attentively listen to their employees, tap into their employees' expertise to address issues, and give their employees a better sense of how individual performance improvement will contribute to overall performance of the firm.

Portions of this chapter first appeared in "Best Practices: Employee Feedback" in the August 2005 edition of *The Bottom Line*, Volume 26, No. 4.

REFERENCES

Aristotle. (n.d.). Aristotle quotes. Retrieved from https://www
.brainyquote.com/quotes/quotes/a/aristotle132211.html

Cappelli, P., & Tavis, A. (2016, October). The performance management revolution. *Harvard Business Review*, *94*(10), 58–67.

Gottman, J. M. (1994). *What predicts divorce? The relationship between marital processes and marital outcomes*. Hove, United Kingdom: Psychology Press.

Kelton. (2013). The Cornerstone OnDemand 2013 U.S. Employee
    Report. Retrieved from https://www.cornerstoneondemand.com
    /sites/default/files/research/csod-rs-cornerstone-kelton-2013
    -employee-survey-results.pdf
Kong, C. (2015, November 23). The real reasons why employees hate
    the performance review. Retrieved from https://www.roberthalf
    .com/officeteam/blog/the-real-reasons-why-employees-hate-the
    -performance-review
Stone, D., & Heen, S. (2014). *Thanks for the feedback: The science and
    art of receiving feedback well (even when it is off base, unfair, poorly
    delivered, and frankly, you're not in the mood)*. New York, NY: Viking.
World at Work & Sibson Consulting. (2010, October). 2010 Study on
    the state of performance management. Retrieved from https://www
    .worldatwork.org/waw/adimLink?id=44473
Zenger, J., & Folkman, J. (2013, March 15). The ideal praise-to-criticism
    ratio. Retrieved from https://hbr.org/2013/03/the-ideal-praise
    -to-criticism

8

Coaching and Mentoring

Champion managers are dedicated to the professional development of their staff and attorneys. They understand that their firm members' knowledge, experience, and skills are valuable assets, and it makes good business sense to invest time, money, and energy in improving them. They know that coaching and mentoring will not only improve a firm member's performance but also engagement and morale. Champion managers don't limit the development of their attorneys and staff to proficiency in matters of procedure and substantive law; they also focus on business development, management, collaboration, technology, and wellness and resilience skills.

Instructional programs and materials have traditionally been the core of professional development activities. They generally offer valuable advice on matters of substantive law, practice skills, and the use of technology. Ample numbers of books, articles, and webinars are available, and online and face-to-face trainings and workshops help firm

members learn how to fully utilize new practice management software and tools. When teaching or simple advice
is sufficient, coaching and mentoring may not be needed.

But an instructional approach doesn't work particularly
well when firm members need to develop and use the kind
of relationship-based skills needed for business development, leadership, and collaboration. Management and professional development would in some respects be simpler
if an instructional approach was all that was needed—just
have smart people read or listen to good content, and professional development is taken care of. But cognitive intelligence and academic performance, though important, are
not the most reliable predictors of lawyer effectiveness and
success.[1] As comprehensive and accurate as information
provided in instructional-based professional development
programs may be, it still leaves firm members with the challenge of putting into practice what they've learned. They
run smack into the "knowing–doing gap"—they know *what*
they should do but not *how* to actually do it. As a result,
they may struggle when it comes to figuring out first steps,
improvising, sustaining momentum or figuring out what to
do when things don't go exactly according to plan. Wellness programs, for example, can offer sound advice on how
to manage stress and build resilience, but they may not be
able to change deeply engrained attitudes and habits that

---

1. Marjorie M. Shultz and Sheldon Zedeck (2011) of the University of California have
found that several noncognitive intelligence factors show a stronger correlation with
lawyer effectiveness than law school admission criteria such as undergraduate grade
point average and LSAT scores. Personality traits, interpersonal and communication
skills, emotional intelligence, practical judgment, and creativity were all found to be better predictors of career performance.

contribute to a firm member's stress and unhealthy life-style. Coaching and mentoring can help firm members over those kinds of gaps.

Champion managers use the feedback and delegation tools described in the previous two chapters to help firm members improve their performance. The *best* champion managers realize that these tools are far more powerful and effective when they are used in the context of a coordinated and integrated plan for performance improvement and career development. Rather than giving firm members isolated bits of feedback and advice, they take a broader and longer-term perspective so they can create a plan that identifies and addresses the most important areas for a firm member's continuing development.

Champion managers also realize that coaching and mentoring are much more than assessing a firm member's strengths and weakness, identifying what they need to do and change, and then telling them to go ahead and do it. That kind of purely directive and prescriptive approach may be appealing, but it only works for relatively simple and discrete matters; for more complex and nuanced matters, coaching is needed. Consider the plight of a lawyer who is told he or she needs to improve their client relationship skills. A simple admonition would probably leave the lawyer wondering what the problem is and what they should do. A directive and prescriptive approach, such as being given a to-do list of actions items (e.g., make a roster of your clients, rank them according to importance, create a schedule for contacting them, and then call them), would tell the lawyer what to do, but would not be much help if the lawyer's core problem is, for example, extreme shyness or how he or she talks to clients on the phone. Feedback from clients could help the lawyer better understand what he or she is doing (or not doing), but it might not be sufficient to help the lawyer actually make needed changes. The more facilitative approach of coaching could help the lawyer not only identify what changes need to be made, but also what he or she needs to do to make and sustain those changes. More importantly, throughout the coaching process the lawyer could receive consistent feedback, support, and encouragement when encountering obstacles in making those changes.

DESIGNING EFFECTIVE COACHING PLANS

Champion managers work together with the firm members they're coaching (their "coachees") to design individualized coaching and development plans. Sometimes they begin by getting input from other members of the firm, such as superiors, peers, and, in some cases, the coachee's reports. Human resources and talent or professional development managers are also often a source of helpful information and insights. Coaching is less effective when managers unilaterally specify goals. When managers and coachees genuinely collaborate in the drafting of goals, coachee commitment, buy-in, and success are far more likely.

Limiting the number of goals is also helpful. If a coachee is given a large number of goals—say ten or twelve—their focus and energy will be spread thin. They will likely focus first on the easiest goals to accomplish, rather than the most important or foundational ones. Limiting a coachee's goals to three or four may require thoughtfulness and prioritization, but taking the time to do so yields better results and more significant improvements.

Care must be taken in the identification and articulation of goals. Many problems come from the way people *establish* their goals, rather than how they well or poorly they *execute* them. Firm members can be set up for underachievement or failure when the goals they're pursuing are ambiguous, unrealistic, or not their most important areas for improvement. To prevent this from happening, goals should be set deliberately, methodically, and in writing. The very act of writing goals helps crystalize a coachee's thinking and enables him or her to perceive previously overlooked opportunities for growth and development. When goals are not written, differing recollections and interpretations of them too often arise. Written goals are also easier to review, share with other people, and modify when necessary.

S.M.A.R.T. GOALS

A useful acronym for setting goals is S.M.A.R.T., which stands for Specific, Measurable, Actionable, Realistic, and Timely. The following guidelines (which can be given to coachees) explain these terms.

Specific. Often we set goals that are so loose, it's nearly impossible to judge whether we've achieved them or not. A specific goal has a much greater chance of being accomplished than a vague or general one. To be specific, state exactly what you want to achieve, how you're going to do it, and when you want to achieve it. Try "who-what-when-where-why" as a way to be specific.

A goal like, "I'll get more referral sources," is too vague. How will you know if and when you've reached your goal? As we'll see, there are many ways to be more *specific* and successful.

Measurable. Whenever possible, use concrete criteria for measuring your progress toward each goal you set. A goal doesn't do you any good if there's no way of telling whether or not you've achieved it. When you can actually measure your progress, you'll find it easier to stay motivated, keep on track, and reach your goals.

Make your goal *measurable*. Change "I'll get more referral sources," into "I'll get *six* more referral sources."

Actionable. You need to ask whether you have been clear enough in setting your goals that you can point to specific actions, tasks, or behaviors. For a goal to be actionable, you also need to be able to "buy into" it. It should be yours and not somebody else's. You need to believe in the value and purpose of the goal, the do-ability of the goal, and yourself.

Make your goal *actionable*: break it down into doable pieces by changing "I'll get six more referral sources," into "I will attend *three* networking events and find at least *two* people at each event who can become referral sources."

Realistic. You also need to ask yourself if you truly have the ability, time, expertise, and commitment to reach your goals. You can't ignore your limitations or external ones.

Make your goal *realistic*: if you recognize that your work schedule will preclude you from attending one of the three networking events you've considered attending, you can replace "I will attend three networking events and find at least two people," with "I will attend *two* networking events and find at least *three* people at each event who can be referral sources."

Time Constrained. Time lines and deadlines are another way to make goals more specific. They make it much easier to monitor our progress, and they foster a sense of urgency, which compels us to take action today and not next week.

Set a *time frame* for when you will attend the networking events: change "I will attend two networking events and find at least three people at each event who can be referral sources," into "I will attend two networking events *in the next seven weeks* and find at least three people at each event who can be referral sources."

IMPLEMENTING A COACHING PLAN

Once goals have been established, it's time to implement a coaching plan, and one of the first questions to be answered is, "Who should be the coach?" It's often assumed that an employee's manager is the best choice, but this is not always the case. If a manager lacks expertise or the time and interest to coach, another person from either within or outside of the firm will be a better choice. External coaches are useful in a number of different situations:

- When a coachee is dealing with challenges that require skills and expertise that may not be found within the firm (e.g., specific writing, leadership, technology, or stress management skills);
- When high-level professional coaching skills are needed to help a coachee overcome particularly difficult obstacles to learning or change; and
- When confidential coaching conversations are needed or preferred because a coachee will be more candid with an objective and impartial person from outside.[2]

Champion managers know that good chemistry and rapport between a coach and coachee are very important, and that experienced and successful lawyers don't always make the best coaches and mentors. There are individuals in all fields that are extremely talented, but lack the ability to coach, lead, manage, or teach others in that same field. There are Nobel Prize–winning professors who are

---

2. For a thorough discussion of how to find and select a coach, please see Chapter 7 of *The Lawyer's Guide to Professional Coaching* (Elowitt, 2012).

notoriously bad at teaching classes or leading seminars and All Star or Hall of Fame athletes who went on to have undistinguished records as coaches or managers. Conversely, some legendary sports coaches and managers were decent but not exceptional athletes when they competed. Because the skill sets for being a lawyer and a coach or mentor are different, success, longevity, and breadth of experience in the legal profession aren't guarantees that a lawyer will also be a good coach or mentor.

The most progress is made when coaching and mentoring are provided on a regular basis within the framework of a structured program. Meeting infrequently at random intervals makes it difficult for both coachee and coach to maintain focus and a sense of urgency. There is no single ideal cadence of coaching sessions that works for all situations; the frequency of coaching sessions can and should change as a coachee makes progress. At the beginning of coaching, for example, weekly sessions may be beneficial to build trust and momentum or to address a critical or urgent issue. It may then make sense to shift to a biweekly or semimonthly cadence so the coachee has time between sessions to reflect, internalize what has been learned, and try new skills or behaviors. Once a coachee is making steady progress in the right direction, monthly sessions may be more appropriate, and after coaching objectives have been met, quarterly check-ins may be all that is needed to sustain changes. Of course, if a coachee is struggling at any time or facing a new, difficult challenge, more frequent sessions can be added.

Champion managers also know that coaching doesn't take place in a vacuum. Sufficient materials and resources should be provided when they can help a coachee meet one of his or her goals. A firm member with a goal of becoming more productive and organized should, for example, be allowed, if not encouraged, to attend a class on time management. While they are being coached, firm members should also be assigned work and given feedback outside of coaching sessions that will help them improve their performance and attain their goals. A wide variety of assessments are also available to help coachees (as well as their coaches and managers) better understand their strengths, weaknesses, personality, and habitual ways of thinking or dealing with conflict. When used skillfully, these assessments accelerate a coachee's progress in making changes and reaching goals.

MENTORING

Mentoring and coaching are similar in many respects and share the common goal of enhancing firm members' knowledge, skills, performance, and satisfaction. Mentoring is also similar to coaching in that it often focuses on identifying specific goals; creating and implementing strategies for achieving them; and emphasizing action, accountability and follow-through.

Mentoring takes many forms. It can be as structured as a highly organized, multi-year program of professional development or as loose as a standing arrangement to get together once a month and talk about work while eating breakfast. Mentoring can be as narrowly focused as advice on one transaction, or as broad as helping a lawyer envision and chart an entire career path. Mentoring that is concerned with a specific issue or case may last for only a few weeks or months, while mentoring around a career or "big picture" issue may continue for several years. With the ever-increasing connectedness that technology provides, a mentor may be someone in another office, city, state, or country.

Mentors play a variety of roles within law firms and other legal organizations. They are most often called upon to share their experience and act as subject matter experts. In this way, they take the role of a more traditional consultant or teacher. When mentors are also a firm member's supervisor, they may spend a lot of their time evaluating work product, giving feedback, and explaining firm policies and professional practices. In these situations, the dividing line between mentoring and managing can be indistinct. Sometimes mentors are called upon to act more as counselors and facilitators whose main responsibilities are advising on matters of firm politics and resolving conflicts. At other times, mentors simply function as sounding boards or supportive figures for less-experienced members of a firm.

In more traditional mentoring relationships, mentors are often regarded as experts or authorities because of their greater experience. While this is understandable, it also carries the risk that mentees[3] may become overly passive and deferential in dealing with their mentors. On a tacit level, mentees may assume that their mentors not only know more about the practice of law than they do, but also

---

3. Etymologists recognize 1965 as the first use of the word "mentee" to refer to a person who is advised, trained, or counseled by a mentor. It is increasingly replacing (and still sometimes used interchangeably with) the word *protégé*, which was first used in 1787.

more about mentoring. All too often this leads to one-way conversations and relationships. In these situations, mentees are often reluctant to raise issues, be entirely candid, or ask for help out of fear of appearing ignorant or incompetent. This increases the likelihood that the mentoring process will be directed by the mentor and not meet all of mentee's needs. This "one-up" power dynamic and the problems associated with it are more pronounced when a mentor is also a mentee's manager. Champion managers minimize this risk by either finding mentors who are not a mentee's manager, or by promoting a more facilitative coaching style approach to mentoring.

By virtue of their training and professional experience, lawyers who mentor are often tempted to automatically give advice and reflexively answer mentees' questions. Giving advice and providing solutions is great in the short term and for simple problems, but it seldom helps mentees learn how to analyze and think through questions for themselves. Though they may get the answer they need to an immediate question, a mentee's learning may remain comparatively shallow. Over the long run, this can actually hinder a mentee's development and lead to overreliance on their mentor.

A facilitative approach to mentoring strives for the kind of active partnership of equals that is found in true coaching relationships. Instead of providing a ready answer or mapping out a set course of action for a mentee, a mentor taking a facilitative coaching approach will raise questions that will help their mentees to:

- Reflect on the problems confronting them;
- Consider their broader context;

- Rethink or reframe the way they're looking at the problems;
- Come up with solutions of their own; and
- Then decide which solution to act upon.

Coaching and mentoring programs are most successful when there is agreement about the objectives and details of a program, and they are aligned with a firm's actual direction, strategy, culture, and values. Haphazardly designed and implemented programs deliver unimpressive results. To avoid this, it is best practice to have a sponsor or champion to drive the process of designing, implementing, and monitoring the program.

CHAPTER SUMMARY

Coaching and mentoring can improve a firm member's performance as well as their engagement and morale. While instructional programs and materials offer valuable advice on matters of substantive law, practice skills, and the use of technology, they do not help develop the kind of relationship-based skills needed for business development, leadership, and collaboration.

Champion managers incorporate a coordinated and integrated plan for performance improvement and career development when they use feedback and delegation tools. They work together with their coachees to design individualized coaching and development plans. Champion managers first obtain input about the coachee's performance from other firm members, including superiors, peers, reports, and human resources and talent or professional development managers.

Goals for a coachee should be limited to three or four of the most important or time critical. Goals should be set deliberately, methodically, and in writing to avoid ambiguity. Remember to use S.M.A.R.T goals:

- Specific
- Measurable
- Actionable
- Realistic
- Time Constrained

When implementing a coaching plan:

- Determine who should be the coach and whether confidential coaching conversations are needed or preferred (and thus whether someone internal or external is best). Use external coaches when needed skills and expertise are not found within the firm, when high-level professional coaching skills are needed to help a coachee overcome particularly difficult obstacles, and when a coachee will be more candid with an objective and impartial person from outside or confidential conversations are preferable.
- Good chemistry and rapport between a coach and coachee are very important, so experienced, successful lawyers who lack the ability to coach, lead, or manage others do not always make the best coaches and mentors.
- Coaching and mentoring work best when provided on a regular basis within the framework of a structured program.
- Coachees should be provided with the materials and resources needed to help them succeed.

When mentoring, consider the following:

- Though similar to coaching, mentoring can be as structured as a highly organized, multi-year program of professional development or as loose as a standing arrangement to meet once a month and talk about work over breakfast.
- Given the technology, a mentor may be someone in another office, city, state or country.
- Mentors are often called upon to share their experience and act as subject matter experts. If they are also the mentee's supervisor, they may spend a lot of their time evaluating work product, giving feedback, and explaining firm policies and professional practices.
- Mentors can act as counselors and facilitators or function as sounding boards or supportive figures for less experienced firm members.
- A facilitative coaching style approach is a mentoring best practice. Mentors should resist the urge to automatically give advice and reflexively answer mentee's questions.
- Mentors should raise questions that will help their mentees to: reflect on the problems confronting them, consider their broader context, rethink or reframe the way they're looking at the problems, come up with solutions of their own, and then decide which solution to act upon.

Portions of this chapter previously appeared in Chapters 7 and 8 of *The Lawyer's Guide to Professional Coaching* (ABA, 2012).

REFERENCES

Elowitt, A. (2012). The lawyer's guide to professional coaching: Leadership, mentoring, and effectiveness. Chicago: American Bar Association, Law Practice Management Section.

Shultz, M. M., & Zedeck, S. (2011, Summer). Predicting lawyer effectiveness. *Law & Social Inquiry, 36*(3): 620–661.

9

Fostering Coordination, Collaboration, and Teamwork

In his book *Taking Your Team to the Top* (2013, p. 7), former Denver Broncos executive Ted Sundquist reminds us that "good teams incorporate teamwork into their culture, creating the building blocks for success." Teamwork and collaboration are not generally the first things lawyers think of as important to their culture. They are by nature autonomous, competitive, and protective of their turf. These traits are reinforced in law school and in the legal profession through firm compensation systems and opportunities for promotion and client development. However, in order to succeed as a manager and better service your clients, you need to learn how to champion collaboration and teamwork in your firm.

As a manager you may be called upon to supervise varying team members in a variety of situations. There may be a dedicated team (other attorneys, paralegals, and your legal secretary) who works with you daily on client matters. Depending on how your firm is structured, the members of your dedicated team may change on a client-by-client basis. If you work in a large firm, you may be a practice, client, or industry group leader or assistant leader with certain management responsibilities for your group. Each member may bring a different style and motivation to the team. Each task may require different skills. It is your job as manager to bring out the best in your team members through coordination and collaboration and to help them develop into champion managers themselves.

For example, a top priority for managers is the ability and willingness to delegate. When you delegate, it is important to match individual people's skills with specific team tasks. Take into account that team members have different strengths, skills, and outlooks, and consider where they are in their careers. If your up-and-coming Millennial associate Carol, who has an undergraduate degree in computer science from Stanford, is looking for a way to contribute to the team effort, add her to your firm's technology committee. Then, assign the initial research for a new document management system to her. Let Carol beta test several options and report back to the technology committee at its next meeting.

BUILDING TRUST

> The only way for the leader of a team to create a safe environment for his team members to be vulnerable is by stepping up and doing something

that feels unsafe and uncomfortable first. By getting naked before anyone else, by taking the risk of making himself vulnerable with no guarantee that other members of the team will respond in kind, a leader demonstrates an extraordinary level of selflessness and dedication to the team. And that gives him the right, and the confidence, to ask others to do the same.

(Lencioni, 2012)

According to Merriam-Webster's Dictionary, "trust" (n.d.) is defined as the "assured reliance on the character, ability, strength, or truth of someone or something." In order to build trust within your team and be seen as someone who is trustworthy, you need to lead by example and exhibit the following traits yourself:

1. As Lencioni suggests, exhibit a willingness to go first and be vulnerable in front of your team. Consider sharing an example of a time you were a new manager when you rushed and made a bad decision by not listening carefully to what your colleagues had to say. Tell them that you need their help and value their opinions.
2. As a team leader and manager, you should be as honest and transparent as possible so that your team understands your motives, concerns, and desired results. The more information you are willing to share, the more your team will reciprocate and be transparent with you.

3. Encourage open discussion at team meetings. As a meeting facilitator, you must allow time for everyone to speak, share information, and actively listen to one another.
4. Understand that communication goes both ways. You should give feedback, both positive and constructive, and encourage your team members to give you feedback as well.
5. Show appreciation by publicly thanking individuals for their contributions and openly give credit to others for their ideas.
6. As mentioned in Chapter 4, your working relationships with others on your team will depend on your ability to create rapport and understand others' values, perspectives, and goals.

Management guru Ken Blanchard (2010, p. 2) talks about the four elements of trust in his ABCD Trust Model:

1. Able: Showing that you have the skills and ability to competently get the job done.
2. Believable: That you are perceived as fair, that you treat people equitably, and that you can be relied upon.
3. Connected: That you focus on other people and identify their needs as well as your own.
4. Dependable: That you follow through with what you say you are going to do.

If you are unsuccessful at building trust with your team, the result is likely to be low productivity and morale, employees who show up for work but lack engagement, and eventually increased turnover.

Trust generates commitment; commitment fosters teamwork; and teamwork delivers results. When people trust their team members they not only work harder, but they work harder for the good of the team.

(Gordon, 2010)

MANAGING MEETINGS

An essential time for collaboration and coordination occurs when the lawyer manager convenes a meeting. Team meetings can be a productive resource for brainstorming and problem solving or they can deteriorate into a waste of everyone's time. Lawyers are good at spotting issues but are often more comfortable debating them than resolving them. This behavior sometimes results in analysis paralysis, particularly when it involves a committee tasked with making a decision. With adequate advance planning and following best practices in meeting management, you can use meetings as an opportunity to build team esprit de corps, resolve issues, and plan for the future.

When you contemplate scheduling a meeting, first decide if you need to hold a meeting at all. Ask yourself if a meeting is the best way to handle an issue or issues. If the information is for one-way sharing, it could be covered in a memo, email, or phone call (with perhaps a short follow-up meeting to answer questions). If team input to reach a decision is called for, then meet.

Patrick Lencioni in *Death by Meeting* (2004) divides meeting types into four categories (see Figure 9.1).

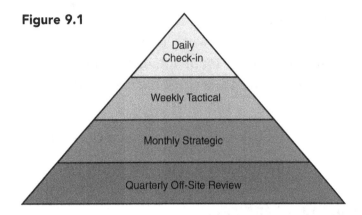

Figure 9.1

1. The Daily Check-In should be a stand-up meeting, last no more than five to ten minutes, and be used to share daily schedules and activities. This is an ideal format for a one-to-one meeting with your secretary or the new associate you are mentoring. It could also be used for a brief meeting to discuss time-sensitive matters, such as a case that's currently in trial or a deal that is scheduled to close in a week.
2. The Weekly Tactical is used to review weekly activities and resolve tactical obstacles and issues, and it lasts 45 to 90 minutes. This is a good format for calendaring and scheduling meetings to make sure no deadlines are missed. Though Lencioni suggests a meeting run time of up to 90 minutes, in a law firm 30 minutes to one hour is a more realistic timetable.
3. The Monthly Strategic is for discussion, analysis, brainstorming, and deciding upon critical issues affecting long term success. It should be limited to one or two topics and last two to four hours. This

type of meeting works best for management, practice group, or other committee meetings. Though Lencioni suggests a meeting run time of up to four hours, outside of executive committee meetings in a mid-sized or larger law firm, a more realistic timetable would be two hours.

4. The Quarterly Off-Site Review should be out of the office; last one to two days; and be used to review strategy, competitors, industry trends, key personnel, and team development. Realistically, in a law firm meetings of this type are more likely to occur on an annual basis and be used by firm management for strategic planning.

Once you decide on the purpose of the meeting, then determine what type of meeting you are going to hold. Are you meeting to brainstorm themes for a potential new website, share information about a case your team is working on, delegate tasks that have been sitting on your to-do list too long, resolve short-term problems in dealing with opposing counsel, or reach a final decision on whether to add a practice group? Understanding the meeting's purpose will assist you in framing the agenda. It will help you determine who should participate in the meeting. You should also set objectives for the meeting to help focus the agenda: "By the end of the meeting, I would like our team to . . ."

The agenda needs to include meeting objectives, topics to be covered, who will address each topic, and the time scheduled for each topic (to keep on schedule). (See Figure 9.2.) Some people better relate to graphic presentations than detailed lists. So, in addition to the written agenda, produce a visual agenda for the meeting that is used to provide

your team with the most important information about the
meeting in a single graphic image. As the meeting facilitator,
you can use the visual agenda to launch the meeting with an
at-a-glance overview of what will be covered.

Figure 9.2

New Actions

Group/Team:
Date:
Time:
Location:

Objective of Meeting:

Key Takeaways:

AGENDA

Time	Topic	Who	Method	Expected Outcome

ACTION ITEMS

Description	Assigned To	Due

© 2015 New Actions LLC

If the purpose of the meeting is to solve a problem, encourage participation by everyone involved by assigning meeting preparation in advance: "Come to the meeting prepared with one possible solution to our problem."

On the day of the meeting, it is crucial for you as facilitator to start and end the meeting on time and stick to the agenda. One of the reasons people cringe at the thought of yet another meeting is that they often start late, ramble on and on, veer off topic, and end late with no real decisions being made.

Before delving into the agenda, establish ground rules for meeting. They should include:

1. One person speaks at a time and no side conversations allowed. This is an important rule, especially in a room full of attorneys bursting with opinions. That said, the facilitator needs to know when someone has had enough time to express his or her opinion and gracefully move on to someone else.

2. All team members need to be given a chance to speak. Allow adequate time for discussion so everyone can be heard and consensus can be reached when required. If the meeting is comprised of attorneys and staff, the staff may be reticent to speak up unless they feel it is safe to do so.

3. Challenge ideas—not people. As Zig Ziglar said, "You can disagree without being disagreeable." Conflict in and of itself is not a bad thing if all sides of an issue are given an opportunity to participate and work through the issue.

4. Find someone to take meeting notes to keep track of issues raised and ideas discussed and make sure they are shared after the meeting.

5. As difficult as it may be to get people to comply, there needs to be a no smart phones rule to limit distractions.

Use a flip chart or white board to summarize important discussions and decisions. Action items should be assigned based on discussions held in the meeting, setting forth responsibilities, tasks, and deadlines. Recap before you wrap up: *What are the most important things we accomplished in our time here together? What went well and what could have been improved?* Before leaving the meeting, determine what should and should not be shared with any team member who did not attend the meeting.

Within a day or two of the meeting, a follow-up memo with action items, deadlines, and who is responsible should be distributed. The date, time, and place of a follow-up meeting should be determined and shared in the follow-up memo. Any unfinished business should be carried over to the agenda for the next meeting. It is your job as manager to follow up with your team and keep track of the status of action items and deadlines to enable you to plan the agenda for your next team meeting.

CHAPTER SUMMARY

As a manager, you are tasked with bringing out the best in your team, developing their individual skills and abilities, and building upon the skills and abilities of the team as a whole. In order to be accepted as a leader, you need to build trust within the team by exhibiting the following:

- Be vulnerable first so others will feel comfortable being vulnerable;

- Be honest and transparent;
- Encourage open discussion at meetings;
- Give feedback to others and encourage them to give you feedback;
- Show appreciation to others; and
- Understand others' values, perspective and goals.

You should follow best practices in meeting management by:

- Determine the purpose of the meeting;
- Decide what type of meeting to hold to best accomplish your goals, whether a daily check-in, weekly tactical, monthly strategic, or off-site review;
- Develop an agenda for the meeting;
- Start and end the meeting on time;
- Develop ground rules for the meeting;
- Recap results at the end of the meeting;
- Provide a follow-up memo to participants with action items, who is responsible for them, and deadlines; and
- Remember to keep track of the status of action items and deadlines to assist in planning your next meeting agenda.

REFERENCES

Blanchard, K. (2010, August 5). *Building trust*. Retrieved from www.kenblanchard.com

Gordon, J. (2010). *Soup: A recipe to nourish your team and culture*. Hoboken, NJ: Wiley.

Lencioni, P. (2004). *Death by meeting: A leadership fable—about solving the most painful problem in business*. San Francisco, CA: Jossey-Bass.

Lencioni, P. (2012). *The advantage: Why organizational health trumps everything else in business*. San Francisco: Jossey-Bass.

Sundquist, T. (2013). *Taking your team to the top: How to build and manage great teams like the pros*. New York: McGraw-Hill.

Trust. (n.d.). Merriam-Webster.com. Retrieved from https://www .merriam-webster.com/dictionary/trust

Ziglar, Z. (2016, August 8). You can disagree without being disagreeable [Advertisement]. Retrieved from www.azquotes.com

10

Managing Conflicts

Conflicts are a normal and inevitable part of everyone's work and personal lives. They exist in any situation where interdependent people have apparently incompatible ideas, needs, interests, goals, values, principles, or feelings. They can be a matter of personality conflicts, communication style differences, power struggles, or people bringing their old psychological and emotional issues into a firm's interpersonal dynamics and dysfunctions. They may find their expression in the words and actions of people, or they may remain hidden. Whether conflicts are patent or latent, developing skill and competence in handling them is useful for all people. For lawyer managers, it is imperative.

People often ignore, defer, and avoid conflicts. They may shy away from the emotional discomfort they expect they will feel or cause in others. They may see conflict as a competition and zero-sum game that they stand a chance of losing. They think of conflict in negative terms such as anger, aggression, loss, violence, disruption, and pain. They feel that talking about a conflict may end up hurting or even ending a personal or working relationship. They remain passive and tell themselves it's not really worth the risk. At times this may be a wise strategy, but at other times it may perpetuate or exacerbate an existing problem and the negative feelings connected with it. When that happens, a new risk emerges: the negative feelings may leak out or explode as a person reaches their breaking point.

Managers (and people in general) can waste a lot of time and energy avoiding inevitable conflicts. Although the temptation to ignore conflicts is a strong one, failing to resolve them can lead to significant costs. Conflicts that remain unaddressed can sap the productivity and morale of firm members. If they are not resolved, firm members may depart, leaving firms to incur the hard and soft costs of replacing them. (The cost to replace a high-performing paralegal or legal assistant, for example, is high—some estimates put it as much as 1.5 times the employee's annual salary [Allen, 2008, p. 3].) Any resources expended in the training of that firm member are lost, while productivity and revenues may suffer until a replacement is hired, trained, and gets up to speed. If conflicts are overt and appear out of control, a firm may also lose clients. In the worst cases, failure to address conflicts can eventually lead to legal actions that must be defended. Productivity, morale, and reputations may suffer as firm members are compelled to expend significant amounts of time and money to defend these claims.

In light of these many possible costs, the better approach is for managers (as well as their fellow firm members) to develop skill and competence, so they can deal with conflicts rather than avoid them. Doing so can reduce the harmful effects of conflicts, while improving interpersonal communication and building trust and stronger working relationships.

High Conflict Employees and Managers

Some people encourage and invite conflict. They habitually engage in behaviors that increase rather than reduce or resolve conflict. Often they have difficulty managing the intensity of their emotions and will have angry verbal or physical outbursts. They tend to think in black-or-white, all-or-nothing terms, and blame others for any problems (real or perceived) that may arise. These people are, of course, a considerable challenge their managers and coworkers.

A very small percentage of managers also exhibit these attitudes and behaviors. Although they may be comfortable with high levels of conflict, they typically create unproductive workplaces with low levels of trust and cooperation. Some of them rationalize a high conflict management style by saying that adversity and competition between employees brings out the best in them. There's little basis for this belief. In high conflict environments, people are understandably more likely to be defensive and self interested. While conflict should not be avoided, it should also not be indulged and exacerbated. The skills and tools described in this chapter are equally useful when dealing with high conflict individuals.

CONFLICT IN LAW FIRMS

Interpersonal conflict in law firms may be more prevalent and tougher to resolve than elsewhere. There are no conclusive data on this, but several factors may make this likely. Every working environment has its share of misunderstandings, personality clashes, and rivalries; in high pressure and high stress environments like law firms, the frequency and intensity of interpersonal conflicts is exacerbated.

Demanding schedules, constant deadlines, and an adversarial system can turn firms into veritable pressure cookers. Lawyers' tendency to be more skeptical, cynical, judgmental, introverted, defensive, pessimistic, and controlling than the general population can also make it harder to deal with and resolve conflicts (Richard, n.d., 1993).

Lawyers often respond to intra-firm conflicts in one of two ways: they may ignore them, feeling that servicing clients is their primary responsibility, and resolving conflicts is someone else's job (typically a managing partner, practice area head, or office administrator); or they may take a "lawyerly" or "legalistic" approach to resolving them. It's not surprising that lawyers will often take a legalistic approach to resolving conflicts within their firm. Because they are so acculturated and proficient in using litigation and negotiation skills to protect and defend their clients' interests, it becomes second nature and the default way they handle intra-firm disputes and conflicts. They seldom do this consciously and intentionally; it just seems to them like the best and natural way to proceed.

However well intentioned lawyers may be, unfortunate and unintended consequences occur when they rely too much on a legalistic approach to intra-firm conflicts. When they are squarely stuck in their lawyer mindset, the following are more likely to occur.

- The adversarial nature of legal practice will have subtly conditioned them to think in binary terms of win or lose, right or wrong, black or white, and all or nothing.
- As a result, they are more likely to assess blame and culpability rather than thinking about how they may have contributed to the conflict.

- In light of their legal training, they may over rely on logic and argument, and get caught up in details rather than examining broader concerns.
- They will advocate and defend their personal interests and positions. Doing so can inhibit learning and growth for both individuals and their firm.
- They will "cite precedent" as a reason for their position (i.e., "This is how we've done it before!") without questioning whether it makes sense now.
- In the best tradition of common law, they will (consciously and unconsciously) try to modify, weaken, or undercut existing policies by finding exceptions, distinctions, and qualifications. As a result, other firm members may feel the stakes in the ground seem to be constantly moving.
- In trying to "win their case," they will focus solely on the immediate conflict, rather than looking at the broader picture and the long-term strategic implications of their positions and decisions.

All this can easily result in unnecessary deadlock and delays. The goal is not to completely do away with a legalistic approach, but to give attorneys an alternate and often more useful way of dealing with their conflicts.

KINDS OF CONFLICTS IN LAW FIRMS

The potential for conflict can be found in virtually every aspect of law practice management. Some of the most common areas for conflicts are:

- The handling of a case, client, or transaction;
- Interpersonal clashes ranging from personality conflicts to bullying and harassment;

- The allocation of budget and resources such as office space or personnel;
- Partnership matters such as selection, promotion, and compensation;
- Staff management and operational matters;
- Employment decisions such as hiring, compensation, and firing of attorneys and staff;
- Reporting relationships and job responsibilities;
- The scope of decision making and supervisorial authority; and
- A firm's direction, strategy, and priorities.

It is a mistake to think of any of the above areas as purely matters for sober analysis, objective discussion, and dispassionate decision making. Emotional factors are in play in each of them. The relationship, status, and power dynamic between those involved in the conflict are usually major contributors to the emotional side of these intrafirm conflicts. Recognizing this is one of the keys to finding that best way to resolving them. Conflicts in the above nine areas can occur among people at the following levels:

- Between peers or equals, e.g., two partners who want to be the head of their practice area, two senior associates who need to use the only available conference room, or three staff members who want to take the same day off when only one can.
- Between superiors and subordinates, e.g., staff member who wants a raise and his supervising attorney who will not approve it; senior associate who has been told by her managing partner that she will not get credit for time spent training two

new hires; or office administrator and legal secretary who can't agree on a new work schedule.

- Among groups of people, e.g., two practice groups who believe their staff and paralegals should have more office space; or two partners committees who feel they should take the lead in creating the firm's new strategic plan.

Whether they want to or not, managers routinely get involved in resolving conflicts. Their decisions, policies, and actions sometimes trigger conflicts with other firm members, while at other times they may be called upon to act as a neutral and objective authority to resolve conflicts in which they have no direct interest. To help chart the best course for dealing with a conflict, champion managers start by asking themselves three questions:

1. Am I part of it? Does the conflict involve me personally or do I have a stake in it?
2. Am I being asked to resolve it? Should my role be that of a counselor, mediator, facilitator, or impartial decision maker?
3. Should somebody else resolve it? Does it make more sense for a third party inside or outside of the firm to handle this conflict?

A FRAMEWORK FOR DEALING WITH CONFLICTS

Regardless of whether they are being asked to resolve a conflict or are a party to one, champion managers need knowledge and skills to be effective. Fortunately, many of

the mindsets and skills discussed in earlier chapters provide an excellent framework for dealing with conflicts.

- See conflicts not just as problems to be solved, but
  also as opportunities to learn. Although it may be
  very difficult when enmeshed in a conflict, try to
  maintain an attitude of curiosity. Ask yourself and
  perhaps others questions like:
    - What can be learned from this situation?
    - What could have prevented this conflict from
      occurring?
    - Is this a new manifestation of an old problem?
    - How may others and how may I have contrib-
      uted to this conflict?
  If you have a point of view or desired outcome already
  in mind, try to hold it less tightly. Be willing to be influenced by what others say and do.
- Take the time to reflect, learn, and know yourself.
  Self awareness and self management can be difficult
  when we find ourselves in the midst of conflict. Prepare ahead of time by discovering your characteristic ways of responding to and handling conflict,
  as well as what your triggers and "hot buttons" are.
  (See more about this in the next section.) After you
  develop this self knowledge, you will recognize that
  other people may have very different triggers and
  responses. Knowing this can help you craft productive conversations.
- Identify who is involved and why. Other people
  may have an interest in the resolution of the conflict but are not willing to voice their views or
  participate in its resolution. And others who are a

party to the conflict may have unwittingly gotten
sucked into someone else's conflict or a related
one. Consider the plight of the office administrator of one of our clients. The heads of his firm's
litigation and real estate practices had a somewhat
antagonistic relationship and battled regularly over
what they felt were their deserved shares of firm
resources. When scheduling space in the firm's few
conference rooms, the office administrator could
seldom please both of them. Try as he might to be
fair, he was often accused of favoritism, ironically
by both sides. Be aware of differences in power
and status: did one of the parties feel they couldn't
express their views at an earlier time because they
rightly or wrongly fear punishment or reprisals?

- Utilize the communication skills described in Chapter 4. Make it a point to separate facts from feelings
  and opinions. Use paraphrasing and summarizing
  to let others know they are being listened to and
  understood. They are also great tools for slowing
  down and cooling off a heated conversation. Realize that non-verbal communication plays a huge
  role in difficult conversations and will contribute
  greatly to you being perceived as patient and
  professional.

- Shift your mindset from winning to problem solving. Few conflicts are simple black-and-white matters. Rather than assessing culpability or blame,
  look at situations in terms of everyone's contributions to them. (You may find some of your DNA
  at the crime scene if you do.) Don't over-focus on
  facts and logic at the expense of recognizing that

relationships and emotions are also in play and are perhaps driving the conflict. Difficult conversations typically have three levels to them.

- Lawyers are most comfortable with the first level, which focuses on facts and the different stories people have about what happened.
- The second level of the conversation, often playing in the background, is about the feelings triggered by and at the heart of the conversation.
- The third, also in the background, is concerned with how the conversation may threaten people's identities and self-esteem.

Progress is slow, if made at all, when people pretend the second and third levels aren't influencing their conversations.

- Find positive ways to deal with the conflict. Constructive responses to conflict typically focus on solving a problem or completing a task. Destructive responses are focused on personalities and negative emotions. (More about this on pages 161–162.) Be willing to apologize and express gratitude when appropriate. Saying "please," "thank you," and "I'm sorry" can go far in creating an atmosphere of mutual respect and trust.

CHAMPION MANAGERS CAN RESPOND TO CONFLICT IN MANY WAYS

We all have our characteristic ways of responding to and handling conflict. You can think of them as the default settings you use in most conflict situations. The Thomas-Kilmann

Conflict Mode Instrument (TKI) describes a person's behavior along two dimensions: their assertiveness (the extent to which they attempt to satisfy their own concerns) and their cooperativeness (the extent to which they attempt to satisfy the other person's concerns). The TKI identifies five basic methods or modes of dealing with conflict along these two dimensions: competing, collaborating, compromising, avoiding, and accommodating (see Figure 10.1).

Figure 10.1

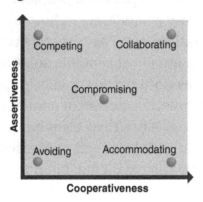

The following descriptions are adapted from Thomas and Kilmann (2015).

- **Competing** is assertive and uncooperative—an individual pursues his or her own concerns at the other person's expense. This is a power-oriented mode in which an individual uses whatever power seems appropriate to win their own position—their ability to argue, their rank, or economic sanctions. Competing means "standing up for your rights," defending a position you believe is correct, or simply trying to win.

- **Collaborating** is both assertive and cooperative—
  the complete opposite of avoiding. Collaborating
  involves an attempt to work with others to find
  some solution that fully satisfies their concerns and
  yours. It means digging into an issue to pinpoint
  the underlying needs and wants of the two individuals. Collaborating between two persons might take
  the form of exploring a disagreement to learn from
  each other's insights or trying to find a creative
  solution to an interpersonal problem.

- **Compromising** is moderate in both assertiveness
  and cooperativeness. The objective is to find some
  expedient, mutually acceptable solution that par-
  tially satisfies both parties. It falls intermediate
  between competing and accommodating. Compromising gives up more than competing but less than
  accommodating. Likewise, it addresses an issue
  more directly than avoiding, but does not explore
  it in as much depth as collaborating. In some situations, compromising might mean splitting the difference between the two positions, exchanging concessions, or seeking a quick middle-ground solution.

- **Avoiding** is unassertive and uncooperative—an
  individual neither pursues his or her own concerns
  nor those of the other individual. Thus he or she
  does not deal with the conflict. Avoiding might take
  the form of diplomatically sidestepping an issue,
  postponing an issue until a better time, or simply
  withdrawing from a threatening situation.

- **Accommodating** is unassertive and cooperative—
  the complete opposite of competing. When accommodating, an individual neglects his or her own

concerns to satisfy the concerns of the other person; there is an element of self-sacrifice in this mode. Accommodating might take the form of selfless generosity or charity, obeying another person's order when you would prefer not to, or yielding to another's point of view.

This model is a way of understanding yourself and those with whom you are in conflict. If, for example, the other person is highly competitive, you may wish to take a collaborative approach rather than going head to head. Or if they frequently avoid conflicts, you would do well to not mistake this for their cooperation. Latent conflicts are sometimes the most dangerous ones, and when they surface the impact can be quite negative.

Each mode of dealing with conflict has its strengths and its weaknesses. Overusing or underusing any one of them can be counterproductive. Knowledge of these five modes can ultimately give you more freedom and range in how you respond to and engage in conflict. To become skilled in handling conflict, champion managers not only know what are their preferred modes, but also have the ability to use any of the other modes when they are better suited for a particular conversation and conflict.

CHAMPION MANAGERS FIND CONSTRUCTIVE WAYS TO DEAL WITH CONFLICT

Champion managers realize that they can respond to conflicts with constructive or destructive behaviors. They understand that constructive behaviors tend to reduce tension and keep the conflict focused on ideas, information, and problem solving. They also recognize that destructive attitudes and behaviors that focus on personalities and negative emotions tend to make things worse and escalate conflicts (Runde & Flanagan, 2007).

	Constructive Responses to Conflict	Destructive Responses to Conflict
Active	Perspective Taking	Winning at All Costs
	Creating Solutions	Displaying Anger
	Expressing Emotions	Demeaning Others
	Reaching Out	Retaliating
Passive	Reflective Thinking	Avoiding
	Delay Responding	Yielding
	Adapting	Hiding Emotions
		Self-Criticizing

As summarized in the table above, both constructive and destructive behaviors can be either active or passive. Passivity should not be dismissed as a form of avoidance when it comes to constructive behaviors. Stopping and remaining silent for a while can be a useful way to slow down and cool off a fast-paced or heating conversation. Doing so can also allow deep thinkers and slow processors the time they need to sort through what has been said.

CHAMPION MANAGERS KNOW THEIR OWN TRIGGERS AND HOT BUTTONS

Conflicts typically begin with a precipitating event or trigger. Frustration is a normal and inevitable part of life and managing people. No matter how calm, collected, and patient you may be, you undoubtedly have some "hot buttons" that irritate you to the point where you may lose your composure and overreact. These triggers may be the situations that are most likely to lead you into conflict or behaviors that cause you to impulsively and at times destructively react without thinking.

Even though every person has their own unique set of hot buttons and triggers, the Center for Conflict Dynamics at Eckerd College has identified nine behaviors that seem to be particularly prevalent or disturbing in workplace settings. They are, in no particular order (Runde & Flanagan, 2007):

- Unreliable—when people break promises, miss deadlines or don't follow through.
- Overly Analytical—when people are perfectionists or focus excessively on trivial matters.
- Unappreciative—when people don't acknowledge the support and assistance they receive, fail to give deserved credit to others, or seldom praise good efforts and outcomes.
- Aloof—when people are condescending, unapproachable, or isolate themselves.
- Micromanaging—when people habitually interject themselves in work delegated to their reports.
- Self-centered—when people care only about themselves and believe their point of view, opinion, or conclusion is the only correct one.
- Abrasive—when people are arrogant, brusque, sarcastic, or hurtful in their language or actions.
- Untrustworthy—when people exploit others, take undeserved credit, or cannot be trusted.
- Overtly Hostile—when people lose their tempers, become angry, or yell at others.

Recognizing your particular triggers and hot buttons can be extremely helpful. Once you understand what they are and to what degree they bother you, you can develop greater control over your reactions. You can also see that your actions may unintentionally trigger other people.

USING A THIRD PARTY TO RESOLVE CONFLICTS

There are times when even champion managers can't or shouldn't take the lead in resolving a conflict. They may feel they lack sufficient emotional distance or skill to handle a difficult dispute. Or they may be so personally enmeshed in the conflict that they fear their actions will be perceived as partial and self-interested no matter how fair and objective they may be. And they may decide that some or all of the other parties to the conflict will only accept the guidance and decision of a neutral, disinterested third party. Some conflicts may involve urgent matters and need quick resolution. If delaying resolution of a conflict will lead to lost revenue or opportunities (or larger conflicts in the future), using a third party may be a very wise and timely decision.

The third party who is brought in should be someone all of the parties will trust, respect, and listen to. The choice of who to bring in depends on the nature of the conflict and its importance and urgency. Obviously, some conflicts will be too small to warrant the assistance of someone from outside the firm. For larger ones, there are professionals who are trained in conflict resolution—mediators, facilitators, and coaches—whose expertise and experience with conflicts of a similar nature can keep conversations from getting stuck. A trusted advisor or practice management consultant who knows your firm and is perceived as impartial may also be a good choice.

Before a third party is retained, his or her role should be clarified: will their services be facilitative, directive, or merely informational? It is also important to determine and agree upon ahead of time whether their decisions will be binding or purely advisory. In some cases, it may make sense to have the parties to the conflict pay all or a portion of the cost of the services of a third party—for example, in a partnership dispute over governance or percentages of equity ownership. When all parties are paying, people are often more motivated to engage and resolve their differences. There are no set rules for how costs should be split, but disparities in wealth or income should be considered so no one party is unduly burdened.

Some firms are large enough to have an ombudsman who functions outside the formal organizational structure and complements existing grievance procedures that are already in place. An ombudsman can be a full- or part-time employee, or an independent consultant or contractor. He or she can provide an additional level of confidentiality, anonymity, and safety when helping firm members raise issues to management. Ombudsmen can act as counselors, helping firm members clarify the conflicts they are experiencing, such as interpersonal disputes, claims of harassment or unfair treatment, and supervisory issues. They can also take an active role in resolving disputes by mediating or facilitating them, although at times they may not be an appropriate choice for conflicts involving potential legal issues. If ombudsmen perceive a pattern or trend of conflicts, they can alert firm management to emerging problems, and they can also help provide guidance in improving grievance and dispute resolution procedures (Cohn, 2010).

CHAPTER SUMMARY

It is imperative for lawyer managers to develop skill and competence in handling conflicts in their firms. If they gain these skills, interpersonal communication will improve and stronger working relationships will result.

Lawyers often respond to intra-firm conflicts by ignoring them or taking a "lawyerly" or "legalistic" approach to resolving them. The lawyer mindset often results in:

- Thinking in binary terms of win or lose, right or wrong, black or white, and all or nothing.
- Assessing blame and culpability rather than thinking about how they may have contributed to the conflict.
- Being overly reliant on logic and argument and getting caught up in details.
- Advocating and defending personal interests.
- Citing precedent without asking if it makes sense.
- Trying to modify, weaken, or undercut existing policies by finding exceptions.
- Focusing on winning the immediate conflict rather than looking at the broader picture.

Emotional factors influence decision making based on the relationship, status, and power dynamic between those involved in the conflict.

Conflicts can occur at the following levels:

- Between peers or equals;
- Between superiors and subordinates; and
- Among groups of people.

Champion managers should ask themselves three questions before deciding how to approach the conflict:

- Am I part of it?
- Am I being asked to resolve it?
- Should somebody else resolve it?

The mindsets and skills discussed in earlier chapters provide a framework for dealing with conflicts:

- See conflicts as not only a problem to be solved but as an opportunity to learn;
- Take time to reflect, learn, and know yourself;
- Identify who is involved and why;
- Utilize the communications skills described in Chapter 4;
- Shift your mindset from winning to problem solving; and
- Find positive ways to deal with conflicts.

The Thomas-Kilmann Conflict Mode Instrument is a tool that identifies five basic methods of dealing with conflict along two dimensions: competing, collaborating, compromising, avoiding, and accommodating. Understanding these five modes can assist you in determining how to respond to and engage in conflict. Champion managers seek to respond to conflicts with constructive behaviors. The Dynamic Conflict Model is a tool to assist you that describes constructive and destructive behaviors and active or passive responses to them.

The Center for Conflict Dynamics at Eckerd College has identified nine workplace behaviors that can trigger "hot buttons" and create conflict:

- Unreliable
- Overly analytical
- Unappreciative
- Aloof
- Micromanaging
- Self-centered
- Abrasive
- Untrustworthy
- Hostile

There are times when even a champion manager should look to a neutral third party to assist in conflict resolution. Before retaining a third party, his or her role should be clarified and a determination made as to who should pay for his or her services and whether the decisions will be binding or purely advisory.

REFERENCES

Allen, D. G. (2008). Retaining talent: A guide to analyzing and managing employee turnover. SHRM Foundation. Retrieved from https://blog.shrm.org/workforce/retaining-talent-a-guide-to-analyzing-and-managing-employee-turnover

Cohn, A. (2010, March 23). Why midsize and large law firms should consider using an ombudsman. Retrieved from http://lighthouseteams.com/ideasatwork/why-midsize-and-large-law-firms-should-consider-using-an-ombudsman/

Richard, L. (n.d.). Herding cats: The lawyer personality revealed. Retrieved from http://www.lawyerbrain.com/sites/default/files /caliper_herding_cats.pdf

Richard, L. (1993, July). The lawyer personality. *ABA Journal.* Retrieved from http://lawyerbrain.com/sites/default/files/the _lawyer_types_mbti.pdf

Runde, C. E., & Flanagan, T. A. (2007). *Becoming a conflict competent leader: How you and your organization can manage conflict effectively.* San Francisco, CA: Jossey-Bass.

Thomas, K. W., & Kilmann, R. H. (2015, August). An overview of the Thomas-Kilmann Conflict Mode Instrument (TKI). Retrieved from http://www.kilmanndiagnostics.com/overview-thomas-kilmann -conflict-mode-instrument-tki

11

Motivating, Engaging, and Maintaining Morale

MOTIVATING

As a champion manager, it's not enough for you to simply delegate work, provide feedback and supervision, and then expect good results. You must also motivate your people if you want them to consistently deliver high quality services. Although most managers acknowledge that motivation is an important management skill, few know that recent behavioral economic studies have challenged much of our conventional wisdom about what motivates people. These studies have shown that traditional carrot and stick motivators, such as external rewards and punishments, are of limited value and at times may even be counterproductive. To get the best out of their people, managers need to understand what their firm members find personally rewarding—that is, what they want to do and will do for its own sake rather than in pursuit of some sort of external reward or avoidance of some sort of punishment.

Law firms have historically relied on two main factors to motivate their attorneys: increases in compensation and the possibility of promotion. Given the economic realities of the post-2008 New Normal, neither of these motivators is as readily available as it once was. The Georgetown Law Center for the Study of the Legal Profession "2013 Report on the State of the Legal Market" noted that since 2008, firms have gone through several rounds of layoffs and have also begun to move toward more flexible staffing models, expanding their use of non-partner track associates, staff attorneys, and contract lawyers. It predicted that to contain costs, "firms will probably be relatively smaller in terms of the number of partners and traditional partner-track associates and relatively larger in terms of the number of other lawyers and non-lawyer professionals" (p. 16).

As the likelihood of making equity partner and sharing in firm profits has become increasingly remote, and contract and non-partnership track attorneys have become more commonplace, what can managers do to motivate their people and keep them engaged and satisfied? What are the new keys to motivation and high productivity? A more sustainable approach is needed and, happily, available. To maintain high levels of motivation, engagement, and productivity, law firms need to shift the emphasis to addressing their members' intrinsic motivations.

Managers need to create firm environments where staff and lawyers (particularly those not on a partnership track) find greater inherent satisfaction in their work. Summarizing several recent behavioral studies, Daniel Pink in his book *Drive* (2009) identifies three elements that contribute to workers' sense of satisfaction: autonomy, mastery, and purpose.

- *Autonomy* is fostered when firm members have greater say-so over what they do, when they do it, who they do it with, and how they do it.
- *Mastery*—a sense of working hard and continually getting better at something that matters—fosters a sense of engagement, professionalism, and pride in one's work.
- *Purpose* appeals to firm members' desire to make a contribution and be part of something larger and more important.

Examples of Extrinsic Motivators	Examples of Intrinsic Motivators
Compensation • being highly paid • getting a raise • receiving a bonus	Mastery • enjoying the challenge of becoming an expert in the use of a complicated practice management software suite
Title, status, or position • becoming a partner, administrator, director, practice area head, or executive committee member	Relatedness • being a member of a firm of people who share common values, goals, interests, and experiences
Perks • a good parking spot • a large, attractive, or well-positioned office or work space	Autonomy • having the latitude to work on a project from a location outside the office • having a flexible work schedule • being trusted to devise your own solution to a legal problem rather than following what's been done before
Formal recognition • awards • prizes • "employee of the month" • being honored in the firm newsletter or on its website	Purpose • understanding your legal research and analysis will lead to an important and long-needed change in case law • knowing your motion is a critical piece of larger litigation strategy

Even though legal professionals may respond better to intrinsic motivators, extrinsic motivators should not be entirely abandoned. Discovering and addressing a firm member's intrinsic motivators is not always possible in every situation; in some cases, people simply have no internal desire to engage in an activity. Extrinsic motivators can be effective in situations when:

- Firm members are engaged in routine, simple tasks;
- Firm members need to be persuaded to try or participate in something that they have little interest in;
- Firm members need motivation to acquire new skills or knowledge; and
- To let firm members know their performance is being recognized.

Managers should be aware that their well-intended external rewards may at times have unintended negative consequences. Researchers have found that offering positive praise and feedback when people do something well can improve intrinsic motivation, but their intrinsic motivation will decrease when they are given external rewards for completing simple tasks or doing minimal work (Pink, 2009). If, for example, you lavishly praise and reward firm members for doing undemanding tasks, they will become conditioned to look for that praise and as a result become less intrinsically motivated to perform those tasks in the future.

For complex, conceptual, and analytical tasks (like those that make up much of lawyering), external motivators may weaken individual and firm performance, hinder innovation and creativity, and encourage short-term thinking. The billable hour is a good example of this. Lawyers' compensation is often based in large part on the number of hours they bill: more billable time generally results in greater rewards (assuming time is not written off or alternative fee systems are not being used). While it makes sense for an individual lawyer to maximize his or her rewards (i.e., compensation), this focus on external motivation can discourage them from finding faster and cheaper ways of completing tasks and solving problems. With increased competition in the legal market, firms with faster and cheaper solutions will find it easier to attract and retain clients. In some cases, reward and compensation systems solely based on billable hours may even encourage lawyers to inflate hours, pad bills, and engage in other unethical behaviors.

ENGAGING

When firm members are highly motivated, there are corresponding high levels of attorney and staff engagement. Engaged firm members are interested in and enthusiastic about their work. They love what they're doing and they want to do an excellent job. They care about their firm's reputation and future, and they are willing to give extra effort to see that it succeeds. They believe their contribution can make a difference. Their enthusiasm and commitment are often contagious, affecting their fellow firm members' mindsets as well as the morale and culture of the firm as a whole.

The term "employee engagement" originated in the 1990s, when studies first revealed a correlation between high levels of employee engagement and organizational productivity. One of the advantages of this concept is that levels of employee engagement can be assessed on an organizational, national, and global basis. The *Gallup Management Journal* publishes a semi-annual Employment Engagement Index. The June 2016 U.S. results indicate that only 32.6 percent of employees are actively engaged in their jobs, 50.7 percent are not engaged, and 16.7 percent are actively disengaged (Adkins, 2016).

To make these figures a little more personal, imagine you have six employees in your firm. If your firm's level of employee engagement is consistent with Gallup's overall figures for the U.S., this means that:

- Half of your employees are not engaged. They show up to work but just put in their time. Their effort and interest are just enough to get by. You have their compliance, but not their commitment.
- On the upside, two of your employees are engaged. They care about and feel connected to the firm. They like their jobs, work with enthusiasm, and are willing to go the extra mile.
- And your sixth employee is actively disengaged, acting out his or her unhappiness, and undermining what fellow firm members are trying to accomplish.

The Benefits of Engagement

In a survey and study of a professional service firm with ten regional offices, the Hay Group (n.d.) found that professionals at the firm's five offices with the most engaged employees were up to 43 percent more productive than their counterparts at the five offices with the least engaged employees.

In addition to improvements in productivity, many studies—but certainly not all—show a correlation between employee engagement and business results such as profitability. Employee engagement is not a simple thing to measure, nor is more of it necessarily a good thing. Some studies suggest there may be a point of diminishing returns with employee engagement, above which there is no significant increase in satisfaction, productivity, and profitability. Surveys of employee engagement and satisfaction can sometimes be poorly designed or administered; in the worst cases, they can be gamed and manipulated by employees to covertly send a message to management.

Rather than trying to quantify the benefits of employee engagement, lawyer managers will be better served by looking at qualitative benefits, some of which may in turn lead to higher profitability. Higher levels of employee engagement:

- Create high morale and a positive culture;
- Boost productivity and collaboration;
- Improve firm members' quality of life and work-life integration;
- Reduce absenteeism, stress-related illness, and burnout;
- Reduce attorney and staff turnover;
- Attract laterals and new attorneys, particularly Millennials;
- Improve client service and satisfaction; and
- Improve the firm's reputation and brand (both externally and internally).

So what can lawyer managers do to improve engagement? The strongest driver of engagement is usually an employee's relationship with their manager. This emphasizes the importance of lawyers being good people managers. They should strive to understand their employees and show that they value them. A healthy dialogue that includes feedback and appreciation is essential. Studies suggest that law firms will benefit when lawyer managers also understand and utilize the following drivers:

- **Good Working Relationships:** Firm members are more engaged when they have strong and genuine positive connections with their coworkers. Champion managers create environments where there arc high levels of trust, teamwork, and cooperation between firm members. They discourage self-interested behaviors and provide opportunities for firm members to collaborate and interact. Firm members don't have to be one happy family, but they should have good working relationships.

- **Clarity:** Firm members are more engaged when they work in environments where there is comparatively little vagueness, uncertainty, and ambiguity. Complete transparency about all firm matters is, of course, unrealistic, but at a minimum, managers should clearly communicate what they expect from firm members. Clear and frequent descriptive feedback is a key to not only driving employee performance but also engagement. Attorneys and staff should understand what their responsibilities are and also the scope of their authority. Examples include which decisions firm members can make on their own, which require input from others, which require approval from others, and which are simply not theirs to make. Clarity about the authority of others avoids situations where an associate or staff member is caught between the conflicting demands of two attorneys.

- **Career and Skill Development:** Firm members are more engaged when they feel that they are offered challenging work that will develop their skills and add to their overall career advancement. It's also helpful for them to have a clear understanding of what is necessary for their career advancement. In providing firm members with these kinds of stretch assignments, it's important that managers also provide the resources, tools, and guidance that firm members need to do their work and achieve their goals.

- **Meaning and Contribution:** Firm members are more engaged when they feel that they not only matter as individuals, but also that their work makes a significant contribution to the overall success of the firm and its clients. It's important, then, for managers to communicate to attorneys and staff the firm's goals, and how each firm member's individual goals and responsibilities support those larger objectives.

- **Recognition and Appreciation:** Firm members are more engaged when they feel appreciated and receive recognition for strong performance. As described in the section on feedback, praise is more effective than criticism in helping firm members change their behaviors and sustain those behaviors. Simple expressions of gratitude, like saying thank you, can build a strong positive bond between managers and firm members.

Champion managers know how to clearly and sincerely express their appreciation and gratitude. Business psychiatrist and executive advisor Mark Goulston (2013) suggests the following three-part approach to giving what he calls a "Power Thank You." First, thank someone for something specific they did for you. It can also be something they refrained from doing that might have hurt or caused problems for you. Second, acknowledge the effort it took for them to do it by saying something like, "I know you didn't have to . . ." or "I know you went out of your way to do . . ." Third, describe the difference it made to you, to your team, or to the firm.

- **Self Direction and Autonomy:** Firm members are more engaged when they have a fair degree of control over how they do their jobs. This may be especially true for professionals like lawyers whose personalities are typically more autonomous than those of the general population. Rather than micro-managing firm members, managers should set clear expectations about desired outcomes and then allow some leeway in how exactly firm members achieve those results.
- **Management Integrity:** Firm members are more engaged when they see their managers walking their talk about the firm's values, rules, and ethics. Doing so sets an example, inspires confidence in the firm, and helps firm members feel pride in their job, performance, and firm.

It's important to recognize that these drivers of engagement may vary from firm to firm, as well as from one firm member to another. Over time, what drives an individual firm member's engagement may also change; what they found absorbing and motivating three years ago may not be the same as what leads to engagement now. Champion managers will recognize and work with these changes.

MAINTAINING HIGH MORALE

Engagement is a large contributor to firm morale, but not the only one. Morale is commonly equated with employee happiness, and managers often assume that morale will be high if they can just keep their staff and attorneys happy. They use any number of tools to boost happiness: holiday parties, fun retreats, casual Fridays, pizza lunches, gift certificates, raises, bonuses, etc. While these are useful ways to acknowledge and reward employees' contributions, their effect on happiness and morale can be short-term and even counterproductive.

Over time, attorneys and staff may begin to expect these additional rewards and even feel entitled to them. If they don't receive them, they may become resentful, unhappy, and worried. They wonder, "What is the message that the firm is trying to send me by ending these perks? Was it something I did or said? Does a shorter retreat mean we're going broke?" By relying too heavily on these kinds of tangible rewards, well-meaning managers can foster unsustainable employee expectations and tie themselves (and their firms) in knots trying to make everyone happy. When hard and slow times occur, necessary cutbacks in these perks can erode employee enthusiasm and happiness.

Thinking in terms of morale rather than happiness is a more useful and durable approach. Morale is the confidence, enthusiasm, and discipline of an individual or group at a particular time. It comes from a sense of shared purpose, mission, opportunity, or predicament. Even in dire situations—perhaps especially in dire situations—morale can be extraordinarily high as everyone sees him- or herself in the same proverbial boat.

In spite of a healthy body of research showing the benefits of high morale, some managers have a hard time believing that something so incorporeal can have profound effects on the bottom line of their organization. For that matter, they may also have difficulty connecting the dots between motivation, engagement, and productivity. For them, we offer a story about morale on sailing ships in the 19th century. (Spoiler alert: floggings are not part of this story, although some lawyer managers encourage us to endorse them as a motivational tool.)

> One day a know-it-all passenger confronted the captain of a clipper ship and asked, "Why are you always so concerned about the wind? You can't see it, hear it, or smell it—so why are you constantly preoccupied by it?" The captain patiently explained to the landlubber that he could read the wind by recognizing the effect it has on other objects. Though it lacked a sound of its own, he could hear it rattle the canvas of the sails. Though it had no visible form, he could see it whip up whitecaps and blow clouds across the sky. And though it had no odor of its own, he knew when it carried the smell and promise of nearby land. It may not have had a substance of its own, but without it, he would never get his passengers and cargo to their destination.

In a similar fashion, an intangible like morale is not perceived directly but rather by the effect it has on firm members' attitudes and actions. It can be read in the ways they communicate, relate, and work together. Some lawyers dismiss firm morale as airy-fairy in much the same way the ignorant passenger dismissed the wind. They can't imagine how something so intangible can have practical importance. They fail to grasp the connection between morale, individual and firm performance, and bottom-line results. And although they may not believe in the "winds" that blow through their firms, they are subject to them and ignore them at their own peril.

Reading the Winds—Signs of Low Morale

How can managers "read" these metaphorical winds of morale in the activities of their firms? What are some of the keys to determining whether morale is high or low? Intuiting firm members' attitudes and moods takes time, practice, and listening, so the best place to start is with the following observable items.

- High turnover.
- Declining productivity and quality of work.
- Unresolved interpersonal conflicts.
- Recurring problems and crises.
- Falling realization rates.
- Repeatedly exceeding budgets for cases and projects.
- Last-minute fire drills and missed deadlines.
- Increasing tardiness and absenteeism.
- Lost business due to lower levels of client service.

Managers should pay attention to whether these signs are appearing at an individual, practice area, or firm-wide level. Though larger scale signs are clearly more serious indicators of weak morale, individual signs should not be ignored—they may reveal emerging morale problems. If staff or lawyers are exhibiting or contributing to any of the above behaviors, it is useful to go deeper and consider their moods and attitudes. Individuals with low morale often show a loss of engagement, enthusiasm, and motivation. They may feel overly stressed and disempowered. They may become more anxious, irritable, and contentious, or they may become withdrawn, resigned, and indifferent to the needs of their colleagues and the firm's clients.

The High Costs of Low Morale

It's relatively easy to find a direct connection between the signs of low morale listed above and the effect they have on firms' bottom lines. When low morale results in high turnover, the hard costs of hiring a replacement (recruiters' fees, advertising, etc.) are often significant, and soft costs (attorney time expended on interviews and training, lost productivity and client dissatisfaction due to inadequate staffing, etc.) can be even higher. It takes considerable time and effort on the part of new hires (and those training and supervising them) before they become fully efficient. While they are coming up to speed, other members of the firm may need to take up the slack and overall firm productivity may drop. The Project for Attorney Retention at UC Hastings College of Law (2007) in San Francisco put the hard and soft costs of replacing a mid-level associate at $250,000 to $400,000.

Employees working in low morale environments are generally less productive and do work of poorer quality. This can lead to errors, gaps, disconnects, and other inefficiencies that result in higher overhead, more written-off time, and falling profits. In extreme cases, this can result in lost clients as well as higher malpractice claims and premiums.

There are also the qualitative and emotional costs of working in an office with low morale. Being in an environment of low motivation and high conflict can be draining and upsetting. Recent neuropsychological studies have confirmed that our emotions are indeed contagious and that low moods and negative emotions can spread throughout a group like a virus (Carter, 2012).

Addressing the Root Causes of Low Morale

Once morale is better understood, it's easier to see why even the most sincere efforts to keep lawyers and staff happy are of limited value. Action must be taken to address the root causes rather than the manifestations of poor morale. To assure that morale is positive and resilient, lawyer managers should:

- Articulate a compelling vision for the firm.
- Make employee development a priority.
- Provide timely and constructive feedback.
- Create a culture of trust and accountability.

Articulate a Vision and Set a Clear Course
It's hard for employees to develop a sense of shared purpose and mission when they lack a clear understanding of the firm's vision and direction. A firm's vision doesn't have to be dramatic or lofty to be compelling: a simple vision

clearly communicated can be far more useful than a grandiose plan that seems overly ambitious and is rarely referenced. Firm members are most satisfied and effective when they understand how their specific responsibilities and tasks contribute to the firm's larger goals and direction. Absent this, they are at greater risk of becoming confused, anxious, and disengaged as they mechanically go through the motions of their day-to-day job.

Having a clear firm direction and strategy also makes it easier to develop career plans for each lawyer and staff person. People generally perform better when they are presented with well-defined expectations that are aligned with larger firm-wide goals. They feel a sense of belonging and importance that makes them want to stretch and do their best. Understanding the bigger picture also helps them learn how to collaborate with and support their peers. Soliciting their input both on firm and individual goals further increases their commitment and loyalty.

In tough times, a firm's vision, direction, and goals may need to change. Managers should not pretend otherwise or slavishly stick to strategies that are no longer useful. Although they may worry that delivering bad news will erode morale, they should nonetheless acknowledge difficult conditions and communicate necessary mid-course corrections to their employees. In uncertain and difficult times, employees often imagine the worst and become fearful and anxious. It is important to listen to employees' concerns and then explain how changes in the firm's goals or strategy will help it weather the storm and return once again to satisfactory levels of profitability and stability.

This reminds employees that all are sharing a common predicament and that by working together they can sail through it.

Invest in Firm Members' Development

Many law firms go to great lengths to carefully select the most qualified lawyers and staff, but then leave their development largely to chance. Without a coherent plan for their development, these employees often end up under-utilized, bored, and stressed. It's no wonder their morale is low. Some firms assume formal training programs and annual performance reviews will satisfactorily address all their employees' development needs. Even though these are helpful, a more frequent and personal approach is necessary.

As mentioned elsewhere: skillful delegation, feedback, and mentoring are the best ways to develop employees and keep their morale high; delegation should be clear and designed to help employees learn new skills, procedures, and substantive areas of the law; and firm members should be provided with the necessary resources to complete an assignment, unless one of the goals of an assignment is to have an employee develop his or her own.

Provide Timely and Constructive Feedback

Employees perform better and have higher morale when they understand not only what is expected of them, but also whether they are meeting or surpassing those expectations. Waiting for yearly reviews can leave them uncertain and confused; without frequent feedback, they are left to assume they're doing okay if they don't hear complaints or get fired. This may be an acceptable policy if a firm's goal is to have employees with "good enough" performance, but it will undercut any efforts to encourage excellence. Worse still, it may send employees unintended messages that improvement is not necessary and their development is not a priority. It is much easier to help employees change or unlearn their behaviors when they haven't been "practicing" them for the twelve months between annual reviews.

Create a Culture of Trust and Accountability

A compelling vision, effective delegation, and constructive feedback are the foundations for a firm culture of accountability and excellence. They let employees know what is expected of them, how well they are doing, and how their work contributes to larger and long-term goals. Morale is robust and resilient in these kinds of cultures.

But even in those kinds of firms, it is virtually impossible to have high morale when trust and accountability are lacking. A very negative and demotivating message is sent when employees believe that inconsistent criteria are being used in evaluating and rewarding their performance. When favoritism exists, employees become cynical, resentful, and seldom give their best efforts. Unevenly applied accountability undermines firm loyalty and the idea that everyone is in the same boat, facing the same obstacles, and working together towards a common goal.

Accountability is not just limited to employees. Firm leaders and managers must "walk their talk" and set a positive example in order to create an environment of trust. Morale is threatened when firm members notice their managers' actions are incongruent with stated firm policies or goals. Consider the confusion lawyers may feel if they're told that it's imperative that timesheets are submitted at week's end, but one of their supervising partners is consistently four weeks late. Or the anger they may feel if they've been told that there will be no bonuses at year-end, but the managing partner arrives the following month in a brand-new expensive car.

Research conducted in the last ten years has not only confirmed the connection between trust and high levels of employee engagement and productivity, but also the neuroscience basis for this. Researchers found that the brain chemical oxytocin promotes trust, collaboration, and teamwork and that the following eight management behaviors (many of which have been described earlier in this chapter) stimulate oxytocin production (Zak, 2017, p. 87–90):

- Recognize excellence, preferably immediately after a goal has been met and when it is tangible, unexpected, personal, and public.
- Induce "challenge stress" by assigning teams difficult but achievable tasks.
- Give employees discretion in how they do their work once they have been trained.
- To the extent possible, let employees choose projects that they find interesting and rewarding, while at the same time providing them with clear expectations, feedback, and accountability.
- Share information about the organization's direction and strategy to reduce uncertainty and chronic stress.
- Facilitate the building of personal relationships to increase social ties and empathy between employees.

- Support personal as well as professional growth to
  improve individual performance.
- Show vulnerability and ask colleagues and employees for help rather than always telling them what
  to do.

Beyond identifying management behaviors that promote oxytocin production and trust, the researchers
found strong, quantifiable correlations between trust and
employee engagement, loyalty, and productivity. Researchers surveyed 1,095 working adults in the United States and
ranked their companies by the extent to which they practiced the above eight behaviors. Based on self-report from
the survey participants, they (Zak, 2017, p. 90) found:

- Companies in the top quartile had employees who
  were 76 percent more engaged, 50 percent more
  productive, and had 106 percent more energy than
  employees whose companies were in the bottom
  quartile.
- Employees working in high-trust companies
  enjoyed their jobs 60 percent more, felt 70 percent
  more aligned with their company's purpose, and
  felt 66 percent closer to their coworkers when compared to those working in low-trust companies.
- Employees working in high-trust companies also
  felt 41 percent more of a sense of accomplishment
  and experienced 40 percent less burnout from their
  work.

These statistics demonstrate the impact of creating a
culture of trust on engagement and retention and, consequently, its potential for improving a firm's bottom line.

Like our clipper ship captain, law firm managers must be able to read the winds of morale blowing through their firm. Failing to do so increases the chances of shipwrecks, mutinies, and excruciatingly slow passages. But unlike our clipper ship captain, champion managers have the power to influence those winds! They can respond quickly and positively when morale ebbs, and better still, they can create a firm culture based on vision, delegation, feedback, trust, and accountability to make sure those winds blow in a favorable direction.[1]

CHAPTER SUMMARY

To be a champion manager, you need to understand what firm members find personally rewarding rather than relying exclusively on the carrot and stick approach. It is your job to create an environment where staff and lawyers find greater satisfaction in their work.

Three elements that contribute to employee satisfaction are:

- Autonomy
- Mastery
- Purpose

Extrinsic motivators can be effective when:

- Tasks are simple and routine.
- Firm members need persuasion to try something they are not interested in.

---

1. A version of this discussion of morale first appeared in "Law Firm Morale—Much More than Smiley Faces" in the February 2013 edition of *The Bottom Line*, Volume 34, No. 1.

- Firm members need to acquire new knowledge and skills.
- Managers wish to provide recognition.

There needs to be a balance between extrinsic and intrinsic motivators. Each has its own purpose depending on the situation and the individual.

High motivation leads to high levels of employee engagement. High levels of employee engagement result in organizational productivity. According to one survey, highly engaged employees can be up to 43 percent more productive than their least engaged peers. Higher productivity can lead to improved profitability as well as employee satisfaction.

Lawyer managers will be more effective if they understand and use the following drivers:

- Good working relationships—foster trust, teamwork and cooperation.
- Clarity—allow transparency and clear communication.
- Career and skill development—provide challenging work and career advancement.
- Meaning and contribution—show how individual efforts contribute to the firm as a whole.
- Recognition and appreciation—remember to say "thank you" and acknowledge strong performance.
- Self-direction and autonomy—set clear expectations but don't micromanage.
- Management integrity—lead by example.

Morale is not about happiness. It is the confidence, enthusiasm, and discipline of an individual or group at a particular time. Morale comes from a sense of shared purpose, mission, opportunity, or predicament. Although intangible, it affects firm members' attitudes and actions. Low morale results in high turnover, declining productivity and work quality, unresolved interpersonal conflicts, falling realization rates, tardiness, lost business, and more. In order to assure that morale is positive and resilient, champion managers should:

- Articulate a compelling vision for the firm.
- Make employee development a priority.
- Provide timely and constructive feedback.
- Create a culture of trust and accountability.

REFERENCES

Adkins, A. (2016, July 25). U.S. employee engagement steady in June. Retrieved from http://www.gallup.com/poll/193901/employee -engagement-steady-june.aspx

Carter, S. B. (2012, October 20). Emotions are contagious—Choose your company wisely. Retrieved from https://www.psychology today.com/blog/high-octane-women/201210/emotions-are -contagious-choose-your-company-wisely

Elowitt, A. (2013, February). Law firm morale—Much more than smiley faces. *The Bottom Line, 34*(1).

Georgetown Law Center for the Study of the Legal Profession. (2013). 2013 Report on the State of the Legal Market. Retrieved from http:// scholarship.law.georgetown.edu/cgi/viewcontent.cgi?article=1003 &context=cslp_papers

Goulston, M. (2013, February 20). How to give a meaningful "thank you". Retrieved from https://hbr.org/2013/02/how-to-give-a-meaningful-thank

Hay Group. (n.d.). *Engage employees and boost performance* (Working paper). Retrieved from http://www.haygroup.com/us/downloads/details.aspx?id=7343

Pink, D. H. (2009). *Drive: The surprising truth about what motivates us.* New York, NY: Riverhead Books.

Project for Attorney Retention at UC Hastings College of Law. (2007). The business case for a balanced hours program for attorneys. Retrieved from http://apps.americanbar.org/labor/lel-aba-annual/2008/pdf/Williams2.pdf

Zak, P. J. (2017, January & February). The neuroscience of trust. *Harvard Business Review, 95*(1), 84–90.

12

Creating and Maintaining a Positive Culture

MANAGING YOUR FIRM'S CULTURE

Whether it is intentional or not, and whether you are aware of it or not, your firm has a culture. Your challenges and responsibilities as a manager are to:

- Become aware of it;
- Determine whether it's optimal;
- Champion it if it is; and
- Change it if it's not.

What do we mean when we say "firm culture"? It is made up of shared behaviors, values, and beliefs that, in turn, form a foundation for how things are accomplished in a firm. It is seen in a firm's actual values, priorities, and decision-making processes. It is constantly expressed in, and at the same time shaped by, the mindsets, conversations, interactions, and relationships of a firm's members (see Figure 12.1).

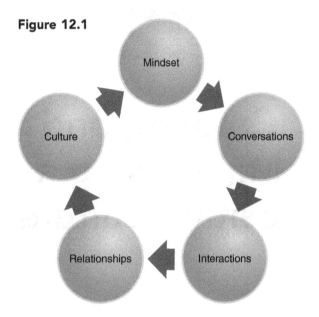

Figure 12.1

Your firm's culture is a lot like a computer's operating system—in may be in the background, but it has a tremendous impact on how things are done. It can encourage both positive and negative behaviors and impact how people in your law firm work together. Firm culture—whether tacit or intentional—can be an obstacle to firm health and growth, or it can be a catalyst for continuous improvement.

Legal scholars and journalists have only recently recognized the importance of firm culture and begun commenting on its role. Legal commentator and futurist Jordan Furlong (2014) provides the following:

> Law firm "culture" isn't that hard to define, really. Culture is what people at the firm actually do every day. In harsher terms, it's what people get away with. Culture is *what actually happens.* A law firm's culture is the daily manifestation of its performance expectations and behavioral

norms—what is encouraged and what is tolerated. So it's not a matter of law firms 'ignoring'
culture—every firm has a culture, and most firms'
cultures are remarkably and depressingly similar.
It's a matter of recognizing that the culture that
a law firm develops and sustains has an impact
on productivity, retention and morale—in many
cases, a catastrophic one.

Even though your firm's culture is an intangible, its influence shows up in tangible measures such as retention,
turnover, productivity, and profitability. Every kind of firm
culture has its own advantages and disadvantages. If you
want your lawyers and staff to grow professionally, stay
with your firm, and work together in harmony; your culture should support those goals and nurture your people.
If profitability and prestige are more important, your culture will probably be more task- and results-oriented than
people- and relationship-oriented.

Firm cultures have many facets and dimensions. Here are
some questions you might want to ask about your own firm
to get your thinking started.

- Are high billable hours the mantra in our law firm
  or do we have a culture that embraces pro bono
  work as well?
- Do we have a lifestyle law firm that is receptive to
  telecommuting and flexible work schedules or do
  we require face time and long hours in the office?
- Does our firm put the success of its individual
  lawyers before the good of the overall firm, or
  is it committed to mutual respect and teamwork
  between firm members at all levels?

- Is ours a culture of consensus or a benevolent dictatorship?
- What is our culture regarding performance? Do we criticize in private and praise in public? How do people in our organization know they are doing a good job?
- How are individuals dealt with if they are having a personal problem? Does the organization pitch in to help, or are people left out on their own to resolve the issue?
- Is the firm actively engaged in creating greater diversity? This includes hiring, promotion, and community involvement and investment.

Step 1. Discover Your Firm's Actual Culture

It may take a bit of digging and reflection to discern your law firm's *actual* culture. Firms often have a *stated* firm culture that has been decided upon at a partners' meeting or retreat during a values clarification or strategic planning exercise. Based on a consensus of the members participating, there may be agreement that the firm will, for example:

- Treat everyone with dignity and respect;
- Have a long-term dedicated commitment to clients;
- Embrace diversity;
- Rely on consensus and collegiality;
- Work as a team; and
- Compensate people fairly for their overall contributions to the success of the firm.

These are great-sounding and worthwhile goals—high fives all around—but as a manager you need to ask whether your firm is actually living up to its articulated culture on a daily basis. There may be a stronger shadow culture undermining the culture you aspire to have. For example, your firm may say it will treat everyone with dignity and respect, but this has little meaning if several of your highest compensated rainmakers are hypercritical screamers who loudly vent their frustrations at associates and staff.

Figuring out a firm's actual culture can be difficult for those working within it. You may unconsciously assume your firm's culture is normal and the only way a culture can be. Or you may be so deep in the forest that is your firm's culture that all you can clearly see are the trees. Or like the fish in Chapter 2 (on page 22), you may not even know you're swimming in the water that is your firm's culture. Fortunately, law practice management consultants and coaches can help you get a clear view.

One approach they may take to discover your firm's true culture is to have everyone complete an individual online self-assessment, such as a DiSC® profile, an HBDI® thinking modes assessment, or a Gallup StrengthsFinder—just to name a few of the many that are available. The results of the DiSC® assessment reveal an individual's style of behavior from among four personality traits (dominance, influence, steadiness, and conscientiousness).[1] The results of the HBDI® assessment uncover an individual's dominant ways of thinking and approaching problem solving from among four preferences (rational, practical, relational, and experimental). Several other assessments can also be used for this purpose, including the Gallup Strengthsfinder and Strengths Based Leadership.

---

1. William Moulton Marston, (a psychologist, attorney, inventor, and creator of the Wonder Woman comic) first explained the DiSC® model of emotions and behavior in his 1928 book *Emotions of Normal People*. It was later developed into an assessment by others.

In order for assessments to be a useful tool, participants need to be comfortable with how results will be shared with the group. Some firm members may be hesitant to share their assessment results, and laws in some states regarding employee privacy may limit sharing. The level of trust and culture in your firm will have an impact on whether people will openly embrace the information contained in the assessment and willingly share it with others. Consider using an outside consultant who is skilled in facilitating the assessment results to minimize discomfort and maximize the results of this exercise.

None of these assessments suggests that one personality trait, thinking mode, or strength is inherently better than another. Their value comes in helping individuals understand both themselves and how they may be different from or similar to other members of their firm. Both assessments allow individual results to be compiled into a group report that reveals the most prevalent personality or thinking styles in a firm.

Another way to examine and better understand your firm's culture is to have an outside consultant interview the members (or key stakeholders) of your firm, analyze their answers, and compile the results into a cultural assessment. One such assessment (Cultural Assessment, Client Services, n.d.) looks at cultural differences in the following areas:

- *Collegiality*: The manner in which people within a law firm deal with each other.
- *Strategic Focus*: The degree to which the firm has a clear identity, both for itself and in relation to other firms.

- *Governance*: The manner in which the firm deals with its people and the way that its lawyers and staff deal with the firm.
- *Values*: The belief systems that represent the collective aspirations of the members of the firm.

A thorough analysis of firm culture can take into account the style or styles of the firm leaders, the most prominent styles within the group, the historical culture of the firm, how well or poorly its members work together, and the goals and objectives that the firm strives to achieve. Firm culture influences the pace at which work is accomplished, the attention paid to details, and how people are treated. It is important to understand this because people who fit into the dominant culture immediately feel a part of the firm, and those who do not may feel uncomfortable working there.

Step 2. Discuss Your Firm's Culture with Other Partners and Stakeholders

Assessments and analyses are helpful only when they provide a starting point or framework for discussions about your firm's culture. If they sit in a drawer or are never acted upon, they are simply a waste of resources. In addition, while they're helpful, they're not strictly necessary; firm culture can and should be looked at and discussed even when an assessment or analysis isn't affordable.

From these discussions, you may find that members of your firm have different and, at times, conflicting views of your firm's culture. You may discover significant differences between your firm's stated culture and the impact it has on some or all its members. Latent issues and disconnects are often revealed in these discussions, and they can then be addressed before they become critical problems. These discussions also help firms reflect on their desired values, direction, and strategy and, when necessary, make changes in them. Overall these conversations make the topic of firm culture discussable—and, as a result, less intangible. They help managers and partners see their firms as complex systems and understand the unintended consequences of some of their actions and policies. Depending on their roles in the firm, people may see firm culture very differently from one another. Any cultural assessment should be validated by including input from both lawyers and staff so a complete picture is provided.

Step 3. Champion Your Firm's Culture if It's Optimal

If you and your partners are satisfied with your firm's culture, then you (and others) should champion it. Your management style and behavior should embody the firm's desired culture and be a model that other firm members can emulate. Leading and managing by example is the most effective way to communicate culture. It is far more powerful than management memos or mission statements.

Problems arise when there is a significant mismatch between a manager's behavior and his or her firm's culture. Firm members get a mixed message: is it do what you say (for example, make bottom line profitability the most important thing) or do what you do (spend firm resources liberally and extravagantly)? These sorts of discrepancies easily lead to widespread cynicism and low morale.

While it's important that your management style and behavior are not antithetical to the firm's culture, they do not have to be in total, lockstep alignment. Some recent research has shown that small- and medium-sized businesses (not law firms) actually do better financially in the short run when their CEO's management styles complement the businesses' culture rather than completely match it (Beard, 2016). In those companies, the CEO provided something the cultures did not.

For example, a manager with a brash, autocratic management style would not fit well in a law firm with a culture that embraced collaboration, collegiality, and consensus decision making. But a manager who could set clear expectations, encourage personal accountability, foster a sense of urgency, and push people to get things done in a timely manner would be a valuable and, at times, necessary balance to the firm's culture.

Step 4. Lead Cultural Change if Your Firm's Culture Isn't Optimal

> Culture is created by leaders. Dysfunctional leaders will foster dysfunctional cultures. The best leaders lead culture; they help followers unlearn cultural assumptions and they help instill new assumptions.
>
> (Grella, 2013)

If there is dissonance between your firm's stated culture and what is actually rewarded through compensation and promotion, the result will negatively impact productivity, retention, and morale. If you are unhappy with any aspect of your firm's culture and you are a firm leader, then work to change it. Firm leadership should be proactive, not reactive, and reward the types of behaviors that will have a positive impact on firm morale. Starting at the top, the partner compensation system should look at over-all firm contributions and reward being a good firm citizen, a team player, placing client needs before one's own, as well as business origination. Compensation systems should encourage collaboration not competition. Beyond compensation, reach out for new ideas from more diverse members of the firm that might positively impact culture. If you are trying to implement cultural change, remember to incorporate culture-related questions in hiring. You want to hire for the culture that you are aspiring to have rather than repeating hiring for your current culture.

CHAPTER SUMMARY

Culture is the foundation of shared behaviors, values, and beliefs that influence how things are accomplished in an organization. It can encourage both positive and negative behaviors and impacts how people in your law firm work together. Though intangible, it has an impact on such tangible measures as retention, turnover, productivity, and profitability.

As a lawyer manager you need to:

- Discover your firm's actual culture by digging below the surface;
- Work with consultants and coaches who use interviews and assessment tools to understand individual styles of behavior as well as cultural differences within the firm;

- Discuss what you have learned about your firm's culture with other partners and stakeholders;
- Champion your firm's culture if it is optimal; and
- Lead cultural change if your firm's culture is not optimal.

REFERENCES

Beard, A. (2016, July & August). CEOs shouldn't try to embody their firms' culture. *Harvard Business Review, 94*(7/8): 28–29.

Cultural Assessment, Client Services. (n.d.). Retrieved from http://www.edge.ai/client-services/law-firm-cultural-assessment/

Furlong, J. (2014, August 19). Category: Management. Retrieved from https://www.law21.ca/category/management/

Grella, T. C. (2013). *Lessons in leadership: Essential skills for lawyers.* Chicago, IL: ABA, Law Practice Management Section.

Marston, W. M. (1928). *Emotions of normal people.* London: K. Paul, Trench, Trubner & Co. Ltd.

13

Building a Champion Management Support System

SETTING UP SUPPORT

Even the most skilled managers need support in order to succeed. All too often we see lawyers chosen to be managers who through no fault of their own are set up to fail or underperform. This is rarely the result of firm politics or a colleague's jealousy or intrigues. More often than not it is simply because both the manager and his or her partners have underestimated or misunderstood the kinds of support managers need to be effective and successful.

Management is a two-way street: managers wield power and authority, but they don't operate in vacuums. Their discretion and resources have limits. Like anyone else, their actions have consequences, and they are responsible to and dependent upon others. They exercise their managerial power in what A. A. Berle referred to as a "field of responsibility," which in the context of a law firm may be a manager's fellow equity holders, peers, administrators, or other stakeholders. Their field of responsibility also includes intangibles such as a firm's culture, historical institutional norms, or rules of good behavior, be they explicit or tacit. When managers operate outside of their field of responsibility, they run the risk of losing cooperation, followers, and even their position.

In the other direction, the constituents of a field of responsibility must provide adequate resources and support for a manager to be able to effectively exercise his or her power. Managers can be ineffectual when they get nominal support but lack the administrative staff, budget, time, and buy-in they need. The presence, absence and degree of the following items make the difference in how successful a manager can be.

1. A Firm Vision, Strategy, and Business Plan

Before stepping into a management position, a lawyer should determine whether the firm has a clear vision and business plan, and whether they are actually referenced from time to time and followed. Managing a firm without knowing its vision, strategy or business plan is like trying to keep the proverbial ship on course without knowing its destination. The skipper may do what seems like a masterful job of seamanship but still end up in the wrong place, disappointing both crew and passengers.

Vision statements help firm owners agree on the direction, strategies and goals of their firm. From them they can create business plans that can be implemented and monitored to assess progress and make changes. Although these planning exercises are extremely beneficial, not all firms go through them. This is especially the case with smaller firms, whose owners mistakenly believe that such plans are only needed by large firms. Even in larger firms, these plans may not be widely shared, understood or followed.

When managers have a clear understanding of their firm's plans, they can align their decisions and actions with them. Vagueness and ambiguity of such plans can make it harder for a manager to appreciate the firm's *actual* values and priorities and operate in accordance with them. (A firm's *espoused* values and goals often differ from the ones they actually practice.) When these are unclear or not understood, a manager's decisions can appear arbitrary and inconsistent, even when they are well intentioned. This in turn can lead to confusion, frustration, disengagement and low morale in the firm. This problem appears more often in firms where a significant number of equity holders or stakeholders fail to agree or operate in accordance with the firm's articulated vision and plan. In these situations, it is more likely that a manager's decisions and actions will be questioned and conflicts will arise.

Flying Blind

This problem became very clear to us while working with a medium-sized firm that had seen high turnover in senior administrative positions and three managing partners in as many years with no one now wanting to serve in that position. Trust was low, dissension high, and the firm environment tense and politicized. Many felt the firm was ready to implode. Our first clue as to what was going on came when we asked for a copy of the firm's vision and strategic plan. While they could find the firm's mission statement (it appeared prominently on the firm's website and promotional materials), no one could find the strategic plan they had created ten years earlier.

One of the senior legal secretaries finally found it a week later in the files of the partner who was managing at the time of the plan's creation. When we asked nine key partners to tell us their understanding of the strategic plan, it became very clear that no one had reviewed the plan anytime recently, and various conflicting interpretations of the plan had arisen. While each managing partners' decisions and actions were consistent with their individual understanding of the firm's vision and strategic plan, they were always at odds with those of a number of their other partners.

Once we brought this to the partners' attention, they understood that the problem wasn't one of management skills and styles, but rather a lack of agreement as to the firm's direction. A number of facilitated discussions led to consensus and a wholesale revision of the firm's strategic plan. Management problems and turnover diminished over the next six months, and the firm made it mandatory for partners to review the strategic plan at least every twelve months.

If a new manager discovers that their firm's vision and business plan are unclear or not followed, they should make it one of their first priorities to get all the equity partners and other stakeholders on the same page. Doing this first will make managerial and leadership tasks much easier.

2. Authority to Manage and Lead

It's not unusual for lawyers to take on or be given management *responsibilities* without commensurate management *authority*. Few things are worse than making a management decision and having people ignore it. This occurs in all sorts of organizations, but seems to be more prevalent in flatter, less hierarchical ones like law firms. Firm managers often face the challenge of leading and managing other lawyers who own the same or a greater percentage of the firm, and are just as powerful, important, indispensable, and well compensated as they are—if not more so. Since lawyers tend to be more autonomous, skeptical and abstract than the general population; on a bad day managing lawyers isn't just "herding cats," it's more like herding feral ones.

Power in law firms is often shared through the use of committees and rotating, short-term appointments to managing partner. Rather than tasking one person with all managerial responsibilities and power, committees are formed to share workload and authority. Important decisions are often made by or upon the recommendation of these management or executive committees. This form of governance is not in itself good or bad: its benefits are that power is shared, checks and balances exist, and there are opportunities for discussion and deliberation before decisions are made. On the downside, partners' deliberations can be protracted,

Figure 13.1

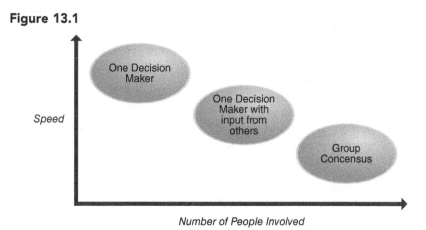

Making the decision:	Description:	Well-suited for situations when:
One decision maker	Leader makes a decision and announces it to either another individual or a group.	The decision is relatively simple. There's limited time for the decision. Few (if any) obstacles to support for or implementation of the decision.
One decision maker with input from *individuals*	Leader gathers input from other individuals, makes the decision, and then announces it.	Information and expertise are needed from some but not all individuals. The individuals giving input represent a sufficient range of stakeholder interests. Support for and implementation of the decision are likely.
One decision maker with input from a *group*	Leader calls a meeting, gathers input from the group, makes the decision, and then announces it.	The decision affects or is important to many people. Information and expertise are needed from many. A meeting offers potential for developing a common understanding of the problem. Implementation of the decision will probably require the coordination, cooperation, and buy-in of many at the meeting.
Group consensus (each person understands, agrees to, accepts, and will implement)	Leader and group reach a decision that everyone understands, can support, and is willing to implement.	Sufficient time is available for the longer process. Information and/or expertise are needed from the entire group. Implementation of the decision will require the complete understanding and buy-in of the group. The group is experienced in the consensus process.

resulting in slow responses if not outright paralysis as issues are revisited without resolution (see Figure 13.1).

Leading and managing can be problematical when lawyers lack sole discretion to make decisions and must work through numerous committees. Managers in these kinds of firms should make sure that there is agreement and buy-in as to decision-making rules and authority. It's important to clarify which decisions are a manager's and which belong to other individuals or committees. Once committees reach agreement on a matter, managers should also have clear guidelines and authority to implement those decisions. The preceding table provides a general framework for determining how many people should be involved in making managerial decisions.

Even when there is agreement as to the number of people who should be involved in making a managerial decision, there can be confusion as to how it should be made (i.e., its process) and implemented (i.e., its execution). When decisions are complex or important, the following DIANA rubric can be used to analyze and clarify them. Doing so more clearly delineates the scope of a manager's authority.

None of this is to suggest that managers should have absolute, unfettered power—they shouldn't—but the extent of their authority should be clearly articulated and agreed to. A few firms function very well with autocratic leaders and managers. They typically wield the most influence and power in a firm because they are its founder, disproportionately its largest equity holder, have the largest and most important clients, or some combination of these three. Even with autocratic leadership, it's important that managerial authority is clearly and widely understood when tasks are delegated to other members of the firm.

D	DECISION	Who is making the decision? • One person? • One person with input from others? • More than one person? • Group consensus?
I	INPUT	Who will be giving input? • Individual input? • Group input?
A	APPROVAL	Whose approval is needed? • Approval beforehand? • Approval afterwards?
N	NOTIFICATION	Who must be notified of the decision? • When the decision is made? • After the decision is made but *before* action is taken? • After the decision is made and action taken?
A	ACTION	Whose actions are necessary for implementing the decision? Have clear instructions, performance criteria, and resources been given to them?

One of the main advantages of autocratic firm leadership is consistency and predictability. These advantages can also be achieved by having firm managers serve for a reasonably long amount of time. There are many reasons some firms like to rotate their managing partners. This can be so no one lawyer becomes too powerful or is too burdened by administrative responsibilities. But when managing partner positions are changed too frequently, lawyers who dislike a manager's decisions may play a waiting game and delay implementation until a new manager is chosen.

There is another subtler phenomenon in law firms that can undermine a manager's authority. Some firms make policies and decisions on what David Maister (2008) has ironically likened to a "common law" model. In these firms, once a policy or decision has been made, lawyers (mimicking the development of common law) will incrementally and continually make distinctions ("this is a different matter") and exceptions ("this time we will do it differently") until a policy or decision is so diluted and ambiguous that the firm's manager feels he or she either has unlimited discretion or none whatsoever. This lack of consistency and predictability can hurt the morale of firm members as well as their managers.

3. Time to Manage and Lead

Law firm managers constantly face the challenge of finding time to manage and lead while maintaining their responsibilities for billable work and client development. Better time and energy management helps managers become more productive and efficient, and (as discussed in previous chapters) once they practice and refine their management skills, they often find they can devote less time to people management. There are however limits as to how much harder and smarter a manager can work. Managers should not forget the importance of also managing the *expectations* of their firm, partners, and family as to how much time they can and will devote to management activities.

Smart firms that recognize the importance of management understand that it takes time and care, so they lower their expectations for managing partners' billable hours and business development efforts while not reducing their compensation. Acknowledging the time commitment and difficulties of managing, some even increase compensation, and a few larger firms now have managing partners who do not bill any hours but instead spend all their time managing the firm. Whether compensation is increased or not, firms need to provide their managers with sufficient staff and infrastructure as well as time. Managing partners should be able to delegate less important matters to other firm members, office administrators, and vendors when necessary. For help in determining what to delegate, when, and to whom; please refer to the table that appears on page 82 of Chapter 6.

4. Internal Resources—The 3 Ps

One of the indispensable resources a manager should have is the mindset discussed in Chapter 3. But beyond that a manager needs some internal resources at his or her disposal. Of these, the three most important are what we refer to as the Three Ps:

- *Passion* is the desire to manage. Some people are management wonks—they love the challenges and triumphs of managing and are energized in this role by working with others. But even if managing doesn't float your boat, the requisite passion for managing may simply come from an appreciation for how effective management will increase your firm's profits and resilience, or from practical necessity if you are the head of a solo or small firm and the only person in a position to manage.
- *Perseverance* rests on a lawyer's the ability to deal with conflict and stress in a healthy manner. Studies have shown that the demands and stress of legal practice take a toll on many lawyers' mental and physical health. (See Chapter 25 for a discussion of this issue.) The additional demands of being

in a management position likely exacerbate those stresses. Lawyers can build resilience and minimize the risk of burnout by developing healthy personal habits, good work-life integration, and competence in handling interpersonal conflicts.

- *Patience* is often overlooked but nonetheless essential. Independent lawyers who are accustomed to moving at a fast pace can become irritated and discouraged by how much time it can take to work with others in making and implementing management decisions. In response, they sometimes check out or go into do-it-myself mode and end up accomplishing less. A manager's drive to achieve is not weakened by developing a degree of patience with others, yourself, and the pace of change. If anything, relationships and resilience improve, resulting in more being achieved in the long run.

CHAPTER SUMMARY

Even the most skilled managers need support in order to succeed. The presence, absence and degree of the following supports help determine a manager's effectiveness.

1. A Firm Vision, Strategy and Business Plan. Managers are most effective when there is a clear firm vision and business plan with which they can align their efforts. When these items are missing, a manager should make the creation of them one of his or her first priorities.

2. Authority to Manage and Lead. A manager's *responsibilities* should be commensurate with his or

her management *authority*. Leading and managing can be problematical when lawyers lack adequate discretion to make decisions and must work through numerous committees. Managers in these kinds of firms should make sure that there is agreement and buy-in as to decision-making rules and authority.

3. Time to Manage and Lead. Finding time to manage is a common problem. Managers need to address the expectations of their firm, partners, and family as to how much time they will devote to management activities. Firms can support their managers by providing sufficient staff and infrastructure and lowering billable hour and client development minimums.

4. Internal Resources. In addition to having the right mindset, managers do better when the have the Three Ps:
   * Passion—the desire to manage;
   * Perseverance—the ability to deal with conflict and stress in a healthy manner; and
   * Patience—with others, yourself, and the pace of organizational change.

REFERENCES

Berle, A. A. (1969). *Power*. New York, NY: Harcourt Brace & World.

Maister, D. (2008). *Strategy and the fat smoker*. Boston, MA: Spangle Press.

PART III

Managing Specific Individuals and Situations

The chapters in this part of the book offer practical advice on how champion managers use the skills and mindset described previously to deal with many of the challenges, situations, and individuals commonly found in today's law firms. Champion managers know the different skills and approaches they need for getting the best out of their underperforming, superstar, and average employees.

For example, they look past facile generalizations about Millennials, treat them as individuals who may or may not be different from older generations, and recognize that there are different keys to motivating them. Champion managers know how to supervise an increasingly diverse workforce that now includes contract attorneys, temps, interns, and employees that may be working on a flextime, part-time, virtual, or telecommuting basis. They also understand that it's good business and ethical to manage for diversity and inclusion, to prevent harassment and bullying, to protect privacy and confidentiality, and to promote individual and firm-wide wellness.

14

Managing Millennials

Kids! I don't know what's wrong with these kids today!
Kids! Who can understand anything they say?

"Kids," from *Bye Bye Birdie* (1960)
Lyrics by Lee Adams

Intergenerational misunderstanding and conflict are nothing new. Baby Boomer managers in today's business and legal communities are often overheard echoing the sentiments expressed in the above song, even though the lyrics are over fifty years old. They find managing Millennials difficult and frustrating, and still wonder, as the song did:

Why can't they be like we were, perfect in every way?
What's the matter with kids today?

To become a champion manager of Millennials (or members of any other generation), it's helpful to first take a closer look at the way we think about "generations" in the workplace. While we can talk clearly about the generations of a product (e.g., iPod Classic 1st through 6th, Mini 1st and 2nd, Nano 1st through 7th, Shuffle 1st through 4th) or of a family (e.g., great-grandparents, grandparents, parents, children), labels like Traditionalist, Baby Boomer, Gen X, or Millennial refer to demographic groups that, by their nature, are less well defined.

Generations in the U.S. Workplace (Fry, 2015)			
Traditionalists	Baby Boomers	Generation X	Millennials
~1925–1943	~1944–1962	~1963–1980	~1981–2000
3.7 million	44.6 million	52.7 million	53.5 million

People born within a few years of one another are, of course, more likely to share the same social, economic, and technological environment and have common experiences; but a person's birth year is only one of many factors shaping how he or she feels, thinks, perceives the world, and behaves. A person's national origin, race, gender, culture, education, work experience, sexual orientation, and socioeconomic status also contribute. Lumping people together in one of these demographic groups without reference to these other factors can easily lead to facile overgeneralizations.

There isn't even agreement on the time frame for the Millennial Generation: some studies refer to Millennials as being born between 1982 and 2002, while others use a date range of 1980 to 2004. Although studies have found common themes, there is also a lack of uniformity when it comes to descriptions of Millennials' beliefs, attitudes, and behaviors. (Interestingly, some of the more nuanced studies actually find differences in the attitudes and behaviors of older and younger Millennials [Rikleen, 2014].) At best, what can be taken from these studies are generalizations about Millennials.

These generalizations can be a trap for an unsophisticated manager. Generalizations about any group of people can too easily lead to stereotyping and pigeonholing. Unsophisticated managers will assume that simply because a person is a Millennial, he or she must think and feel a certain way. Champion managers avoid doing this. Just because a person's birth year falls in the Millennial range doesn't mean they will think, feel, and act like other Millennials. There are Millennials who act more like Gen Xers, and Boomers who act more like Millennials (see text box). It's important to look beyond labels and manage people as individuals with their own unique views, motivators, and behaviors.

Curious About Whether Your Behavior Fits Your Generation?

The Pew Research Center has done a great deal of research into generational differences. They have created a "How Millennial Are You?" quiz that looks at your behaviors to determine in which generation you belong. It can be found at http://www.pewresearch.org/quiz/how-millennial-are-you/.

Studies have shown that some of the attitudinal and behavioral differences between Millennials and older generations lead to misunderstandings, mistrust, and frustration on both sides. Simple demographics make it an imperative for managers to learn how to address these differences and engage, motivate, and retain Millennials. In 2015, Millennials became the largest age group in the United States workforce, and by 2025, Millennials will be 75 percent of the global workforce (Dews, 2014). Approximately one in five lawyers in the United States is a Millennial (McQueen & American Lawyer, 2016), so it is increasingly likely that in the future—if it's not already the case—a Millennial will be your employee, partner, client, or boss.

Champion managers recognize that beyond the stereotypes and jokes about Millennials, there are often differences between them and earlier generations with regard to their perceived work ethic, desire for flexibility and work-life balance, familiarity and facility with technology, and need for meaningful work. Champion managers also know that the ways in which they delegate, deliver feedback, and mentor employees of all generations are particularly well-suited and productive when working with Millennials.

MILLENNIAL WORK ETHIC AND WORK-LIFE BALANCE

Many managers from older generations feel that Millennials—raised on stories of the quick fame and success of some athletes, celebrities, and tech entrepreneurs—often don't understand how hard they must really work and sacrifice in order to succeed. They assume that Millennials aren't working when they're not in the office. Studies suggest this is not the case, with up to 69 percent of Millennials between the ages 25 and 34 bringing work home with them, and 42 percent checking in with work while on vacation (Stapleton, 2014).

Millennials see themselves as working hard but differently than older generations. Compared to Boomers and

Xers, they place greater importance on family obligations, relationships, and personal health and wellness. As a result they want more flexibility of work hours and locations so they can attend to these priorities. Because of their greater comfort and skill with technology, Millennials view the relationship between time and work differently than older generations. They widely believe technology provides them with the means to be productive while working outside of the office. Working remotely can, however, be perceived by older generations as a lack of commitment, loyalty, or work ethic.

Champion managers work with each employee (whether they are a Millennial or not) to find an appropriate balance of time in and out of the office. This balance seldom remains static: as office workloads and client needs change, the balance needs to shift. At the beginning of a Millennial's career, a champion manager may coach him or her on the importance of face time (i.e., being physically present in the office) and building relationships with Gen X and Baby Boomer colleagues.

An employee's performance and productivity are major considerations in determining flex schedules, but not the sole ones. Working remotely or on different schedules can, if not handled properly, result in communication problems and delays. It can also contribute to employees of any generation feeling that they are not an integral part of the office community. Because a feeling of belonging is an important factor in fostering engagement in Millennials, champion managers find ways to include them even when they are working remotely some of the time.

MILLENNIALS AND TECHNOLOGY

Millennials view technology as a tool for working efficiently and effectively while outside of the office, but many of them fear that their managers see it more as a means for 24/7 accessibility. When taken to extremes, constant connectivity can lengthen Millennials' workdays to the point where it exacerbates their stress and makes it more challenging for them to be optimally productive and achieve their desired life-work balance. Champion managers recognize this and set respectful boundaries for how and when firm members should be contacted when outside of the office.

Although Millennials are generally more tech-savvy than their Boomer and GenX managers, they are concerned about being used as unofficial (and at times unpaid) tech support. While they are eager to share their expertise, they want to make sure that helping older generations with technology doesn't take time away from their core responsibilities, particularly their need to bill hours to meet desired targets. Champion managers articulate clear expectations and policies regarding technology, working remotely, and productivity.

MEANINGFUL WORK ENGAGES MILLENNIALS

Millennials are engaged and motivated by work they consider interesting and meaningful. "Meaningful" can mean relevant to their career or personal development, or in line with their core values. As a demographic group, Millennials are more concerned than older generations with global issues, social responsibility, and sustainability. They favor work that gives them a sense of purpose and accomplishment and lets them feel they are making a difference, whether that is for their clients, the firm, or the world as a whole. Pro-bono, charitable, and public service projects often appeal to Millennials' desire for purpose-driven work. Like older generations, Millennials are civic-minded—but they prefer their community involvement and charitable activities to be more hands-on, personal, and direct.

Champion managers already help their delegatees understand the context and importance of an assignment (see page 85 on delegation). This practice works well to address Millennials' desire for meaningful work. For example, a manager might simply ask an attorney or paralegal to "Review our client's emails from the last twelve months and flag any mentions of accidents or workplace safety violations." Although this is a clear and straightforward request, it doesn't explain why this task matters and how it fits into the client's broader legal needs. A champion manager will add, "We need you to do this to show that the steps they've already taken have been effective and that plaintiff's allegations of cover-ups, increased hazards, and injuries are without merit." While this is good practice for delegation to all employees, it is especially important for engaging and motivating many Millennials.

Champion managers don't assume that Millennials' desire for meaningful work means that they are entirely idealistic and altruistic. Studies have shown that high pay is also a key motivator for many Millennials. It is particularly important to Millennials when they have very large student debts to repay or when their job involves an inordinate amount of time and effort. When a job offers little intrinsic meaning and profit is the major motivator within a firm, it's understandable that a Millennial may focus largely on compensation, because that is the main advantage of his or her job.

The best approach to motivating and retaining Millennials is to offer a combination of both extrinsic (e.g., compensation, perks, titles, etc.) and intrinsic (e.g., appreciation, recognition, interesting assignments, etc.) rewards. There is no one set formula for the best combination of these motivators: it will vary from Millennial to Millennial, and may change throughout an employee's career. Managers need to take the time to know their employees and understand their interests and values, so they can discover which motivators will work best.

DELEGATING TO MILLENNIALS

Having been reared by parents who consistently engaged and encouraged them, many Millennials are used to a great deal of adult input into their decisions and actions. Compared to earlier generations who enjoyed ample free time, Millennials are more likely to have experienced a highly structured and scheduled childhood in which most of their activities were planned. As a result, Millennials may be uncomfortable with ambiguity and look to their managers for relatively large amounts of supervision and direction. To older generations, this may create the impression that Millennials are less skilled at problem solving and less savvy about negotiating their way through day-to-day workplace challenges.

To address these differences, champion managers give Millennials clear assignments, specific guidance, and frequent feedback. When delegating work, they avoid vague language such as, "I'll need your analysis of the law relating to this case next week." Instead, provide structure and predictability by saying,

> I need you to analyze the law relating to this case. Start your research now, and let's talk either by phone or in person on Friday. You can share your initial thoughts and concerns at that time, and I will answer any questions you may have. That should allow you to get a draft to me by Wednesday afternoon at the latest. If you run into any obstacles, please let me know by Monday. As you know, our client is concerned about the expense and difficulty of litigating this matter out of state, so please look at issues of venue and jurisdiction, while also considering what other defenses we may be able to raise. Does that sound workable to you? Do you have any questions?

Many Millennials will welcome this degree of specificity and structure, but some may feel that their manager is micromanaging or being excessively directive. Although Millennials often want large amounts of input from their managers, they somewhat paradoxically may also want a fair degree of freedom to figure out new solutions and ways of getting things done. Champion managers initially err on the side of too much guidance as they learn the capabilities and preferences of a specific employee. As their confidence grows, they develop a keener sense of what level of guidance works best with that employee and for a particular assignment.

Millennials generally like challenging assignments that spur their professional growth and development. But if an assignment is a stretch for a Millennial employee (e.g., a pleading or assignment in an area of law they are unfamiliar with, or a more complex case or transaction than they have previously handled), it is of course necessary to provide them sufficient resources and guidance to ensure they will succeed.

GIVING FEEDBACK TO MILLENNIALS

Many Millennials have grown up being encouraged to ask a lot of questions, engage in dialogue, and ask for feedback. In the workplace, their frequent questions and comments are sometimes misinterpreted by older generations as a lack of respect. This is a major disconnect: for older generations, respect is often equated with deference to one's position and authority; for Millennials, respect is equated with being heard and participating in dialogue (Rikleen, 2014).

Given their structured upbringing, high level of adult involvement, and difficulty with ambiguity, feedback is especially important to Millennials. The principles and methods champion managers follow that are described in detail in Chapter 7 work particularly well with Millennials. In short they are:

- Give feedback in the moment if possible. Real-time and frequent ways of providing feedback (e.g., 1:1 weekly conversations) work best. Formal and infrequent means of providing feedback, such as annual or semi-annual performance reviews, are of limited value with all employees, especially Millennials.

- Give feedback in person. Even though Millennials are very comfortable with technology, they see feedback delivered by email, text, or written memorandum as a poor substitute for an in-person conversation. In this regard, they are very much like older generations. Champion managers know face-to-face conversations minimize misunderstandings and provide better opportunities for questions, dialogue, and strengthening relationships.
- Use feedback as an opportunity for learning. Champion managers make time after an assignment is completed to jointly discuss what went well and what didn't. Rather than assigning blame, they are curious about what factors may have contributed to an employee's success or failure. They shift from feedback to "feed-forward" by focusing on what has been learned and what should be done differently in the future.
- Don't overlook what was done right and well. Positive feedback is more effective in changing people's behavior than negative feedback. At the same time, champion managers avoid the "*but* syndrome"—in which they start a conversation with all the positives and then, following the word "but," move onto all the negatives. Feedback recipients of all generations have difficulty listening when they're waiting for the other shoe to drop.
- Avoid sugarcoating or bypassing important messages. Champion managers know that in order to support and develop their Millennial employees

(and those of any other generation), they will, from time to time, need to tell them that their performance was poor. Champion managers understand that doing so may create emotional discomfort (both the employee's and their own), but that diluting or sugarcoating an important message often leads to misunderstandings and missed opportunities for improvement.

MENTORING MILLENNIALS

With their desire to advance and succeed, Millennials respond positively to well designed and implemented mentoring programs. Mentoring conveys the message that a Millennial employee matters and is valued by their firm. The feedback they receive during mentoring is an excellent way to engage them, challenge them, and improve their performance. Regular and skillful feedback can become the foundation for the personal relationships and reciprocal loyalties that Millennials seek.

Mentoring is not only essential in developing Millennials into the next generation of leaders, but also in helping them deal with the stresses and challenges that are part of legal practice today. As noted in Chapter 25 on managing for wellness, mental health and substance abuse are critical issues in the legal profession and the incidence of them is highest in lawyers who have practiced for less than ten years (Krill, Johnson, & Albert, 2016). Attention to these difficult issues can improve the loyalty, engagement, and productivity of Millennials.

MILLENNIAL APPEARANCE & DEMEANOR

Many managers struggle with the ways different generations in their firms act and dress. Older generations often feel that many Millennials dress in a manner that is inappropriate or unprofessional. Flip-flops, tattoos, piercings, and general neatness and hygiene are typical sore points. Millennials, on the other hand, feel that comfortable clothing improves their productivity and satisfaction.

It's important that this issue be proactively addressed, because unconscious bias may exist even when nothing is said. Problems with appearance are exacerbated when there is too little feedback or silent disapproval by older generations. This bias or disapproval may hinder a Millennial's chances of development and advancement.

Champion managers begin by instituting a dress code for their firm. Aside from courts, which do, of course, set standards for how attorneys appearing before them must dress, there is no one-size-fits-all (pun intended) formula for how people should dress in the legal profession. The guidelines champion managers set are usually a reflection of their firm's clients and culture. A conservative client may expect to see his or her attorneys in more formal business attire, while a Millennial client may feel more comfortable working with attorneys in casual attire. Employees who have no face-to-face contact with clients may have more latitude in how they dress.

Champion managers know that clear and reasonable guidelines for attire help, but that they must also be enforced without hypocrisy, arbitrariness, inconsistency, and double standards. Guidelines and standards that are insensitive to employees' gender or finances should be avoided. Policies such as casual Fridays appeal to Millennials' desire for flexibility, comfort, and casual attire.

In working with Millennials, champion managers stress the prime importance of the firm's clients. Attorneys and staff should not only dress but also act in ways that make it easy for clients to relate and work with them. All employees should take into account the communication preferences of clients from different generations. A Millennial client may, for example, prefer to communicate by texts and Skype, while a Baby Boomer may want to receive memos and have face-to-face meetings with attorneys.

MILLENNIAL LOYALTY

Although older generations often feel Millennials lack loyalty to their employers, the reality is more nuanced. Non-Millennials tend to think of loyalty in institutional terms. They are more likely to leave a firm or business when they feel they are not being paid competitively or lack sufficient advancement opportunities. Millennials may be quicker to change jobs than non-Millennials, but most are also interested in developing a long-term relationship with one employer.

Millennials tend to see loyalty in interpersonal rather than institutional terms: their relationships with their managers and superiors are very important, and they want to feel they matter as individuals. Champion managers foster their loyalty by:

- Getting to know them and treating them as individuals;

- Not buying into stereotypes about their generation;
- Making them feel supported, valued, and appreciated;
- Challenging them to grow and develop;
- Providing them with frequent feedback;
- Consciously mentoring and developing them; and
- Providing flexibility in their work environment.

It should be obvious that the above list is a good recipe for fostering the loyalty of employees of all generations. It turns out, lyrics at the beginning of this chapter to the contrary, there's really nothing wrong with kids today. They may be different from older generations in some respects, but they are no less motivated or capable than their elders. Champion managers look beyond labels and manage them as individuals with their own unique views, motivators, and behaviors.

MILLENNIALS AS MANAGERS

Let's not overlook the fact that Millennials in the workplace are becoming managers themselves. Millennials might initially find themselves frustrated with managing Boomers and Xers who approach things differently than they do. If you are a Millennial manager, the first step in managing prior generations is to understand how *they* prefer to communicate and be open-minded in your approach when dealing with them.

To improve communication between the generations, Millennials should consider how Boomers and Xers prefer to communicate. As mentioned in Chapter 18 ("Managing Staff vs. Managing Attorneys"), Boomers tend to prefer to meet face to face or, if need be, by the phone while Xers often prefer communication through e-mail and texts. If you want the attention of a Boomer and need to have a dialogue, then go to that person's office and talk to them (or schedule a meeting if the Boomer is your client). Before you text to communicate with a Boomer, make sure they are comfortable using that medium (and give them some tips if they are not but would like to learn how to use it).

Many Boomers and Xers are accustomed to communicating in a more formal manner for business than you are, so keep that in mind when you send emails to them. When you write emails, they should start with a greeting that is more formal than "hi"—something like "Hello Mr. Smith"—and end with a closing such as "Best regards" or "All the best." Of course, if the email is to a colleague in your firm and on your team, it's okay to use a less formal greeting like "Hi John." The body of the email should be concise and direct, particularly if it is addressed to an Xer. Before hitting "send," you should always proofread your email to check for typos and grammar and to confirm that the tone of the email is suitable for the situation.

To become a champion manager yourself, take time to get to know your direct reports on an individual basis, learn to communicate with them in a way they understand, and get past stereotyping them in the same way you do not want to be stereotyped.

CHAPTER SUMMARY

Intergenerational management has been an issue in the workplace for many years. It is magnified today because there are more generations in the workplace than ever before and Millennials are now the largest age group in the United States workforce.

When managing Millennials, remember that there are differences between them and earlier generations with regard to:

- Work ethic and work-life balance—Millennials want more flexibility of work hours and locations so they can find time for family obligations, relationships, and personal health and wellness. They see technology as a way to remain productive while working remotely.
- Uses of technology—Millennials see technology as a tool for working efficiently and effectively when out of the office, but they do not want to be on call 24/7.
- Meaningful work engages Millennials—Millennials seek work that gives them a sense of purpose and accomplishment where they can make a difference. They want to know why a task matters and how it fits into a client's broader legal needs.
- Delegating to Millennials—Millennials who may have had helicopter parents often look to their managers to provide relatively large amounts of supervision and direction. Champion managers give Millennials clear assignments, specific guidance, and frequent feedback.
- Giving feedback to Millennials—Give feedback in the moment and in person. Use it as an opportunity for learning; avoid sugarcoating, but don't overlook what was done right and well.

- Mentoring Millennials—Millennials appreciate and respond positively to well designed and implemented mentoring programs.
- Millennial appearance and demeanor—Institute a dress code for your firm that is reflective of the firm's clients and culture so Millennials understand what is expected of them. More casual attire may be appropriate for employees who have no face-to-face contact with clients or on "casual" days.
- Millennial loyalty—Millennials view loyalty in interpersonal rather than institutional terms. They want to feel they matter as individuals.
- Millennials as managers—Millennials should communicate with prior generations they manage by understanding how *they* prefer to communicate and taking it into account in their interactions with them. They should not stereotype Boomers and Xers but instead get to know and work with them as individuals.

REFERENCES

Dews, F. (2014, July 17). Brookings Data Now: 75 percent of 2025 workforce will be Millennials. Retrieved from https://www .brookings.edu/blog/brookings-now/2014/07/17/brookings -data-now-75-percent-of-2025-workforce-will-be-millennials/

Fry, R. (2015, May 11). Millennials surpass Gen Xers as the largest generation in U.S. labor force. Retrieved from http://www .pewresearch.org/fact-tank/2015/05/11/millennials-surpass -gen-xers-as-the-largest-generation-in-u-s-labor-force/

Krill, P. R., Johnson, R., & Albert, L. (2016). The prevalence of substance use and other mental health concerns among American attorneys. *Journal of Addiction Medicine,10*(1), 46–52. doi:10.1097/adm.0000000000000182

McQueen, M., & American Lawyer. (2016). Here come the big law Millennials. Retrieved from http://www.loeb.com/~/media/files/pdfs/hurdle_florin_feb_2016.pdf

Rikleen, L. S. (2014). *You raised us—now work with us: Millennials, career success, and building strong workplace teams.* Chicago, IL: ABA Publishing, American Bar Association.

Stapleton, M. (2014, December 30). Motivating Millennials: The 5 key drivers of Millennial engagement. Retrieved from http://www.hr.com/en/magazines/recognition_engagement_excellence_essentials/november_2014_recognition_engagement/motivating-millennials-the-5-key-drivers-of-millen_i4bhv27w.html

15

Managing Underperformers

Managing underperforming attorneys and staff is a good way to see how champion managers utilize the skills and tools described in the preceding part of this book. Underperformers are sometimes referred to as "C players," a term that can be misleading and insensitive. Rather than branding an individual with a low grade, a champion manager focuses on that person's performance of certain tasks or jobs. These individuals may struggle with some of their responsibilities but overall do an acceptable or barely acceptable job. They may have once performed well, but over time their effectiveness has fallen. Managers often wonder what it will take (if anything) to get these employees' performance up to par again.

Managing underperformers is seldom a simple matter. For the few that are grossly incompetent, unethical, or otherwise putting the firm at risk, the decision to terminate them is relatively easy (assuming there is no or little risk of litigation). But if their conduct is not that egregious, managers must determine whether there's a way to help these individuals improve their performance and, if there's not, how to either change their responsibilities or terminate their employment. In those cases, champion managers take the following steps in working with underperformers.

1. CHAMPION MANAGERS ARE PROACTIVE IN ADDRESSING UNDERPERFORMANCE

Champion managers don't wait for things to get better on their own. Many managers hesitate to invest the time and energy needed to manage underperformers. Some wish to avoid the emotional discomfort that comes from discussing poor performance with an employee, while others may feel they lack the skill to be successful in these conversations. They often hope that somebody else will take the lead in addressing an employee's poor performance or the employee will somehow find a way to improve performance without the support or intervention of others. These hopes are rarely realistic.

As described in greater detail in Chapter 7, "Giving and Receiving Feedback," ignoring problems and withholding feedback only makes matters worse. The emotional discomfort managers seek to avoid only gets worse when problems are allowed to fester. Underperformers may mistakenly believe they're doing a good job when they don't receive feedback to the contrary. They will continue to do things poorly while their bad habits become more firmly entrenched. Other firm members who are aware of the underperformance may wonder why it is not being addressed and whether the firm's standards are slipping or favoritism is at play. Either way, morale will decline.

2. CHAMPION MANAGERS THINK BEFORE THEY ACT

Champion managers realize that prompt but not hurried action is needed. They understand that preparation is one of the keys to having a successful conversation with an underperformer. They set a fixed amount of time for preparation so it doesn't lead to procrastination and delay. Champion managers don't narrowly focus on an employee's poor performance: they consider how they or other people or other factors may be contributing to the employee's problems.

If Human Resources records and assessments are available, they may request them to see if the employee's poor performance is an aberration, a recent phenomenon, or part of a longer-term pattern. Champion managers look at the big picture and consider whether other employees are having the same problems and underperforming in similar ways. If that's the case, it may be an indication that problems in the recruiting, hiring, onboarding, or training processes should be addressed.

Champion managers will take time to review everything they know about the underperformer. They consider questions like:

- What training and coaching has the person received?
- Has the person's job description or reporting relationships changed, and is there still a fit with the person's skills?
- What are the person's motivators, triggers, and values?

- Has the person recently lost a mentor or friend in the firm?
- What are my feelings about this person and his or her underperformance?

In preparing, a champion manager will quite naturally have formed an opinion and judgment about the employee but will hold that point of view lightly and be willing to be influenced by what the employee has to say. Champion managers recognize that they will likely learn something from their conversation with an employee. They also avoid "jumping to solutions," thinking they have already figured out the problem and know everything the employee must do to improve. In short, they stay open minded. Rather than relying solely on their assessment of the underperformer, champion managers may at times discreetly ask others about their experiences with the employee. In doing so, they are mindful of the communication skills described in Chapter 4 and will ask questions that encourage others to challenge their existing point of view.

3. CHAMPION MANAGERS TALK WITH—NOT TO—THE UNDERPERFORMER

The semantic distinction between "talking with" and "talking to" may seem petty—but it's not. Conversations with underperformers need to be dialogues not monologues. The guidelines for collaborative feedback described in Chapter 7 should be reviewed and followed. Champion managers begin by explaining the problem or underperformance from their perspective. They describe what they and others have observed and how that has affected other firm members, the firm as a whole, and clients. They cite specific examples rather than making sweeping generalizations. For example, rather than saying "Your legal writing skills are poor," they will say, "There were several grammatical errors, *non sequiturs*, and misspellings of names in the motions you drafted for the Leicester case." They make sure their feedback is clear, timely, supportive, and future oriented. They avoid *post mortems* on problems and instead focus on what can be learned by all and what the underperformer, manager, and firm can do to improve future performance.

In taking a truly collaborative approach, champion managers make sure they listen and encourage underperformers to share their perspectives on the problem. They rely on the paraphrasing and summarizing skills described on pages 56–57 to make sure there is mutual understanding. There are all sorts of things managers may learn when they stop talking and start listening in the expansive way described on pages 54–55. Much to their surprise, they may discover that a firm member feels overwhelmed or undervalued; is having problems with other firm members or at home; doesn't understand what is expected of them; or feels a lack of support, training, or resources. They may also discover that an employee's poor performance is actually a symptom or manifestation of a larger or different problem. And even if they learn little, at least the employee will feel heard and understood.

4. CHAMPION MANAGERS PARTNER WITH UNDERPERFORMERS TO CREATE AN IMPROVEMENT PLAN

Champion managers resist the urge to simply hand an improvement plan to an underperforming employee or unilaterally prescribe a solution. They realize two very important things:

- An employee's participation in crafting an improvement plan enhances its chances of being successfully implemented; and
- Not all employees are willing or capable of changing.

Before co-creating an improvement plan, champion managers make sure that their employee acknowledges the problem and understands its impact. Without that understanding, an employee will likely be unmotivated to change, and managers need to assess whether it is worth their time and energy trying to coach someone who is unwilling to admit that there's an issue. Champion managers also need to assess whether the employee has a growth mindset (believing his or her skills and talents can be developed) or a fixed mindset (believing further development is beyond the reach of his or her innate talents and intelligence). Employees with a fixed mindset tend to just go through the motions of a plan without investing the necessary amount of time and energy to improve.

In jointly creating a plan, champion managers start by asking underperforming employees:

- What they would like to achieve (i.e., what are their goals)?

- What are their priorities (i.e., what are their most urgent or important goals)?
- What is a realistic time frame for achieving their goals?
- What new skills do they need or would they like to learn?
- What resources or support will they need to achieve their goals?
- How will the manager and the employee know if the employee has been successful in achieving these goals?

By having employees share their ideas first, champion managers can test whether an underperformer truly understands the problem and what improved performance will look like. Champion managers can then share their ideas and collaborate with an employee to create an improvement plan based on S.M.A.R.T. goals as described in Chapter 8. When employees feel they have helped design their plans, they are far more motivated to work hard and strive for improvement.

5. CHAMPION MANAGERS COACH AND FOLLOW UP WITH UNDERPERFORMERS

Champion managers realize that creating a performance plan for an employee and not following up with them is like giving someone a map but no compass (or GPS, if you will). Employees can and do get lost unless they have someone to help guide and support them as they work towards achieving their improvement goals. Champion managers monitor their employee's progress or they delegate that monitoring to another person (e.g., an employee's immediate supervisor or mentor) who may be better positioned or qualified to offer support and feedback. They schedule regular meetings to talk about progress; answer questions; offer feedback, encouragement, and advice; and see if timelines for improvement are being met.

If timelines aren't being met, champion managers get curious about why this is happening and discuss this with underperforming employees to hold them accountable. They may check with other firm members to determine whether an employee is making progress. If external events or pressures are obstacles, the plan or timeline for improvement may be modified. If resources or tools are missing, they may be supplied. And if the employee is losing motivation and focus, a firm reminder may get the person back on track. Most employees appreciate this attention and follow-up.

Champion managers provide their employees with feedback on their performance in general and how well they are doing in executing on their improvement plan. They know that focusing on negatives or what an employee hasn't accomplished yet is a poor strategy; positive feedback—letting employees know what they're doing well and what they've accomplished—is much more effective way to help an employee change his or her behavior. When underperformers meet timelines and make progress, champion managers recognize these accomplishments and find ways to acknowledge employees for their efforts and the positive changes they are making. Champion managers may show their appreciation verbally and also through tangible rewards.

6. CHAMPION MANAGERS RECOGNIZE THAT THERE MAY COME A TIME WHEN UNDERPERFORMERS SHOULD BE TERMINATED

Sometimes a champion manager's best intentions and an underperforming employee's best efforts don't produce the needed improvements. Champion managers lay the groundwork for this possibility well before it becomes a reality: they have been clear with their employee about the specific improvements that are needed, they have provided regular feedback to the employee about his or her progress or lack thereof, they have provided any necessary resources, and they have been clear about the consequences for the employee if he or she doesn't improve their performance within the time frame provided. When all this is done, an underperforming employee is not surprised that the conversation has finally shifted from improvement to separation from the firm.

It is equally, if not more, important for champion managers to formally deal with an employee's underperformance. Human resources best practices and relevant employment laws should be followed well before any thoughts of termination. Incidents of underperformance, disciplinary actions, and problems with an employee's behavior or attitude should be documented, including the impact these problems have had on the firm, clients, or other firm members. The firm and manager's efforts to help the employee address problems and improve should also be noted.

Managers are understandably hesitant to terminate an employee. It can be difficult, expensive and time consuming to replace a member of the firm. There can also be the risk of a wrongful termination or related lawsuit.

Managers—even champion managers—can find it emotionally painful to terminate someone who has been a member of the firm. This is particularly true when the person is a well-liked, long-term employee who has made a genuine effort to improve. If a change in job description and responsibilities is not feasible, termination may be the only option.

As difficult as it can be to terminate an employee, champion managers know that keeping an underperforming employee can undermine the morale and performance of their firm's other employees. Not dealing with underperforming employees and not terminating them can send unintended messages that:

- We (the firm's management) are not really monitoring your performance and that of other firm members.
- It's okay to get by with barely acceptable performance and behavior.
- We are not actually serious about espoused values like providing top-notch client service or having a collegial and collaborative firm environment.
- We don't care if you are working twice as hard as the person next to you; you have to pick up the slack and correct that person's mistakes.

Champion managers also know that firm members are often the first to be aware of a fellow firm member's underperformance. Taking corrective action—including termination when necessary—lets them know that their good performance is appreciated and the firm is serious about maintaining its standards of excellence and good behavior.

How employees are terminated also has a large impact on remaining firm members. If they sense that a terminated employee has been treated capriciously or unfairly, they may lose trust in their manager and be more likely to leave.

CHAPTER SUMMARY

Underperformers may struggle with some of their responsibilities, so champion managers should take the following steps to work with them:

- Be proactive in addressing underperformance. Give them timely feedback or they may mistakenly believe they're doing a good job.
- Champion managers think before they act and identify their own feelings about an underperforming employee. They take time to review the employee's performance evaluations and personnel file, consider whether the person's job description or reporting relationship has changed, review what training and coaching the person has received, consider what motivates the person, and determine whether the person has recently lost a mentor or friend in the firm.
- Champion managers talk with—not to—the underperformer. Conversations with underperformers need to be dialogues not monologues. In taking a truly collaborative approach, champion managers encourage underperformers to share their perspectives on the problem.

- Champion managers partner with underperformers to create improvement plans by asking:
  - What would they like to achieve (i.e. what are their goals)?
  - What are their priorities (i.e., what are their most urgent or important goals)?
  - What is a realistic time frame for achieving their goals?
  - What new skills do they need or would they like to learn?
  - What resources or support will they need to achieve their goals?
  - How will the manager and the employee know if the employee has been successful in achieving these goals?
- Champion managers coach and follow up with underperformers by monitoring their progress (or delegating that monitoring to an immediate supervisor or mentor), scheduling regular meetings to talk about progress, offering feedback and advice, and seeing whether timelines are being met. If timelines aren't being met, champion managers discuss this with the employee to hold him or her accountable, and they check with others to determine whether the employee is making progress.
- Champion managers recognize that there may come a time when underperformers should be terminated. They have been clear with their employees about the specific improvements that are needed, have provided regular feedback about their progress or lack thereof, have provided

necessary resources, and have been clear about the consequences for not succeeding. Human resources best practices and relevant employment laws should be followed before terminating an underperformer. An underperforming employee can undermine the morale and performance of the firm's other employees, so taking corrective action, including termination, lets other firm members know that their good performance is appreciated.

16

Managing Superstars

Many managers assume that their superstar employees don't need a lot of guidance and support. Because they're outperforming other members of the firm, a hands-off policy seems appropriate. Managers often think:

> I'll just stay out of their way, keep them happy, and watch them overachieve. They're making money for the firm, so rather than worrying about them, the best use of my time is to focus on clients and help my underperformers.

As superficially logical and appealing as this approach may be, it underestimates the challenges of managing superstar employees. Champion managers know that successfully managing super achievers can be tricky and is seldom as straightforward as helping an underperformer improve. They understand that some superstars are quite secure while others are driven to overachieve and outperform by feelings of insecurity and inferiority stemming from their childhood or other critical parts of their lives. These insecure superstars have their own unique needs and problems that managers need to address if they want to retain these very productive and profitable members of the firm.

Insecure superstars often suffer from low confidence and self esteem. They may have difficulty hearing and taking in the praise they receive. Lacking an internal sense of satisfaction, they may constantly need and look for a great deal of appreciation from others, particularly their managers and superiors. Because they work very hard to please and impress others, they may struggle to say no to projects and assignments no matter how busy they may already be, and yet they manage to get the work done. In their drive to please others and be appreciated, they at times deliver far more than is needed and has been requested, sometimes to the detriment of the firm or its clients. They may also set exacting and at times unnecessarily high standards for themselves and others. These behaviors can leave them feeling unhappy, unappreciated, burnt out, and ready to leave their firm in a quixotic search for a more satisfying work environment.

It can be difficult for managers to discern which of their superstar employees are secure and which are not. Appearances can be deceiving: an air of superiority and smugness can mask a superstar's insecurities and lack of confidence, but those with an innate sense of self-confidence and security typically require less attention and care. Both secure and insecure superstars tend to be narcissistic with large and, at times, fragile egos. An attitude of superiority, which may be grounded in fact, and their need to shine as a superstar can make it difficult for them to form good working relationships with other firm members. They may find it difficult to connect to and collaborate with firm members they feel are not at their same high level of performance or intelligence.

The first step in managing superstars is to recognize and respond to their sometimes hidden weaknesses and needs. Champion managers use the following guidelines and approaches to help their superstars remain productive, engaged, happy, and a member of the firm.

1. CHAMPION MANAGERS ARE AWARE OF THEIR OWN FEELINGS ABOUT THEIR SUPERSTARS

It can be difficult to manage smart, ambitious, and over-achieving lawyers without at times envying their many talents. This can be doubly difficult if they are also narcissistic, condescending, or demanding. Superstars who view a manager as inferior in some respect may challenge that manager's authority and expertise. Champion managers are self aware enough to understand that in situations like these, their own emotions, if unchecked or poorly expressed, can get in the way of effective management.

Champion managers know how to exercise their power and authority in a manner that doesn't exacerbate struggles and tensions with superstars. They don't acquiesce to superstars' demands, but are willing to work with and make concessions to them so long as their own authority and the overall firm objectives are respected. When champion managers push back and set clear boundaries, they do so with finesse so that superstars' egos remain intact and unharmed.

They also realize that it's easy, but a mistake, to take too much credit for their superstars' accomplishments. Doing so can lead to superstars feeling resentful and under-appreciated. It's better to keep the spotlight shining mostly on them for work they've done, while taking credit for being their excellent and understanding manager.

2. CHAMPION MANAGERS OFFER THEIR SUPERSTARS AUTHENTIC, PERSONAL, AND SPECIFIC PRAISE

Champion managers know their superstars' unique talents, needs, aspirations, and motivators. This helps them personalize their praise so superstars can fully internalize it. Rather than offering a generic "great job" or "well done" that superstars will quickly forget or dismiss, champion managers offer praise that specifically identifies what was accomplished, why it was extraordinary, and how it benefitted the firm and client. Superstars, particularly insecure ones, crave frequent praise; but if that praise comes across as rote or insincere, it can actually be demotivating. Champion managers don't rely on tired hyperboles, clichés, and platitudes when giving praise to any of their employees; they know that clear, descriptive, and appreciative feedback is the best approach to take.

Over time, many managers—champion ones included—can begin to simply expect great performance from their superstars. Work they would consider excellent if done by another firm member can be taken for granted and considered average for a superstar. When this occurs, they may unintentionally limit or withhold their appreciation for what their superstar has accomplished. Champion managers avoid doing this: they continue to appreciate their superstars' efforts and accomplishments, while not lapsing into insincere flattery or rote formulas of praise. True and personal recognition works better to motivate superstars to continue their high levels of performance.

3. CHAMPION MANAGERS REWARD THEIR SUPERSTARS THROUGH COMPENSATION AND INTERESTING ASSIGNMENTS

Many superstars like tangible rewards as much as they like accolades. They see their compensation as validation of their self worth and a balm for old or hidden feelings of low self-esteem. If they're paid the same as other firm members, they may assume that their managers value them only as much as they value other firm members. They wrongly believe that their managers don't recognize or appreciate all that they add and do.

If superstars are making an outsize contribution to the firm's performance, visibility, or profits, find a way to recognize that through bonuses, perks, titles, or greater responsibilities if paying them a higher salary is not feasible. Interesting and challenging cases and high visibility transactions are the kinds of plum assignments that superstars will consider an indication of the high regard with which they are held. Complex and demanding assignments also provide superstars with the sort of challenges that keep them interested, engaged, and feeling they're at the top of their game.

4. CHAMPION MANAGERS ARE CLEAR ABOUT DESIRED RESULTS AND THE SCOPE AND EXTENT OF WHAT IS EXPECTED FROM THEIR SUPERSTARS

Overachieving can at times be too much of a good thing. Superstars may do extra work or take on extra responsibilities that are not the best and highest use of their time. In their drive to produce and impress, insecure overachievers in particular may over-deliver. While the work they do may be impressive and exceed expectations, it may not be what a client most needs or is willing to pay for.

Champion managers understand that their overachievers may have difficulty setting boundaries for themselves, so they step in and are explicit about the scope and quality of needed work. Even when champion managers are clear about these boundaries, insecure overachievers may still do excessive work. When this happens, champion managers explain that while they appreciate the overachiever's extra efforts, even more value may be realized by focusing on other important matters. Rather than unilaterally defining or restating the boundaries and parameters for a superstar's work, champion managers take a collaborative approach. They engage the superstar in a highly interactive conversation with the goal of jointly articulating and agreeing to the scope of work. This minimizes misunderstandings and excessive and unnecessary work.

5. CHAMPION MANAGERS HELP THEIR SUPERSTARS AVOID BURNOUT

It's not unusual for superstars and overachievers to push themselves very hard. As noted above, there can at times be deep and unresolved emotional reasons for them doing so. And for some of them, no matter how hard they push and how much they achieve, they are left feeling the need to excel further and be praised and appreciated more. These superstars are especially vulnerable to burnout; their excessive, unrequested, and unnecessary work is often a large contributing factor.

Champion managers are rarely surprised that a superstar—or any firm member for that matter—is approaching burnout. As noted in greater detail in Chapter 25, "Managing for Wellness," champion managers know when a superstar is showing early signs of burnout. If they sense that one of their superstars in uncharacteristically fatigued, angry, erratic, unhappy, or showing signs of self-destructive or addictive behaviors, they get curious and check in.

Some superstars may be quite unwilling to admit a problem or ask for help, in part because they have difficulty with feeling vulnerable or acknowledging what they might perceive as criticism or weakness. But if a champion manager's superstar is willing to acknowledge that something is amiss and stress and burnout are nascent problems, then champion managers can respond in many ways. They may need to reemphasize healthy boundaries for their superstar's work, as described in the preceding section. In some cases, they may even want to reduce the scope of work without letting their superstar feel that they have somehow failed. Or they may need to offer more frequent or personal praise and appreciation. Or they may just need to be a compassionate and interested ear so their superstar feels heard and understood.

Champion managers also know that overachievers who feel burned out and under-appreciated often believe that they can solve their problems and become happier and reengaged in the practice of law by moving to another firm. More often than not, these superstars simply repeat their old pattern of overperformance, exhaustion, and burnout in a new environment. If they are fortunate enough to move to a firm with a champion manager who knows how to handle them, they may break this cycle. Rather than risking their departure, champion managers step up and are proactive in addressing their superstars' destructive behaviors and needs.

Although burnout is a major problem, it would be disingenuous to pretend that some very large law firms don't encourage some of the behaviors that can lead to it. They offer high compensation and great opportunities in exchange for 24/7 availability and grueling workloads. In these firms that have strong name recognition, a high-demand work climate, and a strong interest from candidates, everyone recognizes the deal—it is baked into their business model. It is expected that a large proportion of their attorneys, superstars included, will leave the firm at some point only to be replaced by graduates from top law schools. Departing attorneys leave with excellent legal training and a stellar résumé—hopefully before they burn out.

While some larger firms may tolerate, plan for, and even encourage a relatively high degree of turnover, it is seldom as advantageous for smaller ones. For them, retention is the key to recouping their investment in the training and development of their attorneys.

6. CHAMPION MANAGERS HELP THEIR SUPERSTARS LEARN HOW TO COOPERATE AND COLLABORATE WITH OTHER MEMBERS OF THE FIRM

Some superstars have difficulty collaborating with other firm members. The more narcissistic ones may believe—rightly or wrongly—that they are superior to everyone else. Or they may feel that other firm members, whom they perceive as being less capable or accomplished, will only hold them back. Or they may be so insecure that they don't want to share credit with other firm members. Or their fast pace and exacting work ethic may at times place unreasonable and exhausting demands on other firm members.

Often these kinds of superstars haven't developed the people smarts and people skills they need to work constructively with others. They are solo rather than team players. On basketball teams, they never pass the ball and want to be the one taking every shot. With these particular kinds of superstars, champion managers must first determine whether the practice of law at their firm is a team sport or one where there is plenty of room for "lone rangers." If a superstar can operate independently without damaging firm morale and productivity, it may be better to let him or her continue that way. But if the practice of law at the firm requires high levels of coordination and collaboration, then champion managers need to help their superstars become better team players. There are many ways to encourage collaborative attitudes and behavior.

Champion managers can structure work assignments so that superstars must coordinate and collaborate with other firm members in order to successfully achieve project goals. These managers make it very clear to their superstars that their performance will be evaluated not just on results but also by how well they utilize, assist, and work with other firm members. This can subtly shift a superstar's mindset away from being an individual contributor to being a leader of his or her own team of firm members. As superstars begin to receive praise and recognition for being a team leader, they will be more motivated to take on this role. Champion managers can then be more explicit and direct in giving them management and leadership responsibilities and, as noted in the following paragraphs, can enlist them in coaching and developing other firm members.

7. CHAMPION MANAGERS ENLIST THEIR SUPERSTARS IN COACHING AND DEVELOPING OTHER MEMBERS OF THE FIRM

Superstars often possess a great deal of valuable expertise and experience. The challenge is often in motivating the more narcissistic ones to share it with others, especially if those other firm members are perceived as being less intelligent, experienced, or driven than the superstar. Many self-absorbed high performers will not want to concern themselves with the performance and development of others they consider less capable or senior. They don't see it as the best use of their time and skills.

Champion managers find a way to overcome this problem by appealing to their superstar's motivators, self-interest, and sense of superiority. They make it clear that sharing expertise and acting as a mentor to other firm members is recognition of the superstar's skills and accomplishments and will further enhance his or her standing in the firm. They may also present coaching and mentoring responsibilities as the next challenge a superstar needs to take on in order to be groomed for a more important leadership position at the firm.

CHAPTER SUMMARY

Champion managers recognize that successfully managing super achievers can be tricky and is seldom as straightforward as helping an underperformer improve. They recognize and respond to their superstars' sometimes hidden weaknesses and needs by using the following guidelines and approaches to help their superstars remain productive, engaged, happy, and a member of the firm:

- Champion managers are aware of their own feelings about their superstars and know how to exercise their power and authority in a manner that doesn't exacerbate struggles and tensions with superstars. They are willing to work with and make concessions to them so long as their authority and overall firm objectives are respected.
- Champion managers offer their superstars authentic, personal, and specific praise. Champion managers don't rely on tired hyperboles, clichés, and platitudes when giving praise; they know that clear, descriptive, and appreciative feedback is the best approach to take.

- Champion managers reward their superstars through compensation and interesting assignments. They also find ways to reward superstars through higher salary, bonuses, perks, titles, greater responsibilities, and plum assignments.
- Champion managers are clear about the desired results and the scope and extent of what is expected from their superstars. They understand that their overachievers may have difficulty setting boundaries for themselves, so they are explicit about the scope and quality of work needed.
- Champion managers help their superstars avoid burnout and recognize when they are showing early signs of burnout such as fatigue; anger; or erratic, unhappy, or self-destructive behaviors. They may need to reemphasize healthy boundaries for their superstar's work, reduce the scope of the work without letting their superstar feel that they have failed, offer more frequent or personal praise and appreciation, or just be a compassionate and interested ear so their superstar feels heard and understood.
- Champion managers help their superstars learn how to cooperate and collaborate with other members of the firm. If the superstar is a "lone ranger" and can operate independently without damaging firm morale and productivity, it may be better to let them continue in their ways. If the practice at their firm requires high levels of coordination and collaboration, then champion managers need to help their superstars become better team players

by structuring work assignments so that superstars must work with other firm members in order to successfully achieve project goals, making it clear that their performance will be evaluated not only on results but also how well they work with others.

- Champion managers enlist their superstars in coaching and developing other members of the firm. Champion managers find a way to motivate even the most narcissistic superstars to share their expertise and experience with others by appealing to their superstars' motivators and self-interest.

17

Managing B Players

Many managers overlook the B players in their firm—champion managers don't. They recognize that these solid, good-enough employees make a substantial contribution to a firm's stability and are often an untapped resource for future growth and profitability (DeLong & Vijayaraghavan, 2003). Champion managers know that characterizing an employee as a B performer doesn't mean they believe he or she has reached their full potential with no room for further growth and improvement. They make managing and developing their B players as high a priority as managing their superstars and underperformers, and they know that when B players are ignored they may begin to see themselves as unimportant, underappreciated, or low performing. As a result, their morale, engagement, and productivity may suffer.

It's not too difficult to understand why so many managers spend too little time focusing on their B players. By definition, B players are already doing well enough, so their development is not seen as a high priority. They don't present the same critical risks and problems that underperformers do, so their managers may not feel much of a sense of urgency in managing them. And they don't need the attention and appreciation that some superstars demand, so their managers may feel it's acceptable to leave them be. Some managers may also wrongly assume that their B players simply lack the talent or potential to ever become A players, so investing more time in developing them will yield limited and infrequent returns.

Managers (especially high achieving ones) may simply find it more enjoyable and gratifying to work with their superstar employees and peers. Their conversations and collaborations may lead to impressive results, thus bringing immediate recognition and credit to both. Developing B players, on the other hand, can be more time consuming, and the results may not be quite as spectacular as those achieved by superstars, but over the long run improvements in the performance of B players can be equally, if not more, important to a firm.

WHO ARE THE B PLAYERS IN A LAW FIRM?

B players exist in all sorts of organizations, and the lack of management and development attention they typically receive is nothing unique to the legal profession. Although they are estimated to make up about 60 percent of most organizations, they seldom receive the attention that the top- and bottom-performing 20 percent of their organizations do.

B performers are solid workers and consistent contributors; they exist at all levels of a law firm. They perform well when provided with guidance, follow up, and feedback. They may not be self-starters, or have a strategic perspective, or understand how their work contributes to their firm's overall objectives and operations, but they get things done—well and on time and without a lot of drama. Their ambitions and expectations are often more modest than those of A players, and they may be satisfied with lower compensation in exchange for less stress and a more enjoyable work-life balance. Attorneys are, of course, not the only B players in a firm that deserve attention and development. Champion managers appreciate their B-performing staff members and offer them ways to further develop their skills and talents.

Four Kinds of B Player Attorneys

Former A Players. Some superstars and overachievers eventually slow down and work less intensely. They may wish to start or devote more time to their family, or they may wish to reduce their workload and pressures as they grow older and financially more secure. Or they may wish to use their talents for the benefit of their community or a charitable organization. Some superstars become B players after burning out; their performance may not match previous stellar heights, but they remain productive and valuable members of the firm. The trend towards flextime working arrangements and a higher proportion of non-equity partnerships suggests that we will see more of this kind of B player in the future.

Subject Matter Experts. These attorneys are respected experts in areas of the law that are somewhat tangential but still complementary to their firm's core strategic focus. Even though their practice may not be a seamless fit with those of their fellow attorneys, their firms feel it is better to keep an in-house specialist rather than turn to outsiders for guidance. If they were a superstar or overachiever in their particular practice area, it is likely that they would be a member of a firm with that specialty. Because they are a bit removed from the firm's central practice, they are often perceived as being impartial and objective with few ambitions and personal agendas.

Go-To and Glue People. Although these attorneys may not be the highest performers, their knowledge, skills, experience, and relationships contribute to their firm's success. They understand how things work in their firm: when new people need to be shown the ropes or things need to get done, they are the go-to people. They are usually loyal, long-term firm members who serve as its institutional memory and provide a sense of stability and continuity, especially during tough times and transitions. Their networks of working relationships are the glue that holds firms together and ensures their viability. In many firms, staff members are the most important go-to and glue people. Though they may not be in formal positions of leadership or power, they often have a clear understanding of a firm's interpersonal dynamics and are indispensable in getting things done.

Minders and Grinders. The old paradigm of law firm attorney roles was "finders, minders, and grinders"—in other words, rainmakers who find and develop clients, attorneys who manage those clients' cases and transactions, and attorneys who do most of the actual work on those matters. In the last ten years, this leverage model has evolved slightly in larger firms, with an increasing number of contract and staff attorneys being used for grinding, and an increasing number of finders also doing the minding. Even if these changes continue, B players will be needed and found among the attorneys who mind and grind.

- Champion managers provide their B performers with frequent feedback that is candid, constructive, and future oriented. This helps them to develop to their full potential.
- Champion managers offer their B players authentic, personal, and specific praise rather than generic and insincere expressions. Secure B players usually need less frequent and fulsome appreciation than some of their insecure A player counterparts.
- Champion managers provide their B players with interesting and challenging job assignments to keep them engaged and develop their skillsets. This gives them a sense that they are trusted and valued.
- Champion managers provide their B players with regular training, coaching, and mentoring. This not only accelerates their development, but also helps with their satisfaction and retention.
- Champion managers recognize and reward their B performers' accomplishments; both those that are extraordinary, and those that demonstrate the B player's high degree of consistency, quality, and reliability. Slow and steady producers should not be overlooked.

At the same time, champion managers understand the ways that their B players are different from their superstar and underperformer counterparts. They embrace these differences in the following ways.

- Champion managers are aware of their B performers' individual aspirations and motivations. They don't assume that every B player aspires to be an

A player, but when someone is ambitious, they give them the resources and opportunity to grow.

- Champion managers realize that many of their B performers may be so focused on their individual responsibilities that they lack a broader understanding of their firm's strategic objectives. Champion managers take the time to show them how they fit into the bigger picture and how they add value to both the firm and its clients.

- Champion managers also understand how well their B performers deal with pressure and stress. They realize that some of their B players may not want the high stress and workloads of their superstar counterparts, so they delegate and make assignments accordingly. They realize that some of their B performers may perform very well when workloads increase, but cannot sustain that same high level of productivity over the long run when high work demands and stress are chronic. As a result, they make sure that high-pressure assignments are episodic, so B performers can enjoy their desired work-life balance.

THE HIDDEN POTENTIAL OF B PLAYER TEAMS

Champion managers know another way to develop their B players: when placed on high performing teams, their skills and confidence improve. These dynamic, high-performing teams can be comprised of A and B players, or solely of B players. Synergies between B player team members are important, and teams of B players when expertly managed and led can actually outperform teams of A players lacking that same support (Chamorro-Premuzic, 2015). This doesn't happen automatically; champion managers must be proactive and skillful in their management of the team and particularly its B-performing members. Champion managers need to provide a clear vision and strategy for the team, descriptive feedback on individual and team performance, and an environment with strong purpose and morale.

B players typically need a clear vision and roadmap more than their A player team member colleagues. When strategies, action plans, milestones, and metrics are cleanly defined, Bs can better understand their roles and responsibilities, and see how all the proverbial pieces fit together. They can also assess their performance and see how they are contributing to their team's overall efforts. Champion managers make sure the strategies and objectives they articulate are realistic and attainable. When they're not, B performers may feel they've failed, leading to lower engagement, confidence, and morale.

Less skilled teams that get feedback can outperform more skilled teams that don't receive it. Champion managers provide all of their team members with feedback that is accurate, honest, and not inflated. Rather than making sweeping generalizations or vague assessments, their feedback is based on observable facts and accurate data. Distinguishing facts from opinions helps team members do a faster and better job of discovering and addressing problems. This in turn improves individual and team performance, allowing B performers to work harder and smarter, and thus develop faster.

Champion managers are particularly sensitive to the interpersonal dynamics and morale of their teams. They recognize that these factors are often more important than the aggregate experience, skill, or expertise of the team's individual members. When they assemble teams of B players who are engaged, share common values and drivers, and care about each other; they see their B performers working harder, raising their individual performance, and accomplishing more for the success of the team. When this occurs, they can outperform teams of A players who lack their same high levels of morale and engagement.

CHAPTER SUMMARY

Champion managers don't overlook B players. They recognize their substantial contribution to a firm's stability and potential for future growth and profitability. B players may be one of the following types:

- Former A Players who slow down, want to spend more time with their family, wish to reduce their workloads as they grow older, or want to contribute to their community or a charity.
- Subject Matter Experts who are experts in areas of the law that are somewhat tangential but still complementary to the firm's core strategic focus.
- Go-To and Glue People whose knowledge, skills, experience, and relationships contribute to their firm's success. Staff members are often the most important go-to and glue people.
- Minders and Grinders who manage cases and clients and do most of the actual work on those matters.

Champion managers use their best management and development practices in working with B performers. They:

- Provide frequent feedback that is candid, constructive, and future oriented.
- Offer authentic, personal, and specific praise.
- Provide interesting and challenging job assignments.
- Provide regular training, coaching, and mentoring.
- Recognize and reward their accomplishments.
- Understand their individual aspirations and motivations and provide them with the resources and opportunities they need to grow.
- Understand how they deal with pressure and stress and delegate work accordingly.
- Place them on high performing teams to improve their skills and confidence, providing them with a clear vision and strategy for the team, descriptive feedback on individual and team performance, and an environment with strong purpose and morale.

REFERENCES

Chamorro-Premuzic, T. (2015, July 13). How to manage a team of B players. *Harvard Business Review*. Retrieved from https://hbr.org/2015/07/how-to-manage-a-team-of-b-players

DeLong, T., & Vijayaraghavan, V. (2003, June). Let's hear it for B players. *Harvard Business Review*. Retrieved from https://hbr.org/2003/06/lets-hear-it-for-b-players

18

Managing Staff vs. Managing Attorneys

One of the differences between managing attorneys and managing staff is that attorneys generally have bigger egos and different motivations than staff. To succeed as a champion manager, take a step back before you decide how to approach your team members. How much do you know about their personal style, communication preferences, and motivation? Are there generational differences in how you and your staff communicate? Before you approach them with a project, take their perspective into consideration.

It's also time for some introspection about your own personal style and what motivates or aggravates you. What are your hot buttons? Are you a micromanager? A procrastinator? Does it drive you crazy when there are typos in a document? If your assistant is not at his or her desk when you want something, do you assume they are goofing off somewhere?

USING THE FROMM SIX FOR MANAGING

The former dean of students at Indiana University School of Law – Bloomington developed a competency model for law students called the Fromm Six (with assistance from Professor William Henderson). Though designed with law students in mind, the wisdom shared in the Fromm Six can be successfully applied in your role as a manager of attorneys and staff. Keep these competencies in mind and practice them in your interactions with the people you supervise (Henderson, 2013):

1. SELF-AWARENESS: Having a highly developed sense of self. Being self-aware means knowing your values, goals, likes, dislikes, needs, drives, strengths and weaknesses, and their effect on your behavior. Possessing this competence means knowing accurately which emotions you are feeling and how to manage them toward effective performance and a healthy balance in your life. If self-aware, you also will have a sense of perspective about yourself, seeking and learning from feedback and constructive criticism from others.

2. ACTIVE LISTENING: The ability to fully comprehend information presented by others through careful monitoring of words spoken, voice inflections, para-linguistic statements, and non-verbal cues. Although that seems obvious enough, the number of lawyers and law students who are poor listeners suggests the need for better development of this skill. This skill requires intense concentration, discipline and practice. Smart technology devices have developed a very quick mode of "listening" to

others. Preoccupation with these devices makes it very challenging to give proper weight and attention to face-to-face interactions. Exhibiting weak listening skills with our colleagues/classmates/clients might also mean that they will not really get to the point of telling us what they really meant to say. Thus, we miss the whole import of the intended message.

3. QUESTIONING: The art and skill of knowing when and how to ask for information. Questions can be of various types, each type having different goals. Inquiries can be broad or narrow, non-leading to leading. They can follow a direct funnel or an inverted funnel approach. A questioner can probe to follow up primary questions and to remedy inadequate responses. Probes can range from encouraging more talk to asking for elaboration on a point to even being silent. Developing this skill also requires controlling one's own need to talk and control the conversation.

4. EMPATHY: Sensing and perceiving what others are feeling, and being able to take their perspective, as well as cultivating rapport and connection. To do the latter effectively, you must then communicate that understanding back to the other person by articulating accurately those feelings. That person then will know that you have listened accurately, that you understand, and that you care. Basic trust and respect can then ensue.

5. COMMUNICATING/PRESENTING: The ability to assertively present compelling arguments respectfully and sell one's ideas to others. It also means knowing how to speak clearly and with a style

that promotes accurate and complete listening. As a professional, communicating means to persuade and influence effectively within an interaction without damaging the potential relationship. Being able to express strong feelings and emotions appropriately in a manner that does not derail the communication message is also important.

6. RESILIENCE: The ability to deal with difficult situations calmly and cope effectively with stress; to be capable of bouncing back from or adjusting to challenges and change; to be able to learn from your failures, rejections, feedback and criticism, as well as disappointments beyond your control. Being resilient and stress hardy also implies an optimistic and positive outlook, one that enables you to absorb the impact of the event, recover within a reasonable amount of time, and to incorporate relevant lessons from the event.

By practicing self-awareness, active listening, the art of questioning, empathy, communicating/presenting, and re-silience as outlined in the Fromm Six, you will grow into a champion manager. Before you go into a meeting with a member of your team, prepare for the meeting by going over each competency in the Fromm Six and apply them to what you hope to accomplish in the meeting. If the meet-ing is with your long-time assistant, Lisa, whose job perfor-mance has recently slipped, be self-aware of your own past experiences with Lisa. Do not let them color your behav-ior and reaction to her explanation during the meeting. Use your resilience skills to remain calm. Communicate clearly with Lisa and ask probing yet open questions to learn what has caused the recent performance issues. Listen carefully to her answers, be empathetic, and use the meeting to jointly come up with a performance plan that will encourage Lisa to succeed.

MANAGING OTHER ATTORNEYS

Let's talk about how to manage and motivate attorneys. "You cannot help people perform better by buying a bigger whip and bigger boots" (Gerry Riskin interviewed in Shanker, 2013). In that article, Shanker suggests: "For partners looking to hold onto their best lawyers, the solutions may be surprisingly simple: Treat your associates like adults. Involve them in the business of the firm. Don't be a jerk. Stop yelling. And give positive feedback when it is deserved." As fundamental as this advice appears to be, it is sound and not followed often enough. Attorneys, and particularly young attorneys, are motivated by being sought after for their contributions to the team effort. The more they understand the context of an assignment and how it fits into the overall client strategy, the better they will perform. Think about their strengths when assigning work and treat them as you would like to be treated.

As we mentioned earlier in this book lawyers are often skeptical, argumentative, judgmental, and questioning, with a high sense of urgency and autonomy. Those characteristics are important to remember in dealing with your direct reports and in better understanding your own behavior. How well do you know the attorneys who report to you? Have you taken the time to get to know what motivates them and what frustrates them?

For example, let's say you supervise a second year associate, "John Smith." You have assigned a research project to him via a brief email with little explanation. Because you are busy with far more pressing projects of your own, you only gave John a quick overview of the assignment. Thus, a week later when he emails the completed assignment to you two days after you thought it should have been finished, why are you surprised that his work product is incomplete and he has gone off on a tangent? Rather than jumping to the conclusion that John is useless, remember back to when you were a young associate to recall the type of mentoring and guidance you received that helped you develop your skills as an attorney. This is an opportunity for you to meet face to face with John and explain how he missed the mark on the assignment and specifically what he needs to do to address any problems with his work product. Focus on his strengths as well as his weaknesses. Ask for and consider John's perspective when providing feedback to him.

In addition, the next time you have an assignment for John, call him into your office to go over the assignment in person. Be specific about the assignment, how long it should take to complete, and when it is due. Provide some suggestions to help him get started and explain how this assignment fits into the entire client matter. Ask him if he has any questions and have him repeat back to you his understanding of the assignment and your deadlines. When the assignment is completed, give both positive and constructive feedback so he will know how to improve for the next time.

MANAGING STAFF

Managing staff requires a different approach. They are professionals in their own right and should not be referred to as "non-lawyers." That designation is demoralizing and makes most of them cringe.

Let's say you are a first year associate, "Mary," and you share your assistant, "James," with two or possibly three other attorneys. Consider your assistant an important member of your team who, in all likelihood, will be the one to teach you about the ins and outs of your firm, how to use its document management system, and much, much more. Assistants often have many years of experience and should be valued.

When you first start working together, take the time to sit down and get to know James. Have an open discussion with him about your management style and expectations; similarly, find out about his personal style, ask how he likes to receive projects, and determine the best way for the two of you to communicate. Keep communication lines open between the two of you because James is responsible for the work of several other attorneys and your top priority may not be his. If he seems to place your assignments at the bottom of his list, find out why your work is not getting done. Do not put him in the middle of a power struggle among attorneys. Be proactive in talking to the other attorneys he supports and come up with a plan for getting everyone's work finished on time. Remember the power of appreciation and that a simple "thank you" goes a long way toward building a beneficial relationship with your assistant.

See the box titled "The Invaluable Assistant" for how to establish a positive relationship with your assistant.

The role of legal support staff is changing in large part due to advances in technology. You might find yourself supervising a legal secretary and a paralegal or a hybrid legal secretary/paralegal who performs the functions of both positions. Whatever skills your assistant has, his or her ability to master rapidly evolving technology is an important part of the job. When used effectively, technology can help you and your assistant be more productive and responsive to client needs. A traditional legal secretary may have different motivation and less formal education than a certified paralegal. You should keep this in mind when you communicate with one another and manage your expectations accordingly.

The Invaluable Assistant

A good working relationship with your primary support staff will make your life at the firm much easier. Keep these tips in mind:

❑ Work with your assistant to figure out the ways he or she can best support your practice.

❑ Plan ahead. Give your assistant as much notice as possible about tasks for which you may need help. Emergencies will not endear you to your assistant.

❑ Know how tasks break down at your firm. Typical tasks for an assistant include:

- Managing your calendar.
- Keeping contact information up to date.
- Answering your phone.
- Making contact lists of the key players on major transactions.
- Maintaining organized files.

- Editing documents.
- Distributing documents.
- Organizing materials.
- Assisting with time-entry.

❏ Never ask your assistant to handle personal matters, such as your household errands or bills.

❏ Remember that your assistant is not your therapist and vice versa. Don't engage in firm gossip with your assistant or try to be best friends. Maintain a professional relationship at all times.

❏ Set clear expectations, and hold your assistant accountable.

❏ If you have repeated problems with an assistant, ask another attorney for advice.

❏ Be respectful. Staff members have a number of choices when they come across a potential error in your work. They can fix the error, discuss the error with you, or ignore the error. The way you treat staff members is likely to affect their choices.

❏ Thank your assistant and other support staff regularly.

❏ Remember your assistant's birthday and Administrative Professionals' Day (celebrated annually on the Wednesday of the last full week of April).

❏ Refer to your assistant by any reasonable title that your assistant prefers. Some are fine with the term "secretary"; others cringe.

❏ Introduce your assistant to clients.

❏ Include staff in celebrations on large transactions or litigation victories.

❏ Project enthusiasm about your work. You can't expect your assistant to have a positive attitude if you don't.

The Invaluable Assistant Table reproduced with permission from *Swimming Lessons for Baby Sharks: The Essential Guide to Thriving as a New Lawyer*, Second Edition, © 2016 Grover E. Cleveland, lessonsforsharks.com

When you first establish a working relationship with other attorneys and staff, remember that generational differences among Boomers, Xers, and Millennials will probably have an impact on how well you work together. (Look back at Chapter 14 to refresh your memory about generational differences.) If you and the person you are supervising are part of the same generation, you will have one less communication hurdle to overcome. If you want a new working relationship to get off to a good start, take time to discuss with your direct report how you prefer to be communicated with and learn how he or she likes to be communicated with as well. Boomers tend to prefer face-to-face communication or talking on the phone; Gen Xers prefer email and texting; Millennials incline towards texting and will communicate by email if absolutely necessary. For example, the newly elected managing partner of a mid-sized Los Angeles law firm, a Gen Xer with a full-time legal practice, advised his chief marketing officer that the best way to communicate with him was by texting. He promised he would respond to texts promptly no matter how busy he was. He kept his word. The chief marketing officer, whose office was literally next door to the managing partner's office, often thought it would be more efficient to walk next door and meet in person. However, the CMO honored the managing partner's request to communicate by text, and both of their needs were met.

CHAPTER SUMMARY

In your role as manager, you need to think about the strengths and weaknesses, personal styles, motivation, and communication preferences of the people you supervise before assigning work to them. You also need to exhibit emotional intelligence about your own work habits when you reach out to others. Lawyers and staff may be motivated by different things and may require different amounts of supervision and feedback.

Develop the competencies of the Fromm Six model when dealing with your team members:

- Self-awareness
- Active listening
- Questioning
- Empathy
- Communicating/presenting
- Resilience

Lawyers respond well to being treated as adults, being included in the goals of the firm and understanding their roles in it, being valued for their contributions, and receiving positive feedback when it is deserved. Young lawyers need mentoring and appreciation as well as constructive criticism. Staff members prefer to be treated in the same way. They often have significant work experience and are valuable members of your team.

Consider generational differences when you communicate with the various members of your team. The way in which different generations prefer to communicate will impact your working relationship with them, regardless of whether they are attorneys or staff members.

REFERENCES

Cleveland, G. E. (2016). *Swimming lessons for baby sharks: The essential guide to thriving as a new lawyer.* St. Paul, MN: West Academic Publishing.

Henderson, W. (2013, March). What every law student needs to excel as an attorney. *The National Jurist:* 20–21.

Shanker, D. (2013, January 11). Why are lawyers such terrible managers? *Fortune.* Retrieved from http://fortune.com/2013/01/11/why-are-lawyers-such-terrible-managers/

19

Managing Contract Attorneys, Temps, and Interns

Welcome to the gig economy, where temporary positions are common and independent workers are hired for short-term assignments! In 2016, McKinsey Global Institute surveyed 8,000 companies in the US and EU-15. The results revealed that 20 percent to 30 percent of the working-age population is now engaged in independent work. According to McKinsey, "independent work has three defining features: a high degree of autonomy; payment by task, assignment, or sales; and a short-term relationship between worker and client." The study further breaks down workers into four groups (McKinsey Global Institute, 2016):

1. *Free agents*, who actively choose independent work and derive their primary income from it;
2. *Casual earners*, who use independent work for supplemental income and do so by choice;

3. *Reluctants*, who make their primary living from independent work but would prefer traditional jobs; and the

4. *Financially strapped*, who do supplemental independent work out of necessity.

Free agents and casual earners, who comprise 70 percent of the independent workers surveyed, report greater satisfaction with their work lives than those whose financial situation forces them into it (McKinsey Global Institute, 2016). With the availability of temporary and contract workers in the work force, law firms have an excellent opportunity to leverage their work and potentially improve profitability by using them. Contract and temporary attorneys and staff are less expensive than regular employees because you do not have to pay them benefits and you can retain them on a project-by-project basis. If they are satisfied with the flexibility contract or temporary positions provide, their motivation to succeed increases and your job as their manager and champion becomes easier.

CONTRACT AND TEMPORARY ATTORNEYS

If you are looking for a contract attorney, decide whether you are looking for an independent contractor or employee or whether to turn to a legal staffing agency to fill the position. Be careful about calling contract or temporary attorneys "independent contractors" unless they truly are "independent," perform the work outside of your office, have control over the work to be accomplished, and otherwise meet IRS guidelines for being considered "independent contractors." More often than not, a contract attorney is a temporary employee or there is a shared employer relationship with a staffing agency.

Whether you decide to run an online ad for an attorney, place one in a legal publication, contact a local law school's career services office, or perhaps seek candidates through legal staffing agencies, be very detailed and specific about the project's requirements. One of the advantages of outsourcing the work is you may find a specialist who has experience and expertise that the firm currently lacks. For example, if you are a plaintiff's lemon law firm looking to expand your practice to plaintiff's personal injury and have your first case, a contract attorney with a specialty in personal injury brings tremendous value to the firm. This person could help you create a document management system for personal injury matters, including checklists, file folder hierarchy, and frequently used forms. Depending on the circumstances, the contract lawyer could become a regular employee over time if your practice grows. When interviewing candidates, be clear about your expectations and cover everything from what their role will encompass to what the work entails and how long it should take to complete. These terms, financial arrangements, and anything else relevant should be documented in a temporary employment or independent contractor agreement signed by both parties. The more explicit the agreement is up front the less likely there will be problems later if things don't work out.

Contract attorneys can be utilized for everything from document review to handling motions, depositions, trials, and even appeals. They enable small firms to staff up during busy times, cover leaves of absence, and free up firm attorneys for their highest and best use.

Part of managing contract and temporary attorneys involves managing actual or potential conflicts of interest. If a contract attorney works temporarily for your firm, your firm's clients worked on by the contract or temporary attorney become that attorney's clients as well. Contract attorneys often work for more than one firm at the same time, so it is critical that both the contract attorney and the firm monitor for conflicts. Contract or temporary attorneys should maintain complete and accurate records of any actual conflicts that exist or may arise so they can clear conflicts for every matter on which they work. For more information, look to ABA Formal Opinions and local state bar rules in the jurisdiction in which your firm practices.

To assist you in determining whether a conflict exists or may arise, consider using an incoming personnel conflict of interest form that, at a minimum, asks the candidate for:

- A list of all employers for whom the candidate engaged in legal work during the last five years.
- For each client and matter per employer the candidate worked on in the last five years that gave the candidate direct access to client files relating to legal matters:
  - Name of employer;
  - Position;
  - Client's name;
  - Client's entity type;
  - Client's type of business or industry;
  - Client's location;
  - Matter description;

– What types of activities the candidate participated in, including the level of interaction with
the client and access the candidate had to client
confidential/privileged information;
– Duration of assignment;
– Whether *the candidate's* firm was involved in the
matter in any capacity; and
– Whether the matter involved litigation and, if so,
the case caption and whether the candidate's
employer was working on the plaintiff's side,
defendant's side, or other.

Once you have determined there are no actual or potential conflicts, depending on the situation, scope of work
performed, and state bar requirements, you may consider
giving notice to the client that a temporary or contract
attorney is working on their matter. Whether you need to
do so may depend on how closely the temporary attorney
is being supervised and whether they have access to any
confidential client information.

Managing contract and temporary attorneys is otherwise
not much different than managing regular employed attorneys. Communication is key and mentoring may be needed
if the individual does not have specific experience in your
practice area (e.g., a business litigation attorney brought in
to assist in handling aspects of a legal malpractice defense
matter). If they are going to be housed in your office, on
their first day they should be walked around the office and
introduced to their manager and other team members.
Wherever they are going to be situated, they should be

given an orientation checklist or temporary attorney guide-book that covers such items as:

- Temporary employee job description;
- Office hours, after hours, and weekend building access;
- Parking and public transportation;
- Timesheet submission;
- Office floor plan;
- Office keys and elevator card access;
- Key firm members and contact information;
- Administrative support;
- Compensation schedule and tax forms as needed;
- Information required to add them to professional liability insurance;
- Written procedures on how to use the firm's technology (as well as some one-on-one training as needed);
- Meeting schedule for relevant departmental meetings;
- Emergency information;
- Dress code requirements; and
- Local area restaurants.

Once they settle in, meet with them face to face to set priorities and deadlines and to assign work to them, being as specific as possible about your expectations and what their work product should include. Determine from the outset the best way to communicate with one another. Everything you learned about delegation and feedback in earlier chapters applies to temporary and contract lawyers too. Depending on your culture, the type of project and the length of time they will be working for you, you may want to assign them an internal mentor. Your culture will also dictate whether to include or exclude them in firm, practice area, and/or team meetings and events. If they are working remotely, see Chapter 21 for additional guidance.

INTERN ATTORNEYS

There are two types of attorney interns in law firms—the summer associate and the school year law clerk. Both of them provide an opportunity for your firm to test out potential future associates; their internships are essentially long interviews. You can help them develop legal skills and determine whether they are a good fit for your firm's culture. Of the two, the summer associate position is the one most sought after by law students. Yale Law School (2016) refers to it as the "summer associate dance." Perhaps that's because social events are interwoven between work assignments and summer associates are more likely to be wined and dined than school year law clerks. Social opportunities aside, both types of interns require the same type of champion management by you to help them succeed.

On their first day at the firm, attorney interns should be given substantially the same orientation checklist and guidebook as temporary and contract attorneys. Since they are prospective future long-term employees, assign each an associate mentor and provide a carefully thought-out orientation to the firm. In addition, since they are employees of the firm, they need to be given a copy of the firm's Employee Handbook. Have a formal mentorship program that sets forth the mentor's role, reward mentors for doing a good job, and encourage mentors to be proactive in helping the interns assimilate and develop.

If you want interns to acclimate to your firm culture and eventually embrace it, invest time in orienting and developing them. From a management perspective, if you have more than one intern at a time, they should all start on the same day. This eases the burden on administrative and accounting staff, ensures that initial work assignments will be evenly distributed, and gives interns an opportunity to quickly bond with their colleagues. It also starts everyone out on an equal playing field. During intern orientation (which should ideally be conducted by the HR Director, if there is one, or the Office Administrator), give them the office tour, share work habits and pet peeves of partners they will be working for, offer advice about rest and lunch breaks, outline social events, and so on. When they are given assignments, encourage them to ask questions, take notes, and proofread their work product before turning it in. Expose them to a wide variety of projects and practice areas, so you can match their interests and skills with your firm's requirements.

Once they settle in, apply the champion management skills that work best with your other supervisees to interns too. Communicate, delegate, give feedback, and communicate again. If you make their experience a positive and rewarding one, your interns will become ambassadors for your firm brand at their law schools, and the best of them will return to the firm as your future associates.

TEMPORARY STAFF EMPLOYEES

Many firms hire temporary staff to fill in for vacations, leaves of absence, and occasionally for special projects. When filling temporary staff positions, it is often helpful to use a temporary legal staffing agency. These agencies have access to many qualified candidates, and one of their main advantages is that if the temp does not work out, you can relatively quickly have that person removed and replaced with someone else.

Before you recruit someone, you should prepare a temporary job description which clearly sets forth the essential functions of the position, the anticipated duration of the assignment, as well as the experience and education required. The more detailed you are in your requirements, the better fit you will likely experience in your candidates. Once someone is selected, remember that they are there on a temporary basis, although temping is an opportunity to test someone for a regular position in the event an opening arises.

Temporary staff employees benefit from the same type of orientation as temporary and contract attorneys. The more information and instruction you provide at the outset and the more written guidelines that are available to them, the faster they will become productive. How much time you devote to onboarding, training, and managing temps depends on their prior experience and the amount of time they are expected to work for you. The same best practices used in delegating work, giving feedback, and frequently communicating to your team apply to temps as well. Depending on your firm culture, you may or may not want to include them in internal firm meetings or events.

If, for instance, your legal secretary is about to take a several-month maternity leave, it would be helpful to have a few days overlap between the temporary replacement and your valued assistant. A firm mentor should be provided, as well. In addition, have your assistant put together a desk instruction manual which explains how the temp should handle:

- Visitors to the office;
- Preparation for meetings and depositions;
- Telephone calls and messages;
- How to schedule appointments;
- Setting up new files and obtaining client numbers;
- Entering and scanning documents into the document management system;
- Using preformatted templates;
- How to prepare and file correspondence;
- How to prepare pleadings (if this is a litigation practice);
- How and where to file documents;
- How to process incoming and outgoing mail;
- How to handle messengers and deliveries;
- How to handle faxes;
- When to take rest breaks and lunch breaks; and
- Who to go to with questions.

All staff positions in the firm should have similar desk instruction manuals prepared and kept current. The instruction manuals can be prepared in draft by the incumbent in the position and then reviewed and approved by the individual's direct supervisor and firm administration. They are a valuable tool that assists in ensuring critical job functions are performed by whomever is covering the position in the event an employee takes a sudden, unanticipated leave of absence.

SUMMER STAFF INTERNS

With the arrival of summer often comes the arrival of summer staff interns (aka high school or college-age children of partners who cannot find summer jobs on their own or, preferably, children of partners who are considering going to law school one day). In addition, local bar associations and local chapters of the Association of Legal Administrators support summer intern programs for students of color and underrepresented students.

Once upon a time in a Beverly Hills law firm, the 16-year-old daughter of a named partner suddenly appeared at the office (in a tennis outfit) at the beginning of summer. The surprised firm's administrator, not knowing what else to do with her, sat her next to the receptionist to back up on telephones. She mysteriously vanished after lunch, never to appear again, because she had a pressing tennis match to play. Her father wisely realized that the time it would have taken to motivate and make her productive in the office was not worth the opportunity cost.

Not all summer internships begin and end so abruptly. In fact, if you prepare in advance for summer interns, you can carve out special projects for them and have them provide coverage for vacationing employees. They may even gain an appreciation for what their parent actually does all day at the office. Their roles and expectations need to be managed the same as other temporary staff employees. Giving them preferential treatment, though tempting, will not be well received by the rest of the staff, so do your best to avoid it.

One suggestion for dealing with summer interns who are children of partners is to swap them with another firm's children of partners. That can result in a win-win for both law firms and actually provide a valuable learning experience for the interns. However, if you do engage in such an exchange, be sensitive to potential conflicts of interest and concern for confidentiality.

CHAPTER SUMMARY

The gig economy provides opportunities for law firms to utilize motivated *free agents* and *casual earners* for short-term assignments. By using contract and temporary attorneys and staff, work can be better controlled to manage the peaks and valleys of your firm's practice.

When hiring and managing contract and temporary attorneys, keep the following in mind:

- Be precise in describing the requirements of the position and reach out for specialists who can add value;
- Beware of conflicts of interest and potential conflicts of interest. Use an incoming personnel conflict of interest questionnaire and keep it updated as new matters arise;
- Use an orientation checklist and provide a temporary attorney guidebook to assist in training;
- For longer-term positions, consider assigning a mentor; and
- Follow best practices in how you delegate, give feedback, and otherwise communicate.

With respect to intern attorneys, carefully recruit for potential and cultural fit. Though their positions may be temporary, if you invest time to help them grow and develop, they may return as pre-qualified future associates. Temporary staff employees should be selected for their ability to get the job done. That said, you should still give them an orientation and the tools necessary to be successful. Have desk instruction manuals written and kept current for all staff positions, so you are prepared to adequately cover employee absences when they occur.

Summer staff interns can provide much needed back-up coverage for summer vacations for your employees. However, advance planning of how you will use them and managing expectations, both theirs and the firms, once they arrive is necessary for their summer to be a positive and productive learning experience.

REFERENCES

McKinsey Global Institute. (2016, October). *Independent work: Choice, necessity, and the gig economy.* Retrieved from http://www.mckinsey .com/global-themes/employment-and-growth/independent-work -choice-necessity-and-the-gig-economy

Yale Law School. (2016, May). The law firm summer associate dance. Retrieved from https://law.yale.edu/student-life/career-development /students/career-guides-advice/law-firm-summer-associate-dance

20

Managing Flextime and Part-Time Personnel

Today's employees, particularly Gen Xers and Millennials, value work-life balance often above financial reward. They may have children; want time to travel and enjoy hobbies, volunteer, or continue their education; or provide care to parents, siblings, or grandparents. If you can accommodate their desires by providing a more flexible work schedule, you will engender loyalty and have a more motivated and productive work force. As a champion manager, you will be open to embracing staggered hours, part-time employment, reduced hour schedules, and job sharing in your firm by lawyers and staff alike.

Law firms have generally been more receptive to staggered hours and part-time or reduced hours schedules for their support staff than for their attorneys. Sometimes, particularly in small firms, the rationale is that it is less expensive to juggle part-time employees than hire someone full time with benefits. It is not unusual to see the

working hours of legal secretaries and paralegals staggered
to provide coverage from 8 am to 7 pm to better accommodate attorney and client deadlines. Staggered hours
and reduced hour schedules also work to help commuters
deal with rush hour traffic and responsibilities at home.
Job sharing is more challenging to successfully implement
because it requires extra discipline, written procedures,
and communication among everyone involved.

Part-time college students, especially individuals considering going to law school, have the potential to become
trusted records and office services clerks, legal assistants,
and paralegals, as well as receptionists. They can accomplish the necessary but not exciting or always interesting
tasks and projects that full-time employees never get around
to doing. If they succeed and fit into your firm culture, they
may return one day as a law clerk or as an associate.

FLEXIBILITY FOR LAWYERS

Staggered hours, flex time, job sharing, part-time employment, and reduced hour schedules are more difficult to
arrange for lawyers. Boomers tend to undervalue attorneys
who want their schedules adjusted to allow for work-life
balance. We've seen litigation partners balk at the idea of
a part-time or reduced hours litigation associate because
filing deadlines and last minute court appearances might
not coincide with the associate's limited schedule. Client
demands are 24/7, and they feel their direct report attorneys need to be available at all hours too.

The National Association for Law Placement's most recent survey, published in 2013, revealed that only 6.2 percent of all lawyers at firms typically 250 lawyers and

larger were working part-time, and most of them—over 70 percent—were women. Among female lawyers overall, 13.5 percent work part-time; among female partners, 11.7 percent work part-time; and among female associates, the figure was 10.1 percent. Only 2.7 percent of male attorneys work part-time (Collins & Leipold, 2013).

Despite these statistics, champion managers realize that flexible and part-time arrangements can benefit their firms. They enable firms to retain talented attorneys, improve recruiting and diversity efforts, and attract a more diverse group of attorneys. In order for these initiatives to succeed, firms need to have a formal, written policy that is understood and adhered to by all. Having a formal, written policy also serves as a recruitment tool. As a manager, it is up to you to follow your firm's policy in granting and managing flexible and part-time arrangements. Though you may be tempted to give preference to your favorite attorneys, the policy should be applied evenly and fairly to all attorneys. This does not mean that all requests for part-time or flexible status should be granted, but rather that there needs to be a balance struck between individual requests and firm and client needs. If this is a new initiative for your firm, you may want to initially implement it for a trial period of six months to a year with one or two attorneys going on a flexible schedule or part-time basis. Keep communication lines open with employees during the trial period by encouraging and listening to feedback. Decide what works, notice what needs to be changed, and amend your policies and procedures accordingly.

Deborah Epstein Henry is the founder of Flex-Time Lawyers LLC, a company she initially started in the late 1990s as a network for lawyers to find support and career guidance as well as clients, jobs, and even nannies. In her 2010 ABA book *LAW & REORDER: Legal Industry Solutions for Restructure, Retention, Promotion & Work/Life Balance*, Henry provides a flex-time and reduced hours checklist (shown here and in Appendix D) for firms to follow. It can be used by firms of all sizes and is a good place to start if you are embarking on establishing a flexible and reduced hour policy for the first time at your firm.

The Flexible and Reduced Hours Checklist

The Flexible and Reduced Hours Checklist governs:

1. What information should be contained in a written flexible and reduced hour policy;
2. What topics should be covered at a "flexible sit-down meeting"; and
3. What issues should be addressed in training lawyers working flexible or reduced hours and those who supervise them.

The Flexible and Reduced Hours Checklist includes:

- Eligibility criteria.
- Description of the range of flexible and reduced hour options.
- Proposal process and what it entails.
- Determination of billable hours, percentage, and/or workload.
- Schedule and location for working.
- Timing and transition to and from flexible and reduced hours.
- Mutual flexibility expectations.
- Communication expectations.

- Non-billable contribution expectations.
- Work/life supervisor, affinity group, and support.
- Assignment process.
- Promotion eligibility and process.
- Compensation, including bonuses.
- Training.
- Travel restrictions, if any.
- Childcare or eldercare coverage, if applicable.
- Strategies to ensure work flow does not negatively impact colleagues and clients.
- Information provided about schedule to clients.
- Technology expectations of responsiveness and accessibility.
- Emergency contact information.
- Applicability to non-equity and equity partners.
- Benefits.
- Vacation.
- Annual review of workload, schedules, and feedback.

Reprinted by permission of the author.

In 2002, Williams and Calvert published in *William & Mary Journal of Women and the Law* a report from the Project for Attorney Retention titled "Balanced Hours: Effective Part-Time Policies for Washington Law Firms." It included the following finding and recommendations:

> A key finding of the report is that a communication gap exists between managing partners, who often feel they have addressed the demand for part-time, and lawyers who feel that existing policies are neither usable nor effective. To help close this gap, the PAR usability test gives firms a quick

read on whether or not their existing policy is usable and effective.

PAR also has developed recommendations for effective balanced hours' policies that are based on best practices currently in use in law and accounting firms. The key recommendations are:

- *The Principle of Proportionality:* Attorneys on balanced hours' schedules should receive proportional salaries, bonuses, benefits, and advancement. This means the budgeted hours for a balanced hours' attorney should include billable and non-billable time; their assignments should include interesting and high-profile work comparable to that of standard hours' attorneys; and they should be promoted to partnership based on the same criteria as other attorneys.
- *Flexible and Fair Policies:* The potential retention benefits will not be attained when reduced hours are available only for a few superstars. While each attorney seeking balanced hours must present a viable business plan, balanced hours should be available to any attorney who does so and should be tailored to meet the attorney's individual needs. Balanced schedules should not be limited only to women, or to parents, or to primary caregivers.
- *Effective Implementation:* Implementation is the key to success. Critical aspects of implementation include: clear and consistent support from the top; an effective implementation plan that

includes training and a part-time coordinator who monitors benchmarks to assess whether the program is fair and effective; and planning processes for attorneys and the firm to create balanced schedules that meet the needs of both.

BEST PRACTICES IN ESTABLISHING WORKPLACE FLEXIBILITY

As noted in the above study, having a plan in place will be more successful if you follow best practices in setting it up, implementing it, and allocating resources to manage it. This applies to flexible and part-time policies for support staff employees too. Other research, such as World at Work's 2015 Trends in Workplace Flexibility Study, suggests a correlation between flexibility and turnover. It found that the more flexible an organization is, the lower its turnover. It also shows that for organizations with an imbedded culture that embraces workplace flexibility, there is a positive effect on employee engagement, motivation, and satisfaction.

Before you implement such a policy, survey employees and ask what type of flexibility they want. Review the alternatives and consider the strengths and weaknesses of all options. Develop written policies and procedures for implementation and monitoring. Set clear performance goals up front. Then, communicate, communicate, communicate about the changes. The resultant policy is more likely to succeed due to employee buy-in than if management came up with a policy with no employee input. As a champion manager, check back in after a trial period, obtain

Figure 20.1

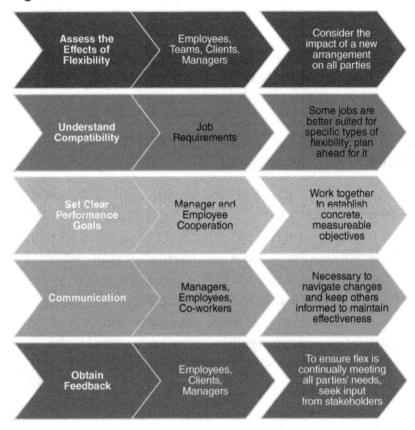

employee feedback, and make any needed modifications to the program. Then communicate, evaluate progress on a regular basis, solicit feedback from participants, and make periodic changes as needed (see Figure 20.1). Setting up policies to support these programs and embedding them in your culture are your big-picture approaches. In addition, consider the following tips to assist you in managing workplace flexibility day to day (Kossek, Hammer, Thompson, & Burke, 2014):

- Keep an open mind, experiment and evaluate how the arrangement is working; do not rush to make a yes or no decision.
- If you are uncertain about workplace flexibility or concerned about managing someone working flexibly, try to put your assumptions aside and look at the evidence.
- Be clear about the business objectives that must be met by individuals and teams.
- Do not ask why a person is seeking a flexible work arrangement; ask whether the work can be done and whether the employee will be able to be just as effective working flexibly as not.
- If the flexible work arrangement needs to be revised, identify areas that require additional information or modifications.
- Remember that you play a key role in successful implementation.
- Recognize that employees and teams may have different working styles and preferred hours.
- Trust that your team is managing its work responsibly, and empower your team to meet business objectives.
- Help your employees think about all the components of working flexibly, so they are more likely to succeed.
- Share best practices, so employees can learn from the experiences of others.
- When considering supervision of employees working different hours than you work or at a different location, think about how much of each employee's time/work you actually personally observe when

he or she is in the office during traditional working hours and how much is already conducted via
e-mail and other information and communications
technology options.

- When appropriate, hold meetings by phone rather
  than in person.
- Establish core hours for your team if everyone
  needs to overlap for several hours each day.
- Set reasonable deadlines, so you do not force
  employees to abandon their flexible arrangement.
- Schedule regular check-ins, allowing both you and
  the employee working flexibly to touch base and to
  discuss how the arrangement is going.

For some additional ideas on workplace flexibility, see
also Deloitte's "The Corporate Lattice" (Benko, Anderson,
& Vickberg, 2011).

FLEXIBILITY FOR STAFF EMPLOYEES

When considering allocation of work, staff-level part-time
workers are ideal for projects and certain tasks like filing
that do not have to be completed at a particular time or
on a daily basis. It is a mistake to assign time-critical tasks
to part-time employees unless the work can be accomplished on a job-sharing basis. One small boutique law
firm used a part-time college student with flexible and frequently changing hours to open new files and assign client
numbers for *all* new firm matters. His lack of regular daily
availability created a backlog in opening new files and pre-
vented attorneys from billing time to those matters until he

caught up again. This caused lost billable time and considerable frustration among attorneys, paralegals, and legal secretaries at the firm. If the job were shared between two part-time employees whose hours were staggered, this allocation of work could have worked.

Whether a job is shared or not, all support staff positions should have written job descriptions and detailed procedures about how to accomplish the essential duties and responsibilities of the position so that coverage can be provided when someone is on vacation or on a leave of absence. When a job is shared between two people, the allocation of their duties needs even more documentation, such as:

- Who works which days/times each week;
- Whether there is any overlap in their schedules;
- Which people they support;
- How work is assigned to each of them;
- How they will communicate with each other, their supervisor, co-workers, and clients;
- How they should communicate their status on accomplishing work to one another;
- Who finishes work when a project cannot be completed in the same work day;
- Who provides back-up when one of them takes sick or vacation time;
- How each person will be evaluated, both individually and as a team;
- Whom they report to; and
- What happens if the job share arrangement does not work or one of the job share partners leaves?

Frequent communication between the attorney or other manager assigning work to employees who job share and the part-time employees is critical. There needs to be a system for communicating the status of an assignment in place among the parties involved. Otherwise, tasks can be overlooked and deadlines missed when two employees share a job because each person may assume the other has performed it. This can occur when paralegals and legal secretaries job share as well, so make sure the appropriate structure is in place to deal with rushes and last-minute crises.

New part-time support staff should receive a tailored orientation to the firm that includes policies about benefits, time off, and any other information that will help them succeed. In addition, as employees they should be given and asked to sign an acknowledgment of receipt of a copy of the firm's Employee Handbook. Include them in relevant team meetings so they become part of the firm culture. As their manager, give them ongoing feedback and include them in the firm's evaluation process.

CHAPTER SUMMARY

Work-life balance is important to today's employees, both lawyers and staff alike. As a champion manager, make every effort to accommodate requests for flexible work schedules and you will be rewarded with less turnover and higher employee engagement, motivation, and satisfaction.

In order to have a successful flexible and part-time arrangement with your team, you need to prepare a formal, written policy that is understood, administered fairly, and adhered to by all. Look to "The Flexible and Reduced Hour Checklist" in *LAW & REORDER* by Deborah Epstein Henry for guidance in creating your firm's attorney plan. Also refer to "Balanced Hours: Effective Part-Time Policies for Washington Law Firms," put together by Williams and Calvert for The Project for Attorney Retention for best practices in creating and administering these policies for attorneys.

Before implementing a flexible workplace plan in your firm, survey employees to find out what type of flexibility they want, develop procedures and policies consistent with their input, set clear performance goals up front, and monitor their performance. After a trial period, seek feedback from stakeholders and modify the plan as needed. See Figure 20.1 from the SHRM Foundation on page 312 for assistance as well as their tips for managing workplace flexibility (Kossek et al., 2014). Remember to include support staff team members in the flexible workplace documentation. Plan and tailor assignments and projects to suit their interests as well as firm and client needs.

REFERENCES

Benko, C., Anderson, M., & Vickberg, S. (2011). The corporate lattice: A strategic response to the changing world of work. Retrieved from https://dupress.deloitte.com/dup-us-en/deloitte-review/issue-8 /the-corporate-lattice-rethinking-careers-in-the-changing-world-of -work.html

Collins, J., & Leipold, J. (2013, February 21). Rate of part-time work among lawyers unchanged in 2012—Most working part-time continue to be women most. Retrieved from http://www.nalp.org/

Henry, D. E. (2010). *LAW & REORDER: Legal industry solutions for restructure, retention, promotion & work/life balance*. Chicago: American Bar Association.

Kossek, E. E., Hammer, L. B., Thompson, R. J., & Burke, L. B. (2014, September). Leveraging workplace flexibility for engagement and productivity. Retrieved from http://www.shrmfoundation.org/

World at Work. (2015, September). Trends in workplace flexibility. Retrieved from https://www.worldatwork.org/home/html/home.jsp

Williams, J., & Calvert, C. T. (2002). Balanced hours: Effective part-time policies for Washington law firms: The Project for Attorney Retention (PAR), final report, Third Edition. *William & Mary Journal of Women and the Law, 8*(3). Retrieved from http://scholarship.law .wm.edu/cgi/viewcontent.cgi?article=1186&context=wmjowl

21

Managing Virtual and Telecommuting Personnel

BENEFITS AND CRITERIA FOR TELECOMMUTING OR WORKING VIRTUALLY

Based on the latest statistics from a GlobalWorkplace Analytics.com survey (2016) on the work-at-home/telework population in the United States, 50 percent of the U.S. workforce holds a job that is compatible with at least partial telework and approximately 20 to 25 percent of the workforce teleworks at some frequency. In addition, the survey says that 80 to 90 percent of the U.S. workforce would like to telework at least part-time. The most prevalent model is one in which employees work at home for two to three days a week.

The definition of a remote or virtual worker covers a broad range of situations, from a full-time employee allowed to telecommute from home a few days each week to employees who work virtually all the time in geographically dispersed locations. It might even mean a firm that is entirely virtual with no brick-and-mortar office or a very small presence in an executive suite for client meetings and depositions.

Telecommuting is increasing in law firms because technology exists to enable employees to work anywhere and at any time. Though these arrangements are more frequent, law firms are challenged with developing telecommuting policies, effectively managing off-site employees, and also ensuring that the technology used is secure and confidential client information is protected. The first obstacle you and your other managers may have to overcome is the philosophy that attorneys must be seen sitting in their office chair in order to be working. Shifting that mindset will significantly improve your ability to manage a virtual workforce. As a champion manager, it is your job to implement and oversee virtual and telecommuting policies so that they benefit the firm, your employees, and your clients.

In its report on "Leveraging Workplace Flexibility for Engagement and Productivity," (Kossek, Hammer, Thompson, & Burke, 2014) the SHRM Foundation recommends that before adopting a telecommuting arrangement for individuals or work teams, you should discuss and evaluate:

- How work will get done and how meetings and joint projects will be handled.
- How communication with co-workers, supervisors and managers will continue within core hours.
- How much time will be spent in the office and when.

- What equipment and technical support will be needed and who will provide it.
- How the arrangement will be supervised and evaluated in comparison with onsite workers to ensure equity.
- Which employees or teams should be available during core work hours.

To assist you further in implementing a telecommuting policy, the federal government's website for small businesses (FindLaw, 2016) suggests that you:

- Identify jobs best suited to telecommuting—Determine which positions are compatible with a remote working arrangement, keeping in mind that telecommuters typically work in the office one or more days per week.
- Choose the best candidates for telecommuting—Not all employees are well-suited to working from home, while others prefer the camaraderie of working in an office.
- Check state and federal incentives—The cost of establishing a home office sometimes can be offset by incentive programs at both the state and federal level (often through the state's environmental protection agency).
- Set up a trial period—Start a six-month or one-year pilot program with a small group of employees, keeping track of successes and failures.
- Adjust management techniques accordingly—Use the trial period as an opportunity to both acclimate supervisors and test new management techniques with respect to telecommuters.

- Track results—At the end of the pilot program, review the results; interview employees who participated in the program and determine how it worked or didn't work, (determining and implementing) ways to improve the program.
- Set goals for expansion—(Determine the feasibility of a) Plan for a firm wide implementation of the telecommuting program (based upon pilot outcomes and a strong risk/benefit and cost analysis).

Your job as a champion manager is to determine which people are the best candidates for virtual work and telecommuting. To assist you in reaching your decision, consider people who:

- Are self-directed, able to productively work by themselves and without close supervision.
- Are self-motivated and independent.
- Manage their time well.
- Are comfortable working alone for long periods of time.
- Have a low need for in-person social interaction.
- Have the communication skills necessary to effectively interact with co-workers, clients, supervisors, and subordinates while working remotely.
- Perform tasks that are well suited for telecommuting such as telephone-intensive tasks, computer-oriented tasks, rigorous thinking and writing tasks, project-based work, and document review.

As a champion manager, before you grant any telecommuting requests, you might want to ask your firm members who seek an opportunity to telecommute to complete a self-assessment like the "Telework Employees Self-Assessment" below (and also in Appendix E). It allows them to be interactive and introspective about their work preferences and support their case to you. As a best practice, you should complete the assessment as well to see whether an employee's self-assessment matches your expectations for a successful telecommuting experience.

Telework Employees Self-Assessment

A good telecommuting arrangement starts with a good self-assessment. Employees are encouraged to consider the following factors in making an honest determination about their telework capabilities. Record any concerns you may have and how you will address them in order to telecommute.

General
- Do you have sufficient portable work for the amount of telework proposed?
- Are you comfortable working alone for the amount of days you have requested to telework? Will you miss the social interaction of the office?
- Will your teleworking impact your coworkers? Do they need you in the office to complete work? Will they be doing extra work because you are teleworking?
- (In what ways) are you willing to be flexible about the telework arrangement to respond to the needs of (our clients, your) manager, (your) workgroup, and (your) work?

Self-Management
- Do you have the ability to do work with minimal direct supervision?
- Do you have organized work practices?

- Do you have good planning skills?
- Do you have effective time management skills? Are you able to meet schedules and deadlines?

Technology
- Do you feel comfortable with the technologies, if any, that will be needed to telework?
- Are you willing to learn any new technologies required to telework?

Communication
- Do you have the ability to ensure good communication with your manager, co-workers and clients?
- Will you return e-mails, calls and other messages in a timely manner?

Appropriate Space
- Is the telework office space conducive to getting your work done?
- Is the telework office space safe?
- Are dependent care (i.e. child care, elder care, or care of any other dependent adults) arrangements in place?
- Will you be distracted in the telework office space (e.g. by children, friends, television, or other responsibilities)?

(Telework Employees Self-Assessment, 2016)

CHOOSING AND MANAGING TELECOMMUTERS AND VIRTUAL EMPLOYEES

Once you determine who good candidates for telecommuting might be, you need to consider whether your policy should be limited to exempt attorneys and staff. Oversight of non-exempt hourly employees is more difficult due to wage and hour laws that govern overtime, meal, and rest periods. Some firms take a hard line that no non-exempt employees can work remotely at any time and block them from even accessing email after work hours and on weekends.

With the right policies and procedures in place, there may be exceptions made for certain non-exempt employees whose positions and job duties are more independent than others. For example, one boutique family law firm in Los Angeles had a long-time trusted administrative staff person who handled collections. She moved out of state but had the skills and professionalism to do the job remotely without supervision, and she performed it well. The clients were accustomed to dealing with and speaking to her and because of the technology in place, they did not realize she had switched to always working virtually from out of state. For specialized positions like collections coordinators and experienced paralegals in niche practices that are valuable to the firm, you may want to consider bending the rule and allowing them to telecommute or work virtually if they move away. You still need to comply with wage and hour laws and have them keep track of their time the same ways any other non-exempt employee will. If they work in another state, you need to comply with that state's local wage and hour, tax, and other employment laws, too.

Champion managers establish an approval process so that lawyers and staff are not allowed to grant special telecommuting arrangements on an ad hoc basis. Best practices suggest that employees fill out a written application form to request permission to telecommute and that the Managing Partner, Human Resources Director, someone else in management, or some combination thereof be charged with reviewing and approving requests. There should be clear approval criteria for determining who can telecommute so no favoritism is allowed and no ADA or EEOC protected categories are inadvertently denied permission to telecommute. The criteria should be based on the job requirements and whether they lend themselves to working remotely (such as extensive phone contact, computer work, document review and drafting), as well as the employee's work habits, motivation, and ability to work with limited supervision. The policy should be applied fairly and consistently based on objective factors, such as the type of work performed, to avoid any potential claims that an employee was discriminated against.

The firm's Employee Handbook should include a section on telecommuting that describes:

- What equipment will be provided by the firm to a telecommuting employee;
- Who pays for the business expenses of telecommuting employees, such as mileage, telephone and Internet expenses, supplies, shipping costs, computers, and office furniture;
- Timekeeping, meal, and rest period requirements; and
- Which positions are eligible for telecommuting and the position's requirements regarding time that must be spent in the office.

Beyond the Employee Handbook, each telecommuter should be given and asked to execute a telecommuting agreement that identifies the responsibilities of both the telecommuter and the firm. The terms of the agreement should include at a minimum:

- Scope of agreement, stating that employee agrees to telecommute on a voluntary basis and that the agreement may be terminated at any time by either the employee or the firm, with or without cause.
- Term of agreement: the effective date and duration of the agreement.
- Termination of agreement, stating that telecommuting is available only to eligible employees at the sole discretion of the firm and that either party may terminate the agreement with or without cause upon reasonable notice in writing to the other party.
- Salary, job responsibilities, benefits, and performance reviews.
- Work hours, overtime, sick time, and vacation.
- Work schedule, stating that the daily work schedule for days spent working at home is subject to negotiation with and approval by the firm and that the employee may be required to work certain fixed hours and be accessible by phone and/or email during those hours.
- Equipment, including whether the firm will provide computer, software, Internet access, and other equipment needed for telecommuting.
- Office, including that the telecommuter will designate a workspace within the employee's home for the equipment to be used when working. That the employee agrees to maintain the workspace in a safe condition and that the employer can make on-site visits with reasonable advance notice for the purpose of determining that the site is safe and free from hazards and to maintain, repair, inspect, or

retrieve firm equipment, software, data, or supplies. If an employee uses an office outside their home, such as renting space in an executive suite, then state who authorizes this and who will pay for it.

- Office supplies, including who will pay for them.
- Workers' compensation, including that the firm will provide workers' compensation coverage to the employee for work performed in the designated work area.
- Income tax, noting that the employee is responsible for determining any income tax implications of maintaining a home office.
- Employee must comply with all of the firm's policies and procedures contained in the Employee Handbook and the terms of this agreement.
- If the telecommuter is fully working virtually, then the terms of the specific working arrangement need to be spelled out as well.

COMMUNICATING WITH TELECOMMUTING AND VIRTUAL EMPLOYEES

When managing remote employees, a champion manager establishes a system for how to best communicate with them. How often do you need to connect? What method works best? Do you and your virtual worker prefer to communicate by phone, email, texts, video, or some combination of all four? A champion manager recognizes the importance of routinely reaching out to telecommuters and virtual employees to stay connected with them since they do not have the opportunity to casually run into their virtual colleagues in the office.

It is important to build trust between yourself and your virtual employee. Frequently staying in touch will build that trust over time. Try not to micromanage your virtual worker by checking in too often to see if they are actually working, since that is potentially disruptive and counter-productive for both of you. Build trust by being transparent with one another about expectations, work hours, and accountability.

Team Meetings

A best practice is to include telecommuters and virtual employees in regular team and department meetings. The use of video conferencing like Skype, GoToMeeting, Google Hangouts, or more advanced video conferencing systems for those meetings will improve the working relationships among virtual employees and team members who are physically at the meeting. Meetings and conversations become more personal when you can see someone rather than just hearing them over the phone or communicating by email.

Consider using the beginning of each team meeting to casually catch up with one another before launching into the meeting agenda. Publish a meeting agenda in advance and designate a start and end time so everyone can come to the meeting focused and prepared. As with any meeting, end it by summarizing actions taken and putting in place next steps and expectations in advance of the next team meeting.

Participation by video conference keeps everyone more engaged in the conversation and discourages multi-tasking that might occur if the meeting were held over a conference call, provided the technology is robust and works well. It encourages information sharing and builds a team esprit de corps.

Security Concerns

It is important to minimize or completely restrict remote employees' use of personal devices, personal servers, or personal e-mail while conducting firm work to reduce the risk of possible security breaches. If your firm has a BYOD (Bring Your Own Device) policy and allows employees to use personal devices, make certain that adequate controls, software, and procedures are in place to protect the firm's online security. If your system is difficult to log onto remotely or is too slow when working from home, your creative associate is likely to email a confidential client document he or she plans to work on at home to a personal, unsecure email address. Have the right protocols and procedures in place to prevent that from happening.

Require telecommuters to follow the same password protection and encryption procedures that are used when they work in the office. To the extent that you still maintain paper files for clients, instruct them to keep client files and other paperwork in a secure place with the understanding that these files are firm property and must be returned immediately when their employment terminates. Remind them that work equipment must be used for work only and that the telecommuter must follow the same firm policies and procedures set forth in the Employee Handbook as if they were working in the firm's office.

CHAPTER SUMMARY

Telecommuting and virtual workers are increasing in law firms due to available technology and employees who want flexibility in their schedules to enhance work/life balance. As a champion manager, you are charged with developing policies to enable employees to work virtually, effectively managing off-site employees, and ensuring that the technology used is secure so that confidential client information remains protected.

Before implementing a telecommuting policy, you should do some advance planning that includes reviewing recommendations from the SHRM Foundation and the federal government's business website (business.usa.gov) on what to consider. Further, you should think through the job functions, skills, and motivation levels of people who seek out virtual work. Encourage them to complete the Telecommuting Employees Self-Assessment from www.tele work.gov (see box in this chapter) to assist you in selecting individuals who are most likely to succeed as virtual or telecommuting employees.

You should establish a fair approval process with specific criteria for determining which lawyers and staff are eligible for telecommuting. Include a section on telecommuting in your Employee Handbook and have each employee execute a written telecommuting agreement that sets forth the terms of his or her individual agreement.

Communication with remote workers can be tricky unless you establish a system for how best to communicate with them and make them part of the process in determining that system. Include virtual workers in team meetings through the use of video conferencing. Implement policies and procedures to ensure client confidentiality and minimize the risk of security breaches by remote workers.

REFERENCES

FindLaw.com. (2016, October). Telecommuting policies. Retrieved from http://www.findlaw.com/

GlobalWorkplaceAnalytics. (2016, January). Latest telecommuting statistics. Retrieved from http://www.globalworkplaceanalytics.com/

Kossek, E. E., Hammer, L. B., Thompson, R. J., & Burke, L. B. (2014, September). Leveraging workplace flexibility for engagement and productivity. Retrieved from http://www.shrmfoundation.org/

Telework Employees Self-Assessment. (2016, October). Retrieved from http://www.telework.gov/

22

Managing for Diversity and Inclusion

WHY DIVERSITY AND INCLUSION MATTER

A 2015 research report, *Diversity Matters*, by McKinsey & Company (Hunt, Layton, & Prince, 2015) indicates that "gender diverse companies are 15 percent more likely to outperform their respective national industry medians and ethnically diverse companies are 35 percent more likely to have financial returns above their respective national industry medians." Although financial success is one reason to embrace diversity, law firms should make diversity a priority because it is the right thing to do in an increasingly global workplace. If you are still not convinced, then you will be when your clients demand it in order for them to continue working with your firm.

When we think of diversity, we tend to primarily focus on the visible aspects of diversity such as race, gender, age, and physical ability. The Deloitte research study "High-Impact Talent Management" (Bersin, 2015) reminds us not

Figure 22.1

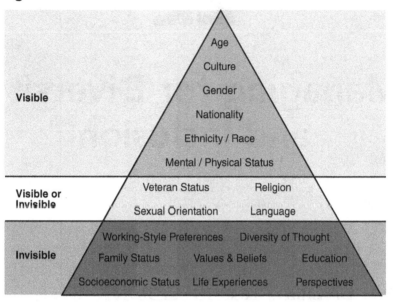

to overlook the invisible traits of diversity, such as diversity of thought, life experiences, values, beliefs, and socioeconomic status (see Figure 22.1).

We need to go beyond even this broadening of our ideas of diversity; having a diverse workplace is not enough without emphasizing inclusion. Attracting diverse talent alone will not lead to increased productivity and retention. Your newly hired employees need to feel that they will fit into your firm, have their ideas and opinions valued, and be embraced by its culture.

WHY DIVERSITY AND INCLUSION INITIATIVES FAIL

As a champion manager, you should ask, "What do we need to do to ensure our firm becomes more diverse and that our initiatives do not fail?" Deloitte, in "Global Human

Capital Trends 2014: Engaging the 21st-Century Workforce" (Bourke, Smith, Stockton, & Wakefield, 2014) advises that organizations need to broaden "their understanding of diversity to focus not only on the visible aspects of diversity, such as race, gender, age, and physical ability, but also diversity of thinking. This means deriving value from people's different perspectives on problems and different ways to address solutions. It's a complex world, it's a global world, and maximal participation is required from every workplace participant from the bottom to the top. Thinking of diversity in this way helps organizations to see value and to be conscious of the risk associated with homogeneity, especially in senior decision makers. And this means that diversity is no longer a 'program' to be managed—it is a business imperative."

In the past, law firms have undertaken diversity initiatives only to have them barely make an impact—if not completely fail. According to the DRI Law Firm Diversity Retention Manual (Morris, 2005), among the reasons for failure are:

- Missing or inadequate commitment at the top— senior management must be supportive (and senior management must champion initiatives and measure outcomes).
- Emphasis only on recruitment—increased recruiting without changes in the work environment will result in excessive attrition among women and attorneys of color.
- Failure to acknowledge the firm's culture—firms need to assess their past and present hiring practices and views of the firm's attorneys about diversity and promotion practices.

- Lack of understanding of diversity phases—a diverse law firm develops over time and is an ongoing effort that involves identifying opportunities and challenges, providing education and awareness and developing a diversity plan with clear benchmarks.
- Failure to establish specific tactics—firms need to establish tactics to achieve objectives such as revising policies and practices on how work is assigned to lawyers and staff.
- Ignoring the importance of training and development—both need to be linked to firm-wide diversity objectives (at all levels in the firm from staff through partnership).
- Failing to understand the implications of a changing workforce—client demand is a key driver here.

HOW TO GET STARTED ON YOUR OWN DIVERSITY AND INCLUSION POLICY

If you are unclear about how ready your firm is to embark on a more robust diversity and inclusion policy, you may need to assess its attitude, culture, success criteria, and expectations. One way to get started is to use an assessment tool such as "Inclusion/Diversity and Pluralism—An Organizational Diagnostic" (Davis, 2016) from The Ryan Group (or something similar with the help of a different diversity and inclusion consultant). This assessment defines inclusion as "the means by which we optimize the benefits inherent in our diversity"; diversity as "the similarities and differences in the individual and the organizational characteristics that shape our workplace"; and pluralism as "the encounter of shared engagement that permeates our workplace." The diagnostic itself (Davis, 2016) focuses on surveying your observations in your workplace on inclusion, diversity, and pluralism including:

- Your understanding and awareness;
- Your perceptions of supervisors and managers;
- Your perceptions of senior leaders;
- Your personal work experiences;
- Your awareness of diversity and inclusion information and initiatives;
- Your ratings of overall effectiveness; and
- A section about you.

Another tool you can use is the *Diversity Best Practices Guide* (McKinney, Maury, Hester, & Rucker, 2016), which is published and updated annually by the National Association for Law Placement (NALP). Its primary audience is large law firms that employ an in-house diversity and inclusion professional who can "serve on the Diversity and Inclusion Committee, facilitate the implementation of the firm's diversity and inclusion initiatives, serve as a resource for diverse lawyers and assess whether minority, female and associates with disabilities have access to opportunities and are working on matters for clients with the most sought-after work." Even if you are a champion manager in a small law firm, you can obtain guidance from these materials. Their recommendations can be scaled down to fit your firm and its culture. It includes links to many helpful website resources, including relevant ABA committee materials, U.S. government websites, and diverse national bar associations.

To heighten your awareness of trends for female, minority, and LGBT lawyers and lawyers with disabilities, you should read NALP's recently published first-ever findings on *Diversity through Infographics: From Law School to Partnership* (2016). The data is organized into four demographic buckets that combine data from NALP's major annual reports and surveys. It includes statistics on each of these demographics—for example:

- In 2015, women made up 44.68 percent of associates and just 21.46 percent of partners at major law firms—of which only 17.4 percent are equity partners.
- Minorities were almost 22 percent of the associates in large law firms but only 6 percent of equity partners.
- Of the 38 percent of graduates who self-reported sexual orientation, 4 percent self-identified as L, G, or B. Fifty-seven percent of the reported openly LGBT lawyers are accounted for in just four cities: New York City, Washington, DC, Los Angeles, and San Francisco.
- Between 1 and 2 percent of graduates self-identify as having a disability; they account for just over 0.39 percent of associates in law firms.

MOVING YOUR FIRM FORWARD

In order to move your firm forward toward an inclusive and diverse culture, a champion manager needs to consciously work on changing the status quo. In an article "Diversity in the Practice of Law: How Far Have We Come?" (Cuyler,

2012) Marci Rubin, the former long-time Executive Director of the California Minority Counsel Program, challenged that organizations that achieve this cultural shift will be those that:

- Recognize the impact of the implicit, or hidden, biases we all have—those attitudes, memories, and stereotypes that are outside of our conscious control—and the hidden barriers they raise for diverse attorney advancement, and take steps to understand those implications at every decision-making opportunity;
- Move from counting numbers to looking at the advancement opportunities for every attorney, assuring every attorney has equal access to work assignments that develop critical skills and to high-profile work assignments;
- Value diverse teams in reality by holding everyone accountable for making certain teams are diverse and all voices are heard;
- Involve senior management in all diversity efforts—leadership from the top is imperative for success;
- Make compensation, partnership or promotion expectations, and skills matrices transparent;
- Provide equal access to mentors and sponsors to all attorneys at all levels; and
- Involve women and attorneys of color in all levels of firm leadership.

As a champion manager, your role is to take on this challenge within your firm. Where you start depends on where you are on the road to diversity and inclusion in your firm. If you look around the room at a partners' meeting and all you see is a group of middle-aged white men, you have a long road ahead of you. Some of the ideas below were suggested by NALP's *Diversity Best Practices Guide* mentioned above.

- To start, encourage firm members to participate in women's and minority bar associations and external corporate legal organizations by sponsoring memberships in these organizations. Then partner with minority bar associations to identify and hire diverse laterals. Reach out to law schools beyond the ones you typically recruit from to include those with a larger percentage of diverse students. Attend and exhibit at job fairs, particularly minority job fairs, to recruit both lawyers and staff. Be more focused in your recruiting efforts to intentionally seek out diverse attorneys. These efforts may take time to realize results, so there needs to be a multi-year commitment in order to see changes in your firm's demographics.
- Prepare and conduct diversity training programs for all current employees, lawyers, and staff members alike, and roll them out as a strategic initiative that supports the firm's business plan. Everyone must understand the importance of diversity and inclusion within the firm and as a means to better support diverse clients. Include existing women attorneys, LGBT attorneys, attorneys of color, attorneys with disabilities, and diverse support staff as committee members in putting together the program to understand their perspective. Commit-

tee members should also include white and male attorneys who need to buy in and be accountable for the results.

- After you hire a diverse lawyer, onboard them thoughtfully to weave them into the culture of your firm. Assign both a partner and associate as mentors and make the mentorship meaningful by holding mentors accountable for helping to assimilate your diverse attorneys. Adopt a similar mentorship program for diverse support staff to help them acclimate to the firm and its culture. The formality of the mentorship programs will depend on your firm size and culture. In a small firm, an informal program may be just as effective as a formal one so long as it is understood as a priority.

- Take a fresh look at existing systems and policies for unintended and/or historic bias, including the firm's work allocation system, the process for inclusion at firm events, the internal training programs, and the committee appointment process. Keep diversity and inclusion top of mind.

- Provide reasonable accommodations for individuals with disabilities to ensure maximum productivity. Make sure that they have adequate access in the office building, parking facility, and their work space.

- Finally, hold firm leaders and managers accountable for progress on diversity and inclusion. Contributions to diversity and inclusion should be encouraged and rewarded through compensation and recognition within the firm.

HANDLING GENDER-RELATED ISSUES

Despite the large number of women lawyers in the workplace, there remains gender inequality in compensation and men still control most of their firms' leadership positions. Women are held to a higher standard and must exude confidence, display emotional intelligence, listen carefully to others, have excellent communication skills, and develop business before they are considered for major roles in their firm's leadership. Recent articles in the *New York Times* highlight women's compensation gap as partners and women law students' under-representation at top tier law schools (Olson, 2016b).

In 2016, the Women in Law Empowerment Forum released its sixth annual Gold Standard Certification winners (Lawdragon News, 2016). The firms selected are those that have successfully demonstrated that women represent a meaningful percentage of their equity partners, of their highest leadership positions, of their governance and compensation committees, and of their most highly compensated partners. Only 31 firms with 300 or more attorneys practicing in the U.S. qualified and won by meeting their requirements.

Gender pay equity has come to the forefront recently due to legislation and several class action lawsuits by female partners against large law firms. In 2016, for example, California established the "Equal Pay Act" for men and women performing substantially similar work. Starting in 2017, the law expanded to include race and ethnicity and prohibits "prior salary" as being a basis to perpetuate wage differences. Further, the legal search firm Major, Lindsey & Africa conducted a survey in 2016 of big-firm partners that revealed that there is a 44 percent difference in pay between female partners and their male colleagues (Olson, 2016a).

In the 2013 ABA report "Closing the Gap: A Road Map for Achieving Gender Pay Equity in Law Firm Partner Compensation" by the Task Force on Gender Equity, principally authored by Lauren Stiller Rikleen, there are 12 recommended practices to make the compensation process more fair and transparent and create a level playing field for female, male, and minority partners. Implement them or adapt them for your firm as you go down the road to diversity and inclusion. They are:

- Build transparency into the compensation process— factors upon which compensation decisions are made should be in writing and communicated to all partners. "Internal equity" should be analyzed to ensure consistent application of compensation criteria.
- Include a critical mass of diverse members on the compensation committee.
- Develop systems to promote fair and accurate allocation of billing and origination credit.
- Require diversity in pitch teams and related business-development efforts and ensure that diverse lawyers become a part of the client team when successful.
- Reward behaviors that promote institutional sustainability.
- Implement formal client succession protocols.
- Measure and report results.
- Develop a process to resolve allocation disputes promptly and equitably.

- Implement training for all involved in the evaluation and compensation process.
- Engage the client's role in gender equity.
- Implement systems to ensure equitable compensation for partners on a reduced-hours schedule.
- Maximize the effectiveness of affinity groups (i.e., groups of individuals with shared common goals or interests).

As you progress along the road to diversity and inclusion, you need to push yourself and your firm harder uphill to continue to reap the benefits of your efforts. Legal talent consultant Ida O. Abbott, in the ABA's *Law Practice Today* article, "Come in and Make Yourself Uncomfortable" (2016) encourages men and women to get over initial inhibitions so that successful sponsor-protégée relationships can form readily. She suggests the following to increase your chances for that to happen:

- *Teach men and women to communicate*—especially about topics that might make them uncomfortable. Help them understand how gender dynamics, including gender bias and power differences, affect male-female communication.
- *Put yourself in social situations where you feel uncomfortable*—at your next networking event approach a stranger—someone of a different gender, race, status, age or other characteristic and introduce yourself.
- *Practice empathy.* Suspend assumptions about the other person and approach them with an open mind.

- *Facilitate discussions about gender.* Invite a small group of men and women to discuss gender-related issues. Make the discussion informal; have it led by a skilled facilitator who can keep the conversation focused and make people feel safe when they speak honestly.
- *Get to know potential sponsors and protégées in your network.*
- *Expand beyond your immediate network.* Ask for suggestions and introductions to people you may want to meet.
- *Work together on non-work projects.* Look for activities and organizations such as specialty bar associations, nonprofit or community organizations, the symphony board, an alumni association or political campaign to work on together.
- *Include men in women's initiatives.* Include men in some of your firm's women's initiatives and events.

DIVERSITY AND YOUR FIRM'S CLIENTS

A 2015 *New York Times* article (Olson) mentions mounting evidence that:

> corporations are putting more pressure on law firms to make diversity a central factor in their hiring decisions. When corporations request formal bids from law firms to represent them in legal cases, they are asking for lawyers with more varied experience and backgrounds—and proof that firms have such people in place.

To retain current business and obtain future business from corporate clients, you must be able to track the information they request and staff projects with diverse attorneys.

As a large firm, Seyfarth Shaw is typically asked at least one question about diversity efforts on prospective clients' requests for proposals. They also answer 45 to 50 more in-depth requests from client companies and participate in various industry/media surveys each year, according to a 2015 article their members wrote for the Association of Corporate Counsel (Spratt, Maechtlen, & Pauling, 2015). The article mentions how Allstate, one of the firm's largest clients and a leader in both legal and corporate diversity, asked "How would you, as a law firm, want to be evaluated by your clients on diversity and inclusion?"

Regardless of firm size, that's a question you as a champion manager should be asking your firm. In response to Allstate's question, Seyfarth developed metrics and created shared incentives that connect fees to service levels of diversity. At risk is 5 percent of the overall annual fee from Allstate. Successes and challenges toward achieving the benchmark goals for diversity are shared with Allstate during overall client service progress and planning sessions.

One aspect of diversity training within your firm is to instruct your attorneys, particularly your new associates, on how to work with diverse clients who may come from a different culture with different values, business and personal etiquette, and even business language. You certainly do not want to inadvertently offend a client who may then refuse to work with that attorney or your firm again. If you need help, there are consultants who specialize in teaching the nuances of how culture shapes business practices and protocols around the world.

CHAPTER SUMMARY

Consulting firms like McKinsey & Company and Deloitte, through their studies and reports, remind us that diversity and inclusion matter and should be a priority for you and your law firm. Consider both visible and invisible diversity traits before you embark on a diversity and inclusion initiative. Look beyond the obvious to gain an understanding of how diverse people can work better together and strengthen your law firm.

Diversity and inclusion initiatives may fail due to lack of commitment by leadership, emphasis only on recruiting and not retention, failure to acknowledge the impact of the firm's culture, lack of understanding diversity phases, expecting results too quickly, not having a long term plan with expectations that are appropriate for the input and commitment level, failure to establish specific tactics, ignoring the importance of training and development, and failing to understand the implications of a changing workforce. If you are uncertain how ready your firm is to embark on a more robust diversity and inclusion policy, consider using an assessment tool, referring to various guides published by NALP, and/or working with an external diversity consultant to get you started.

Moving toward an inclusive and diverse culture requires that you consciously work on changing the status quo and place a high value on diverse teams by holding everyone accountable; involve senior leadership and management as well as diverse firm members in all diversity efforts; provide targeted orientation, mentoring, and training to all attorneys and staff; and recognize historic or unintended bias and change it.

You need to acknowledge that gender inequality may exist in compensation systems and leadership positions in your firm, and as a champion manager make it a priority to rectify it. The ABA's Task Force on Gender Equality has 12 recommended practices to level the playing field for women, men, and minority partners. Consultant Ida O. Abbott encourages men and women to get beyond their initial inhibitions and make themselves uncomfortable for a while so successful relationships can develop.

Finally, you must not forgot that your large and/or diverse clients expect you to make diversity and inclusion a central factor in your hiring decisions, retention, and staffing of their legal work. It is increasingly a central factor as to whether they will hire and continue to work with you and your firm.

REFERENCES

Abbott, I. O. (2016, March 14). Come in and make yourself uncomfortable. Retrieved from http://www.lawpracticetoday.org/

Bersin, J. (2015, December 06). Why diversity and inclusion will be a top priority for 2016. *Forbes*. Retrieved from http://www.forbes .com/home_usa/

Bourke, J., Smith, C., Stockton, H., & Wakefield, N. (2014). Global human capital trends 2014: Engaging the 21st-century workforce. Retrieved from https://dupress.deloitte.com/

Cuyler, A. (2012, September & October). Diversity in the practice of law: How far have we come? *Legal Publisher, 29*(5).

Davis, W. (2016). Inclusion/diversity and pluralism: An organizational diagnostic. The Ryan Group. Retrieved from http://www.ryangroup inc.com/

Hunt, V., Layton, D., & Prince, S. (2015, January). Why diversity matters. Retrieved from http://www.mckinsey.com/business -functions/organization/our-insights/why-diversity-matters

Lawdragon News. (2016, June 24). Women in Law Empowerment Forum announces awards. Retrieved from http://www.lawdragon .com/2016/06/24/women-law-empowerment-forum-announces -awards/

McKinney, K., Maury, J., Hester, K., & Rucker, A. (2016). Diversity best practices guide 2016 edition. Retrieved from http://www.nalp.org /diversitybestpracticesguide

Morris, H. P. (2005). The DRI law firm diversity retention manual. Retrieved from http://www.dri.org/

NALP. (2016). NALP Diversity Through Infographics: From Law School to Partnership. Retrieved from http://www.nalp.org/

Olson, E. (2015, August 18). Many Black Lawyers Navigate a Rocky, Lonely Road to Partner. Retrieved from http://www.newyorktimes .com/

Olson, E. (2016a, October 12). A 44% pay divide for female and male law partners. *New York Times*. Retrieved from http://www .newyorktimes.com/

Olson, E. (2016b, December 30). More law degrees for women, but fewer good jobs. *New York Times* Retrieved from http://www .newyorktimes.com/

Rikleen, L. S. (2013, August). Closing the gap: A road map for achieving gender pay equity in law firm partner compensation. Retrieved from http://www.americanbar.org/aba.html

Spratt, J., Maechtlen, L., & Pauling, G. (2015, October 16). Three smart strategies to advance law firm diversity and inclusion. *Association of Corporate Counsel*. Retrieved from http://www.acc.com/

23

Managing to Prevent Harassment and Bullying

WHAT CONSTITUTES HARASSMENT AND BULLYING?

In the United States, harassment in the workplace is employment discrimination that violates Title VII of the Civil Rights Act of 1964, the Age Discrimination in Employment Act of 1967, or the Americans with Disabilities Act of 1990. The U.S. Equal Employment Opportunity Commission (n.d.) defines harassment as:

> unwelcome conduct that is based on race, color, religion, sex (including pregnancy), national origin, age (40 or older), disability, or genetic information. Harassment becomes unlawful where (1) enduring the offensive conduct becomes a condition of continued employment, or (2) the conduct is severe or pervasive enough to create a work environment that a reasonable person would consider intimidating, hostile or abusive.

In some states, such as California, employers with 50 or more employees are required to provide anti-harassment training, which must include anti-bullying training to its supervisors. In the past and before anti-harassment training was considered a best practice (if not a mandatory requirement), employees who complained of being sexually harassed occasionally filed law suits against firms who looked the other way when harassment first occurred. We have all likely heard of, witnessed, or been a party to situations where a female associate or staff member was promised a promotion or threatened with losing her job if she did not submit to her male supervisor's advances. The tacit acceptance of such behavior has changed over time and is neither legal nor acceptable. However, it still can occur and must not be tolerated.

Workplace bullying is a newer concept. It is also considered a form of workplace harassment but it is not yet always illegal. While all states in the United States have laws and most have policies against bullying, cyberbullying, and related behaviors to protect school-age children, these laws and policies do not necessarily extend to protecting adults in the workplace. However, bullying can be illegal if the activity otherwise violates federal or state laws prohibiting discrimination and harassment at work. Recent emphasis against bullying at school has made many adults realize that they face bullying at work. In many Canadian jurisdictions, there are laws prohibiting workplace bullying and psychological harassment.

The Workplace Bullying Institute (WBI, formed in 1997 by two psychologists) conducted a U.S. Workplace Bullying Survey in 2014. In it, Namie, Christensen, and Phillips (2014) define workplace bullying as:

repeated, health-harming mistreatment of one or more persons (the targets) by one or more perpetuators. Workplace bullying is abusive conduct that is

1. Threatening, humiliating, or intimidating, or
2. Work interference—sabotage—which prevents work from getting done, or
3. Verbal abuse.

The WBI (Namie, Christensen, & Phillips, 2014) compares workplace bullying to domestic violence:

> Being bullied at work most closely resembles the experience of being a battered spouse. The abuser inflicts pain when and where she or he chooses, keeping the target (victim) off balance knowing that the violence can happen again on a whim, but dangling the hope that safety is possible during a period of peace of unknown duration. The target

Figure 23.1

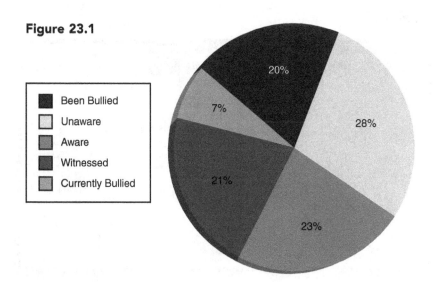

Been Bullied
Unaware
Aware
Witnessed
Currently Bullied

20%
7%
28%
21%
23%

is kept close by the abuser by the nature of the relationship between them—husband to wife or boss to subordinate or co-worker to co-worker.

Their survey results show that 27% of Americans have suffered abusive conduct at work; another 21% have witnessed it; and 72% are aware that workplace bullying happens (see Figure 23.1). They also reveal that those who have witnessed the bullying vicariously by seeing the bullying of others or knowing that others were bullied experienced emotional injuries similar in severity to injuries suffered by bullied individuals.

The Crisis Prevention Institute (CPI) (Solon, 2014) offers specific examples of workplace bullying to watch out for, which include repeatedly and intentionally:

- Withholding essential information.
- Failing to invite a person to meetings that are essential to that person's job.

Figure 23.2

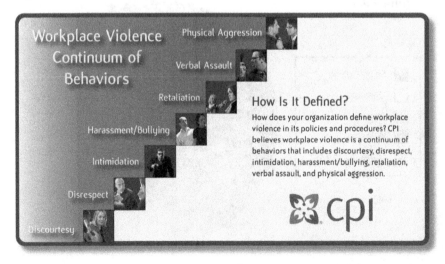

- Ignoring a person who disagrees with you.
- Making gestures or invading personal space to cause fear or concern for safety.

CPI describes bullying/psychological harassment as "workplace violence which is comprised of a continuum of behaviors ranging from discourtesy and disrespect, intimidation, harassment/bullying, retaliation, verbal assault, and physical aggression" (see Figure 23.2).

Other acts of bullying to watch out for that can be added to this list are:

- Grossly and unrelentingly micromanaging someone you supervise.
- Setting unrealistic deadlines, giving meaningless tasks, and overloading work.
- Stalking or cyber-stalking.
- Use of profanity, name calling, or yelling at someone you supervise.
- Any conduct that a reasonable person would find offensive, hostile, threatening, and unrelated to the firm's business.

HOW TO PREVENT OR STOP HARASSMENT AND BULLYING

As a champion manager, it is your job to implement and manage policies and procedures to prevent workplace harassment and bullying. If you are a manager in a small law firm and have no formal policies or procedures in place, where do you begin? If you are a manager in a large law firm where formal policies and procedures exist, how do you enforce them?

The CPI (Solon, 2014) recommends that organizational leaders respond to bullying by:

- Review(ing) current policies and procedures. Do your policies and procedures address respecting one another in the workplace? Have you provided clear expectations regarding interactions among coworkers? Is there a clear channel for reporting workplace incivility and bullying?
- Provid(ing) easy access to communication channels and support systems. Implement a clear method—that doesn't have recourse—for reporting incivility and bullying. Some organizations have toll-free hotlines that employees can call to report instances of incivility or feeling targeted. Also consider implementing employee and customer surveys.
- Process(ing) complaints fairly. Implement a standard investigation process to evaluate every reported incident. Establish a universal disciplinary policy for instigators of bullying. Be cautious in making exceptions for any internal or external customer who has been accused of incivility or bullying, and ensure a thorough evaluation of the information gathered.
- Implement(ing) training. Provide training for all employees in respectful communication protocols and the consequences for not adhering to them. Many organizations go a step further and train employees in skills to prevent, recognize and respond to incidents of incivility, aggression, and bullying in their workplaces.

The CPI (Solon, 2014) further suggest that, as a manager or supervisor, you should:

- Keep your ear to the ground. Listen to employee concerns both formally and informally, and be aware of sudden shifts and pattern changes in behavior.
- Address concerns and all forms of aggression. Respectfully attend to employee concerns about incivility and disrespectful verbal aggression when-ever it occurs. When necessary, follow through on progressive discipline.
- Walk the talk. Treat your employees respectfully, and encourage respectful interactions at all times through all communication channels. Managers and supervisors set the overall tone for workplace behavior, and your employees are watching you for cues.
- Arrange, support and attend training. Provide ongo-ing training on respectful workplace interactions. Having employees acknowledge a policy during orientation isn't enough. Employees need to know specific behaviors that are acceptable or unaccept-able and be trained in how to handle incivility and bullying when it occurs.

With respect to other types of employment discrimi-nation and harassment, similar policies and procedures should be put into place that address the specific federal and state legal issues in your jurisdiction and consequences of harassment in the workplace. This is an area complicated by differences that may occur between federal and state law in your respective locale. In some areas, such as California, the state regulations are more stringent and supersede federal regulations. Sample written anti-discrimination and harassment policies that can be adapted for your firm can be found through the Society for Human Resource Management (SHRM) and many local Chambers of Commerce. SHRM also has a sample Workplace Bullying Policy available (Workplace Bullying Policy, 2014).

Before we leave this topic, remember to be introspective about your own behavior. Make sure you are walking the talk because, as a champion manager, you set the tone for your direct reports and others in the firm and clients with whom you interact. In a recent article in the *Harvard Business Review* (Mawritz, Greenbaum, Butts, & Graham, 2016), "We're All Capable of Being an Abusive Boss," the authors mention that "abusive supervision costs U.S. corporations $23.8 billion annually." That's a staggering number, and their research suggests that:

> given the right conditions, just about any of us can be an abusive boss. Abuse can be an unintentional, impulsive reaction that results from a lack of willpower due to depleted emotional and cognitive resources. Supervisors who are sleep deprived or who experience work-family conflict, for example, are especially likely to lash out.

Mawritz et al. (2016) go on to suggest:

> If you find yourself on the verge of treating an employee poorly, find a quiet place and take a breather. If possible, avoid interacting with your employees until you have cooled off and feel

recharged. Also, consider using functional self-talk. Tell yourself in advance that you will not lash out at employees in the wake of employee deviance or low employee performance. By being thoughtful about these situations and working to improve your willpower, you can more effectively avoid the high costs of abusive supervision and improve your effectiveness as a manager.

CHAPTER SUMMARY

Federal and state laws regulate what constitutes harassment (and sometimes bullying) in the workplace and what employers must do to eliminate it from their firms. It is your job as a champion manager to stay abreast of these frequently changing laws and to implement policies and procedures to prevent and stop workplace harassment and bullying.

To assist you in better understanding and eliminating workplace bullying, look to guidance from The Workplace Bullying Institute and the Crisis Prevention Institute (CPI). Their examples of conduct that constitutes workplace bullying will heighten your awareness of what can go wrong. CPI provides recommendations that firm leaders and firm managers and supervisors should follow to stop workplace bullying as soon as it occurs and try to prevent it from happening in the first place.

As a champion manager, remember to model this behavior for others, encourage firm leaders to follow your lead, and keep best practices in mind. We all have stressful days, but there is no excuse for becoming an abusive boss.

REFERENCES

Mawritz, M., Greenbaum, R. L., Butts, M., & Graham, K. (2016, October 14). We're all capable of being an abusive boss. Retrieved from http://www.hbr.org/

Namie, G., Christensen, D., & Phillips, D. (2014). 2014 WBI U.S. workplace bullying survey. Retrieved from http://workplacebullying.org/multi/pdf/WBI-2014-US-Survey.pdf

Solon, R. (2014, January). Strategies to stop workplace bullying. Retrieved from http://www.crisisprevention.com/

U.S. Equal Employment Opportunity Commission. (n.d.). EEOC Harassment Definition. (n.d.). Retrieved from http://www.eeoc.gov/

Workplace Bullying Policy. (2014, May 23). Workplace bullying policy. Retrieved from https://www.shrm.org/

24

Managing for Privacy, Confidentiality, and Cybersecurity

To maintain the requisite knowledge and skill, a lawyer should keep abreast of changes in the law and its practice, *including the benefits and risks associated with relevant technology.*

(American Bar Association, 2016;
Rule 1.1 of the Model Rules
of Professional Conduct
[emphasis added])

When anti-virus software and firewall protections by themselves were considered the gold standard in information and Internet security, the task could be delegated to the IT manager or department. Today, a firm's response to privacy, cybersecurity, and confidentiality risks requires a more strategic and holistic approach. Firm management must take the lead to ensure that cybersecurity is a priority, allocate funds to reduce the risk of cyber threat, and have systems and procedures in place in the event of a cybersecurity breach. Managers must also make sure that their emphasis on protecting client information doesn't result in overlooking the necessity of protecting information about their employees.

> The need for vigilance never stops. You cannot secure your data once and think you're finished; the rules of information security change on close to a daily basis. Certainly, someone in the firm needs to keep up with the changes on a regular basis or the firm needs to engage a security consultant to do periodic reviews.
>
> (Nelson, Ries, & Simek, 2012)

CYBERSECURITY

If you happen to be your firm's managing partner or a partner in charge of the firm's technology committee, there are four steps you should take to address cybersecurity if you have not already done so:

- Obtain a third-party assessment from a security consultant who can benchmark the firm against law firm industry standards and recommend needed actions.
- Develop an incident response plan in advance of any breach so your firm has procedures and responsibilities defined and in place should a security incident or breach occur.

- Since new threats and the ways to deal with them are constantly changing, the firm needs to update its security systems and incidence response plan on a regular basis. Make a plan that defines 'regularity' and implement on schedule.
- Cybersecurity training programs need to be updated and rolled out firm wide periodically throughout the year.

This section is not intended to be a deep dive into information security for law firms and how to address it in detail. There are excellent resources already out there published by the ABA, such as *Locked Down: Practical Information Security for Lawyers, Encryption Made Simple for Lawyers*, and the *Solo and Small Firm Legal Technology Guide*. You can also go online to the ABA's Legal Technology Resource Center for webinars and other resource materials. In addition, the International Legal Technology Association (ILTA) publishes white papers and surveys to keep you abreast of best practices.

There is, however, information from ILTA's 2016 Technology Survey (Corham, 2016) worth considering if you wonder how your firm compares with its peers:

- The top three technology issues or annoyances reported by respondents are security compliance/risk management (39 percent), users' acceptance of change (38 percent), and managing expectations of users and management (27 percent).
- Respondents said the three biggest security challenges they face are balancing security with usability (34 percent), user acceptance and

behavior (25 percent), and (in a tie) user education and awareness (21 percent) and firm culture (21 percent).

- Security issues ranking lower than expected were client security requirements (14 percent), BYOD/mobile devices (12 percent), and cloud apps/data security (4 percent).
- Security awareness training programs are dramatically up, with 62 percent of firms now having them in place (up 13 percentage points over 2015).
- Respondents said that besides encryption and common antivirus software, the top three security measures used are removal of administrative rights on the desktop (65 percent), intrusion detection systems (56 percent), and two-factor authentication (49 percent).

A lawyer shall make reasonable efforts to prevent the inadvertent or unauthorized disclosure of, or unauthorized access to, information relating to the representation of a client.

(American Bar Association, 2016; Rule 1.6(c) of the ABA Model Rules of Professional Conduct)

Following Internet security best practices, knowing the Model Rules of Professional Conduct with respect to client confidentiality and privacy, and learning the corresponding rules in the jurisdictions in which your firm practices do not prevent you from human error or intentional insider threats. Nor will they prevent your firm and its clients from being targeted by cybercriminals. They also do not ensure that your firm will adequately invest in technology infrastructure to better serve and protect its clients.

> Joseph Abrenio, vice president of commercial services at Delta Risk previously told Legaltech News that "the most prevalent cause of data loss is human error and negligence. Let's face it, productivity is king, and lawyers, paralegals and assistants; all of the staff are constantly under great pressure to produce," he said. "When you're doing that at such a high rate, ultimately it's bound that human failure is going to happen. And I've seen numerous inadvertent disclosures of data that are either to opposing counsel, to counsel not even involved in the case, or people that have no relationship to the case."

> (Dipshan, 2016)

As a champion manager, you need to consider your firm's culture in establishing and enforcing confidentiality, privacy, and cybersecurity policies and procedures. A hard line approach allowing only the use of firm-issued notebook computers, iPads, and smart phones for firm business may work well in certain firm cultures. Some firms may have BYOD policies in effect and expect attorneys and staff to use their own devices. Yet others may provide more flexibility and allow a combination of both. In order to get attorneys and staff to comply with client confidentiality, privacy, and cybersecurity policies and procedures, the policies and procedures should be perceived as reasonable and in line with your firm's culture. Even with the best of policies and intentions, human error is likely to occur. At some point, one of your team members will click on an attachment that unleashes malware onto your firm's network. Here's where your management and delegation skills and your firm's incident response plan come into play, get the network up and running in short order, and save the day, limiting lost productivity and billable time.

If you want to update and improve your firm's existing client confidentiality, privacy, and cybersecurity policies, form a data privacy and security task force that includes Millennials. They often use information sources and technology more comprehensively and differently than the generations before them. Your role as champion manager to design, implement, and manage new procedures will become easier by reaching out to attorneys and staff who will be innovative and aware of the latest tools and technologies to protect your firm.

At the first meeting of your task force, set the tone by sharing a war story or two of firms that have been hacked, had bank accounts stolen, and/or client data stolen. Move on to the agenda, which should include:

- Making cybersecurity a firm priority.
- Email security and use of encryption for emails and documents.
- Encryption of hard drives, removable media, and smart phones.
- Use of social media and limits to what can be shared about clients on the firm website and on Facebook, Twitter, LinkedIn, and other social media.

- Software add-ons to limit inadvertently sending emails to the wrong recipient.
- Whether to allow USB thumb/drives for sharing documents and transferring files from home or while traveling.
- BYOD policies and procedures.
- Mobile device management.
- Cyber liability insurance.
- Consumer online file-sharing options and encryption.
- Best practices for backing up onto cloud services and on-location physical drives.
- When and how to use cloud-based services and, if your firm still maintains its own network file server, whether to move it entirely to the cloud or just use cloud services for back-up.
- Whether to use a password manager, stronger passwords, or dual factor authentication and how to implement these cyber security measures.
- Establishment of mandatory cybersecurity training on incoming email protocols, document management, use of public WiFi, use of mobile devices, and remote access from home computers.
- How to respond to client requests for a security audit and compliance with client security requirements.
- Opening and maintaining a bitcoin account so you are ready in the event you are attacked by ransomware and your back up cannot be restored.

OFF-LINE CONFIDENTIALITY AND PRIVACY

Before leaving this topic, not all issues of client confidentiality and privacy occur through the use of computers. Your firm's basic client confidentiality and privacy policy and the training you provide to reinforce it should remind team members:

- Of their duty to preserve and protect confidential client information.
- To follow HIPAA guidelines to assure that all information such as client social security numbers and medical records (should your firm have that information) be protected and safeguarded.
- No client files should be left in an unsecured area, such as conference rooms, at the reception desk, or on work station counter tops.
- Not to discuss confidential client matters in public places like hallways, elevators, and restaurants.

Confidentiality must also be observed with respect to certain types of employee information that are typically maintained in an individual's personnel file. The information contained in these files should not be discussed within the firm except on a limited need-to-know basis by firm management. A separate confidential file should be established and maintained for:

- Medical records, including family/medical leave requests, if the employee has disclosed the nature of her/his illness; return to work releases; workers' compensation records; medical information related to reasonable accommodation under federal and state laws; and any other medical information.

- Equal employment opportunity records.
- I-9 files.
- Other confidential files, including investigative files for harassment, discrimination claims, and background and reference checks.

At a plenary session "Can They Hear Me Now? Practicing Law in an Age of Mass Surveillance" held at the 2016 ABA TECHSHOW and mentioned in an article by David Lat (2016), lawyer Marcia Hoffman gave good advice to law firm managers: "Security is never perfect." Hoffman continued, "So don't stress yourself out by aspiring to perfection. But you can, and should, try to do better over time. You—and your clients—will be very glad you did."

CHAPTER SUMMARY

The rules of information security change almost daily. Four things firms need to do to address cybersecurity are:

- Obtain a third-party assessment from a security consultant.
- Develop an incident response plan before a breach occurs.
- Update systems and the incident response plan on a regular basis.
- Update and roll out firm-wide training periodically throughout the year.

In addition, obtain resources from the ABA and ILTA to educate yourself and other firm managers about best practices in cybersecurity, client confidentiality, and privacy. Before you implement any new policies, consider your firm culture and the best way to roll out and enforce policies and procedures.

Be prepared, for the day will come when your firm's cybersecurity will be breached. Select a diverse group of professionals to participate on the firm's cybersecurity, client confidentiality, and privacy task force to assist you in managing this important area in your firm. Advance planning and including other team members in the process will protect you, your firm, your employees, and, most importantly, your firm's clients.

REFERENCES

American Bar Association. (2016). Model rules of professional conduct. Retrieved from http://www.americanbar.org/groups /professional_responsibility/publications/model_rules_of _professional_conduct/model_rules_of_professional_conduct _table_of_contents.html

Corham, T. (2016, December). ILTA's 2016 Executive Summary. Retrieved from http://www.iltanet.org/

Dipshan, R. (2016, August 09). Insider threats rise in 2016 and legal's data security is in danger. Retrieved from www.legaltechnews.com

Lat, D. (2016, April 02). 7 cybersecurity tips for lawyers. Retrieved from http://www.abovethelaw.com/

Nelson, S. D., Ries, D. G., & Simek, J. W. (2012). *Locked down: Information security for lawyers.* Chicago, IL: American Bar Association, Law Practice Management Section.

25

Managing for Wellness

This long-overdue study [on substance use and mental health concerns among American attorneys] clearly validates the widely held but empirically under-supported view that our profession faces truly significant challenges related to attorney well-being. Any way you look at it, this data is very alarming, and paints the picture of an unsustainable professional culture that's harming too many people. Attorney impairment poses risks to the struggling individuals themselves and to our communities, government, economy and society. The stakes are too high for inaction.

> Patrick R. Krill, attorney, clinician and lead
> author of the 2016 ABA & Hazelden
> Betty Ford Foundation Study

Until fairly recently, employee wellness was not considered a very high management priority. Managers assumed that some of their employees would at some point have medical and emotional problems, and that it was largely the employees' responsibility to deal with them. At best, some form of health insurance coverage would be offered, and employees would take it from there. Aside from encouraging flu shots and complying with occupational safety standards, little if any thought was given to how organizations and managers could take a preventive approach to employee health and well being.

Over time, statistics have revealed the magnitude and ubiquity of problems such as alcoholism and mental illness in the United States and their impact on the workplace. Organizations began to understand how significantly their employees' health affected overall productivity and profitability. It was hard to disregard statistics like the following:

- The Centers for Disease Control and Prevention (2016) found that losses in workplace productivity in the United States in 2010 due to excessive alcohol consumption amounted to more than $179 billion.
- A study published in 2015 in the *Journal of Clinical Psychiatry* found that from 2005 to 2010 the economic burden of major depressive disorder on U.S. workplaces was between $83 and $103 billion per year because of absenteeism and reduced productivity while at work. This figure did not include medical costs shared by employers (Greenberg, Fournier, Sisitsky, Pike, & Kessler, 2015).
- Studies have shown that anxiety disorders affect 18.1 percent of adults in the United States (approximately 40 million adults between the ages of 18 to 54), and U.S. adults with anxiety lose an average of 4.6 to 5.5 days work days per month because they are unable to work or have to cut back their work

due to their disorder (National Institute of Mental Health, n.d.).

Now that there is widespread recognition that employee wellness correlates with higher productivity, retention, engagement, and morale over the long term, all kinds of organizations, including businesses, professional firms, not-for-profits, and government agencies have begun taking a proactive approach. The dramatic rise in health care and insurance costs (often borne or shared by employers) has further encouraged action in addressing employee impairment and derailment problems.

Statistics for the legal profession are more worrisome and sobering than those for the general U.S. economy. The 2016 Hazelden Betty Ford Foundation and American Bar Association report on substance abuse and mental health in the legal profession mentioned in the quote at the beginning of this chapter (Krill, Johnson, & Albert, 2016) found that:

- 21 percent of licensed and employed attorneys qualify as problem drinkers;
- 28 percent struggle with some level of depression;
- 19 percent demonstrate symptoms of anxiety; and
- Younger attorneys in the first ten years of practice exhibit the highest incidence of these problems!

MANAGING FIRM MEMBERS WITH SUBSTANCE ABUSE OR MENTAL HEALTH ISSUES

Given these statistics, it's very likely that you as a manager will at some point deal with an attorney, professional, or support staff member with a mental health issue or

addictive behavior. This is one of the most difficult situations for managers both in and outside of the legal profession. According to another survey conducted by the
Hazelden Foundation, "54% of HR professionals believe that
getting employees to acknowledge or talk about substance
abuse is their toughest challenge" (National Business Group
on Health, 2007). Managers who see wellness-oriented programs and practices purely as expenses are less likely to
implement them. Champion managers, on the other hand,
see them as an investment in the maintenance of their most
important asset—their people—and know they make good
business sense.

Managers must consider several factors in addressing
these sorts of workplace issues. They must balance their
desire to help an individual employee with the overall well
being of the firm and its other members. At the same time,
the relevant employment, privacy, and disability laws of
their jurisdiction may also impose responsibilities and limitations upon them. If, for example, they label and treat an
employee as having an alcohol problem rather than a performance problem, they may be accused of perceiving that
employee as "disabled" as defined by the Americans with
Disabilities Act. Rather than including further discussion of
the complex legalities of addressing substance abuse and
mental health issues, we refer you to the resources provided at the end of this chapter.

Champion managers take a proactive approach to
employee wellness. They realize that these days the proverbial ounce of prevention is worth far more than a pound
of cure. They educate themselves about these sorts of
problems; become aware of their warning signs; focus on

their employees' performance problems before jumping to broad or premature conclusions about derailment behaviors; and then, when possible, partner with their employees to address underlying problems. They recognize that problems like substance abuse and addictive behaviors are often tied to underlying mental health issues like depression and anxiety, and they understand the role chronic stress can play in triggering or exacerbating all of these sorts of problems.

Even though each employee presents a unique set of circumstances and challenges, champion managers keep several general principles in mind.

- Mental health and substance abuse problems rarely, if ever, go away when they are ignored. If anything, they tend to worsen over time.
- Even if you're a champion manager, you have limitations. You alone don't have the power to help someone or fix their problem—they need to step up.
- Mental health professionals and addiction specialists know more than you do and are more skilled and experienced at dealing with these sorts of problems. Champion managers refer their employees to them, as well as to sobriety programs, lawyer assistance programs (LAPs), and employee assistance programs (EAPs).
- As a manager, you are in an excellent position to create and promote a firm culture that pays attention to wellness. You are also in an excellent position to set an example by modeling healthy behaviors.

- Wellness is becoming a way to differentiate your firm and attract attorneys and staff, particularly Millennials, who often value wellness and work-life integration more than previous generations.
- Even though you are a manager, you are not immune to these sorts of problems. If you have higher levels of chronic stress, you may be more susceptible than other firm members.

Managing Employees with Substance Abuse and Addiction Issues

It can be difficult for a manager to detect signs of alcoholism and substance abuse. Some addicts are relatively high functioning (pun definitely not intended) and many are skilled at lying and concealing signs of their addiction. Champion managers know that the following behaviors may indicate that an employee has a substance abuse problem.

- Obvious signs of intoxication, such as slurred or unintelligible speech or odors of alcohol and other intoxicants.
- Increased absenteeism, tardiness, or unexplained breaks and absences.
- Inconsistent and diminished job performance—for example, taking more time to accomplish familiar tasks; making errors and bad decisions; exercising poor judgment; and failing to meet deadlines or show up for hearings, meetings, and appointments.
- Sudden and uncharacteristic changes in behavior or personality, such as displays of forgetfulness or confusion; a lack of concern over personal

appearance and hygiene; increased defensiveness or overreaction to feedback and suggestions;
erratic, manic, or hostile behaviors; or increased
secretiveness and withdrawal from interactions.
- Sudden changes or onsets of physical conditions,
  such as dramatic weight loss, unsteady gait, or den-
  tal problems.

Alternate and innocuous reasons for each of these
behaviors may certainly exist. Each one of them, in and
of itself, is hardly a compelling reason for suspecting substance abuse; but the greater the number of them, the
greater the likelihood that a problem exists. Keep in mind
that substance abuse and dependency are rarely a delib-
erate choice; people consciously decide to take drugs and
engage in risky behaviors, but they seldom, if ever, do so
with the intention of becoming addicts or abusers.

Before talking to an employee, it's important to follow
best human resources practices, update yourself on relevant employment laws, and document any performance
problems by specifically describing what was seen and
heard. Rather than simply recording your conclusion that
an employee arrived at work intoxicated or high, you must
tie this to that employee's job performance and describe
when this occurred, who witnessed the behavior, what you
and other firm members actually observed the employee
saying or doing, and the effect his or her behavior had on
other firm members or clients. It's also a best practice to
already have a substance abuse policy that has been communicated to all employees, preferably through your firm's
employee handbook.

Conversations with an employee about suspected substance abuse should be handled with great care. It is important that these interactions don't deteriorate into you as the manager monopolizing the conversation or patronizing or preaching to the employee. (The guidelines for constructive and collaborative feedback described in Chapter 7 provide a more effective approach.) You can expect the employee to be defensive, resistant, or shut down. To minimize the chances of this happening, the conversation should take place in a private space and at an appropriate time. Talking to an employee while they are intoxicated is seldom useful and at times a recipe for disaster. It may also make sense to have a third person, such as a human resources manager, join the conversation.

During your conversation, assure the employee that your focus is on their performance and the impact it is having on the firm, its clients, and their fellow firm members. Avoid judging or diagnosing the employee—leave that to professionals. If an employee acknowledges that he or she is struggling with addiction or abuse, offer your support and partner with him or her in identifying next steps, such as a referral to a mental health professional or an addiction treatment specialist. Some employees may wish to involve you in their treatment and recovery; others will wish to handle it privately. If an employee feels there is no problem or it's well under control, avoid arguing. Instead, return to the topic of the problem behaviors and the need to address them regardless of their cause. However the employee responds, continue to monitor his or her performance and take appropriate corrective and disciplinary actions when necessary.

Managing Employees with Mental Health Issues

The most common mental health problems affecting employee performance are depression and anxiety. They may occur separately or in combination with one another. They may also underlie problems with substance abuse when employees unconsciously attempt to self-medicate. Because many of the signs of substance abuse and depression are similar, managers may be confused as to the reasons for changes in an employee's behavior and productivity. Rather than trying to divine or diagnose causes, keep the focus on an employee's performance problems.

In many respects, a champion manager's handling of employee mental health disorders will be similar to their handling of substance abuse issues.

- Champion managers focus on performance problems rather than their causes;
- They learn about depression and anxiety but leave diagnoses to professionals;
- They comply with relevant laws and follow best human resources practices by documenting problems and changes in an employee's performance;
- They offer concern and support; and
- They recognize their limitations as a manager, albeit a champion one.

The key to recognizing an employee's possible depression and/or anxiety is to focus on changes in their behavior, attitude, or performance. If they suspect an employee is depressed, champion managers will consider the following changes, especially if they are sudden, dramatic, uncharacteristic, or continue over time:

- Increased absenteeism.
- Decreased productivity, increased errors, and difficulty finishing tasks and projects.
- Forgetfulness, indecisiveness, and difficulty in concentrating.
- Frequent irritability, low moods, and difficulty in working with others.
- Slower movements and frequent complaints of fatigue.
- Withdrawal and a loss of interest in work or socializing with friends and firm members.
- Complaints of unexplained aches and pains.

Like depression, anxiety can show up in many ways and in different degrees. Being anxious about a single looming deadline is not a sign of an anxiety disorder, but being anxious about all deadlines—some real and perhaps some imagined—may very well be. If a champion manager suspects an employee is suffering from an anxiety disorder, he or she will consider the following changes in the employee—again, especially if they are sudden, dramatic, uncharacteristic, or more pronounced over time.

- Increased tenseness, restlessness, and agitation.
- Becoming easily overwhelmed, sometimes to the point of not being able to complete work or meet reasonable deadlines.
- Looking, acting, and/or talking about being constantly worried.
- Magnifying the severity of problems and challenges.
- Having trouble focusing and understanding and following instructions.

- Spending a disproportionate amount of time looking for possible errors.
- Increased irritability and impatience.
- Becoming socially withdrawn and losing interest in activities previously enjoyed.
- Sudden changes or onsets of physical conditions, such as appetite, smoking and drinking habits, or the ability to perform fine motor functions.

Talking with Employees about Possible Mental Health Issues

Regrettable as it may be, in many places there is still a stigma attached to having mental health disorders like depression or anxiety. Champion managers understand that people struggling with these problems may be reluctant to acknowledge and talk about them, especially with their managers and employers. Creating a firm culture where conversations about employee wellness and mental health are normal can help overcome an employee's feelings of shame and a reluctance to talk. Champion managers often overcome their employee's resistance by, as always, focusing on observable performance problems rather than jumping to conclusions and layperson diagnoses. They don't judge their employees or offer fixes; instead, they find that listening and open-ended questions (see Chapter 4) are the best ways to encourage employees to talk candidly.

No matter how smart you are, no matter how compelling an advocate, trying to talk a person out of being depressed and anxious doesn't work. Champion managers don't challenge or depreciate an employee's feelings. They avoid offering unsolicited advice and saying things like:

- It's all in your head.
- You just have the blues; they'll pass.
- You're worrying about nothing.
- I know how you feel. My best friend Bill was pretty depressed/anxious last year when he . . .
- Stop feeling sorry for yourself.
- You just need a break.
- You have to try harder and give yourself a chance to be happy.

Champion managers choose a private and distraction-free place for these conversations, so employees can feel calm, comfortable, and safe. They assure each employee that conversations will remain either confidential or shared with as few people as possible. They ask the employee what information they may share and with whom. Champion managers are sensitive and supportive without bypassing or sugarcoating serious issues. Rather than blaming or judging, they provide clear and descriptive feedback about how the employee's behavior and performance have changed. Most important, they listen to what the employee is saying, how they're saying it, and what they may not be saying. They try to understand the employee's perception of their performance problem and how they may see their depression or anxiety contributing to it.

Many people can manage their mental health issues and perform to acceptable standards, while others may require individualized support, especially during acute episodes. Depression and anxiety may be considered disabilities in some circumstances. If the employee is amenable, his or her manager will work with him or her to develop a plan for addressing the problem, including the specific ways the manager and firm can provide support. It's important that the employee know what additional resources (such as referrals to mental health professionals) are available through the firm's health insurance coverage or employee assistance program. External resources may also be available. Before ending the conversation, the manager and employee should agree on a time to discuss improvements, if any, in the employee's performance and mental health. Managers should be very clear that the employee is welcome to make contact again before that time should the need arise.

The management of employees with substance abuse or mental health problems should begin well before these conversations take place. Champion managers take a proactive and preventive approach. They create a firm culture that promotes understanding and reduces the stigma associated with these problems by fostering an open and supportive environment where people can talk about wellness and disclose mental health or substance abuse problems if they wish. They make sure their firm has clear policies on substance abuse and mental health, and they educate their firm members on these problems. Depending on their firm's size and resources, they may also establish firm wellness programs. They personalize the support they offer because anxiety and depression affect people in different ways. They recognize that while some of their employees may be able to continue working, others may need temporary or permanent accommodations, such as time off each week to attend treatment programs, limited or flexible hours, movement to another area of the office, a change of job description and responsibilities, or even a leave of absence. Champion managers also understand the role chronic stress plays in contributing to these conditions.

MANAGING STRESS AND DERAILMENT BEHAVIORS

Many lawyers, professionals, and support staff—managers included—buy in to the belief that they must accept constant high levels of stress as a necessary and unchangeable part of their work life. Feeling and admitting to being stressed are seen as signs of weakness or a lack of professionalism. Champion managers know that toughness and resilience don't come from ignoring stress; they come from learning how to manage it!

Dealing with Stress before It Becomes Chronic

Champion managers know that stress is an inevitable part of living and practicing law, so attempts to totally eliminate it are unrealistic, ill advised, and a waste of time and energy. They also realize that not all stress is bad: relatively brief episodes of stress can actually be healthful and stimulating, resulting in improved performance and productivity. Champion managers understand that stress can be acute, episodic, or chronic; and that chronic stress is the kind that is most damaging to our physical and mental health.

Chronic stress is not a psychological diagnosis or a form of mental illness, but it does affect the functioning and structure of the brain, leading to a reduced capacity for learning and memorization, and heightened susceptibility to stress and anxiety. Although it is not the *cause* of addiction, substance abuse, or mental disorders, it has been found to be a powerful *trigger* for their initiation, continuation, and relapse, even after long periods of wellness or sobriety. This is true for tobacco use as well as drugs and alcohol.

Chronic stress can also affect the physical health of firm members and their ability to productively practice law and do their jobs. It has not been found to be the cause of any disease or disorder, but it has been shown to contribute to the onset, severity, and duration of several them (e.g., cardiovascular disease, high blood pressure, obesity, diabetes, asthma, cancer, HIV/AIDS, digestive disorders, and headaches). It not only affects how healthy people are but also how long they live, by suppressing their immune system and making them more susceptible to diseases and infections.

Champion managers don't try to create a stress-free firm culture; they instead create a *stress-smart* culture. They delegate work and assign cases and transactions so stress, though it may be high, will be episodic rather than chronic. Paralleling their efforts to educate firm members about substance abuse and mental disorders, champion managers help their employees learn more about:

- The inevitability of stress and the distinctions between pressure, stress, and chronic stress;
- How individual employee behavior can contribute to stress across the firm;
- How to manage stress by developing new habits and attitudes that mitigate the impact of chronic stress; and
- The importance of dealing with stress before it becomes chronic.

Observing External Stressors and Internal Stressors

Champion managers help their employees understand that stress can originate from outside and within us. The state of the general economy, deadlines, and time pressures stress almost everyone. Additional external stressors abound in the legal profession, such as an adversarial system, narrow margins for error, aggression and competition in practice areas such as litigation, and public hostility towards lawyers.

Internal stressors, by contrast, are determined by a person's emotional intelligence (self-awareness, self-control, adaptability, resilience, optimism, and self-confidence), personal beliefs and attitudes (e.g., perfectionism or stoicism), cultural values (such as respect for an elder or deference to a superior even when they are clearly wrong), and genetics and neurobiology that may predispose him or her to respond to external stressors in a particular way or to a specific degree.

Champion managers teach firm members that this isn't a mere theoretical distinction. People generally have more control and influence over their internal stressors. They may not be able to change an external cause of their stress, but they can choose how they respond to that stress. Champion managers encourage firm members to:

- Determine which of their stressors are external and which are internal;
- Distinguish between what they can control and what they can't;
- Decide whether their beliefs, attitudes, and habits are contributing to their stress;

- Dedicate time each day to monitoring their levels of stress; and
- Develop regular practices and habits to build their resilience and renew their energy.

Perhaps the single most important thing champion managers can communicate to their employees is that learning how to deal with chronic stress is essential to the early detection and prevention of substance abuse. Using drugs or alcohol as a way to self-medicate is a very limited and potentially dangerous way of responding to chronic stress, burnout, and underlying depressive and anxiety disorders. Addiction and abuse take stress to a whole new level.

CHAPTER SUMMARY

Employee wellness should be a management priority because problems such as alcoholism and mental illness affect overall productivity, profitability, and firm morale. Champion managers see wellness-oriented programs and practices as an investment in the maintenance of their people. However, they must balance their desire to help an individual employee with the overall well-being of the firm and its other members. They also need to be aware of relevant employment, privacy, and disability laws in their jurisdiction before they address individual wellness concerns. Below are suggestions for how to manage employees with substance abuse and mental health issues.

- Look for signs that an employee may have a substance abuse problem such as obvious intoxication;

increased absenteeism, tardiness, or unexplained breaks and absences; inconsistent and diminished job performance; sudden changes in behavior or personality; and sudden changes or onsets of physical conditions. Follow best HR practices and your firm's substance abuse policy and document and tie their behavior to job performance. Focus on performance and its impact on the firm and its clients when you meet with the employee. Take corrective and disciplinary actions when necessary.

- Depression and anxiety are the most common mental health problems affecting employee performance. In many respects, a champion manager's handling of employee mental health disorders is similar to their handling of substance abuse issues and should focus on performance problems, leave diagnoses to professionals, comply with relevant laws and follow HR best practices by documenting problems, and offer concern and support and recognize the limitations of that support. Pay attention to changes in an employee's behavior, attitude, or performance.

- Champion managers understand that people struggling with depression or anxiety may be reluctant to acknowledge and talk about them with their managers. You can help overcome their reluctance to talk by focusing on observable performance problems, listening, and asking open-ended questions. These conversations should be held in a private and distraction-free place so employees

can feel calm, comfortable, and safe. Provide the
employee with additional resources available
through the firm, such as health insurance coverage or employee assistance programs.

* Champion managers understand that toughness
  and resilience don't come from ignoring stress;
  they come from learning how to manage it. Chronic
  stress is the kind that is most damaging to our
  physical and mental health and can result in triggering addiction, substance abuse, or mental disorders. Champion managers help their employees
  learn more about the inevitability of stress and
  the distinctions between pressure, stress, and
  chronic stress; how individual behavior can contribute to stress across the firm; how to manage
  stress by developing new habits and attitudes;
  and the importance of dealing with stress before it
  becomes chronic. They help employees understand
  that stress can be externally caused (by deadlines
  and time pressures) or be internally created (by
  cultural values, self-awareness, adaptability, personal beliefs and attitudes, and genetics).

Champion managers encourage firm members to determine which stressors are external and internal; distinguish
between what they can and can't control; decide whether
their beliefs, attitudes, and habits are contributing to their
stress; dedicate time each day to monitor their stress levels; and develop regular practices and habits to build their
resilience and renew their energy.

REFERENCES

Centers for Disease Control and Prevention. (2016, January 12).
Excessive drinking is draining the U.S. economy. Retrieved from
https://www.cdc.gov/features/costsofdrinking/

Krill, P. R., Johnson, R., & Albert, L. (2016). The prevalence of
substance use and other mental health concerns among American
attorneys. *Journal of Addiction Medicine, 10*(1), 46–52. doi:10.1097/
adm.0000000000000182

National Alliance on Mental Illness of Massachusetts. (2015, March).
BAD FOR BUSINESS: The business case for overcoming mental
illness stigma in the workplace. Retrieved from http://ceos
.namimass.org/wp-content/uploads/2015/03/BAD-FOR-BUSINESS.pdf

National Business Group on Health. (2009, August). *An employer's
guide to workplace substance abuse: Strategies and treatment
recommendations* (Rep.). Retrieved from https://www.business
grouphealth.org/pub/f3151957-2354-d714-5191-c11a80a07294

National Institute of Mental Health. (n.d.). Any anxiety disorder among
adults. Retrieved from https://www.nimh.nih.gov/health/statistics
/prevalence/any-anxiety-disorder-among-adults.shtml

RESOURCES

Goren, W. D. (2013). *Understanding the Americans with Disabilities Act*
(4th ed.). Chicago, IL: American Bar Association, Solo, Small Firm
and General Practice Division.

Greenberg, P. E., Fournier, A. A., Sisitsky, T., Pike, C. T., & Kessler,
R. C. (2015, February). The economic burden of adults with major
depressive disorder in the United States (2005 and 2010). *Journal of
Clinical Psychiatry, 76*(2): 155–62.

Gurchiek, K. (2015, January 20). Coping with employees' mental
illnesses can be challenging. Retrieved from https://www.shrm
.org/resourcesandtools/hr-topics/risk-management/pages/coping
-employees-mental-illnesses.aspx

Society for Human Resource Management. (2014, October 14). Disability accommodations: Conditions: Does the Americans with Disabilities Act (ADA) provide a list of conditions that are covered under the act? Retrieved from https://www.shrm.org/resources andtools/tools-and-samples/hr-qa/pages/cms_011495.aspx

Society for Human Resource Management. (2015, March 25). EEO: Disability: Are employees undergoing treatment for drug and alcohol addictions covered under the ADA? Retrieved from https://www.shrm.org/resourcesandtools/tools-and-samples/hr-qa /pages/adadrugsandalcohol.aspx

PART IV

Becoming the Complete Champion Manager

It's easy for attorneys at all levels to become so focused on client matters that they ignore their own wellbeing and professional development. For lawyers who manage, the additional responsibilities of developing employees and meeting strategic objectives make this balancing act all the more difficult. Time allocated for managerial activities and the continued development of managerial skills is often sacrificed just to "stay on top of things." Managers can become so focused on their employees that they neglect their own welfare and needs. When this occurs, a manager's development often stops or regresses.

Scheduling and zealously protecting time for management activities and learning is the most effective way to counter this tendency. In addition, Part IV of this book explains four practical ways managers can continue to improve their people management skills by learning how to assess their progress, finding and refining their own management style or styles, maintaining authenticity and integrity, and using various practice management resources.

26

Assessing Your Progress as a Manager

As lawyers become more skilled and comfortable with managing, they often want to know if they are making true progress towards becoming a champion manager. As with any other set of essential skills, it's necessary for them to pause periodically and reflect on the level and development of their managerial skills. It's important for them to ask, "Am I doing a good job of managing?" To answer that question, it's also necessary for them to ask, "How do I know if I'm doing a good job of managing?" or, more precisely and formally, "What have I seen or heard that lets me assess the quality of my people management?"

SELF-ASSESSMENTS

There are two ways to approach these questions. The first is largely through self-assessment; the second is by asking others. Each method has its advantages and disadvantages. Self-assessments are often flawed, because confirmation bias—our tendency to interpret new evidence as confirmation of our existing beliefs or assumptions—is real. Attorneys and managers, like all other people, tend to see what they want to see and interpret events and facts so as not to contradict the views they already have of themselves. In short, self-assessments don't help us see past our blind spots. If we feel we're horrible managers, we will be prone to overlook our management successes; if we feel we're god's gifts to our firm's employees, we may not recognize our managerial weaknesses.

To mitigate these problems, it's necessary to ground self-assessments to the greatest extent possible in observable facts. The Management Self-Assessment Checklist (shown here and in Appendix F) of 17 questions includes both subjective and objective factors. As you will see, it's important to provide examples for your answer to each question.

Management Self-Assessment Checklist

1. Do I feel that I am more effective now as a manager than I was 6 or 12 months ago? Examples?
2. Do I have a better idea of what to do and how to respond when a problem arises? Examples?
3. Am I anticipating people management issues before they become critical and/or urgent? Examples?
4. When people management problems arise, am I less reactive and more proactive? Examples?
5. When people management problems arise (as they undoubtedly will no matter how good I may be), how quickly and well am I responding to them? Examples?
6. Over the last 6–12 months, have I been proactive in creating policies and procedures for the management and development of firm members? Examples?

7. What have I done in the past 6–12 months to improve or change my firm's culture? Examples?

8. Over the last 6–12 months, has there been a change in how employees are hired and on-boarded? If there has been a change, can it be linked to my management?

9. Over the last 6–12 months, has there been better retention of staff and attorneys? If there has been a change, can it be linked to my management?

10. Over the last 6–12 months, have there been changes in absenteeism and productivity? If there has been a change, can it be linked to my management?

11. Over the last 6–12 months, when and where have I observed good firm morale and engagement? Examples?

12. Over the last 6–12 months, have we implemented new cybersecurity, privacy, and confidentiality policies, procedures, and software? If there has been a change can it be linked to my management?

13. Over the last 6–12 months, have we implemented any new policies or procedures to manage contract attorneys, temps, and interns? Examples?

14. Over the last 6–12 months, have we implemented or updated our anti-harassment and anti-bullying training?

15. Over the last 6–12 months, have we made diversity and inclusion a firm priority? Have we implemented any new policies or programs to support that goal? Examples?

16. Over the last 6-12 months, have we worked to improve communications between employees working remotely and the firm? Examples?

17. Over the last 6–12 months, have we looked at adding flextime or part-time personnel to our attorney, professional, and support staff, or implemented best practices to improve productivity and communication for existing flextime or part-time personnel? Examples?

ASSESSMENT BY FIRM MEMBERS

The above questions are a useful tool for reflection and assessment, but at best they only provide one perspective—yours. Getting the views of others can be extremely helpful, but simply asking for feedback can be complicated. Subordinates may be reluctant to share negative or critical feedback with their managers out of fear of retribution or damaging relationships, and peers may have personal or political reasons for not being fully candid. Even a manager's closest and most trusted friends may withhold information and opinions that, although helpful, might hurt the manager's feelings.

This phenomenon is not unique to law firms. All too often managers and leaders in all kinds of organizations (e.g., political, governmental, military, business, academia, and non-profits) become isolated and out of touch because subordinates, peers, and even their bosses are hesitant to give them honest feedback. There are often good reasons for reluctance: some people just don't take kindly to being told they're not doing a great job. Champion managers, on the other hand, are as skilled at receiving feedback as they are at giving it. Even when they feel defensive, they maintain a sense of curiosity and inquiry. They become active recipients in the kinds of constructive and collaborative feedback dialogues described in detail in Chapter 7.

Better methods of gathering feedback on managerial performance exist. They yield far more superior and useful information. They go by a number of different names, the most common being Upward Reviews (Beard, 2012) or 360 Assessments. 360 Assessments solicit views from a manager's leads, peers, and reports, while Upward Reviews gather information from a manager's reports. In a law firm, that is usually the attorneys and staff that report to a manager.

With both of these assessments, participants' answers must be kept confidential and anonymous to reduce any apprehensions or concerns they may have. If confidentiality and anonymity are not provided, the results are seldom very useful or robust. These assessments can be implemented online or through one-on-one conversations with a management consultant or other outside neutral party. Conversations, whether by telephone or face-to-face, typically yield better data than online assessments, but they can be costly and time consuming, especially if a large number of people are participating. Online assessments are scalable and their cost usually does not increase significantly when more firm members participate.

Whether virtual or in-person, both assessments typically use a predetermined set of questions about the manager's performance. Some online assessments use a stock set of questions that leave little or no room for customization, while others allow more flexibility. In-person assessments have a clear advantage in allowing the highest degree of customization. For example, portions of the question sets can be varied for participants depending on whether they are attorneys or staff members. It is very important that the questions are broad and open-ended. Narrow questions often fail to capture important information, particularly about firm wide issues like strategy execution, culture, morale, and engagement. They can also "lead the witness" in eliciting answers to what a manager may want to hear rather than what participants may feel is more important. Managers and other key stakeholders usually work with their practice management consultant to create the best

set of questions and determine who in the firm will participate in the assessment.

Online assessments that rely solely on numerical evaluations (e.g., rate your manager from 1 to 10 on how well he
or she delivers feedback) offer limited information. They
may give a general sense of how well a manager is doing in
a specific area, but without room for further comments and
explanation they barely scratch the surface. As a result,
interpreting a manager's scores can require a lot of specu-
lation as to the underlying reasons for the scores.

The manager who is the subject of either of these assessments answers the same set of questions so his or her perception of their performance can be compared to that of
the other survey participants. When there are significant
disparities between how a manager sees him- or herself
and what participants are saying, it is almost always good
evidence of a blind spot and an area for improvement.

Once the data has been collected, it should be analyzed and interpreted by a competent and experienced
professional. Executive coaches, practice management
consultants, and human resources specialists who are
not members of the firm bring the required objectivity
and independence to these tasks. They can also modify
and "sanitize" participants' comments so that anonymity is preserved. These professionals should also present the assessment results to the manager and use that as
the springboard for discussions about where and how the
manager can improve his or her performance. Often these
assessments and initial discussions are a catalyst for very
productive long- or short-term coaching engagements.

Upward Reviews and 360 Assessments are wonderful
tools when conducted properly. They can be invaluable

in helping managers develop into champions. Some managers choose to share their assessment results with their partners, key stakeholders, or entire firm. This level of transparency can transform a firm's culture. It's a powerful demonstration of leading by example, sending the message that "I (the manager) am serious about and committed to improving—and you should be as well." It can also serve as a model for an effective performance review process for other key firm members.

The only significant downside with these assessments occurs when participating firm members feel their views have not been heard. When this happens, cynicism and distrust can grow. Participating firm members want to feel that their input has been considered and will make a difference. Ignoring their feedback can make them feel undervalued and that the whole process was an empty exercise and waste of their time. When assessment results clearly demonstrate a substantial need for improvement and none follows after a reasonable amount of time, morale and engagement suffer.

CHAPTER SUMMARY

Managers should periodically pause to reflect on the level and development of their managerial skills. This can be accomplished in two ways—through self-assessment or by asking others. Self-assessments should be based as much as possible on observable facts. Use the Management Self-Assessment Checklist to consider objective and subjective factors about your performance as a manager.

Champion managers are as skilled at receiving feedback as they are at giving it. They rely on Upward Reviews or 360

Assessments to obtain feedback from others. A 360 Assessment obtains views from their leads, peers, and reports while an Upward Review gathers information from a manager's direct reports. Participants' answers should be kept anonymous and confidential. The assessment can be implemented online or through one-on-one conversations with a management consultant or neutral party. Both types of assessments typically use a predetermined set of questions about the manager's performance, which can be stock questions or customizable. The manager who is the subject of either of these assessments answers the same questions so his or her perception of their performance can be compared to answers from the other survey participants.

Once the data is collected, it should be analyzed and interpreted by a competent and experienced professional such as an executive coach, practice management consultant, or human resources consultant to preserve confidentiality and anonymity. Firm members who participate need to feel that their views have been heard and that areas that need improvement are addressed with the manager. If not, morale and engagement will suffer.

REFERENCES

Beard, N. (2012, Sept. & Oct.). Tools to improve morale, promote retention and train mentors. *Law Practice*, *38*(5).

27

Refining Your Management Styles

Managers over time tend to acquire their own personal, identifiable style of managing. They find ways of communicating and interacting that become instinctive, comfortable, and hopefully effective. They develop certain ways of delegating, giving and receiving feedback, motivating, and holding firm members accountable that turn into habits. Firm members come to expect their managers to act in that manner and can sometimes be confused when they don't.

The elements or building blocks of champion management (as described in Part II) can be expressed in a number of different styles. Champion managers don't share a single management style any more than they all dress or talk alike. They find a style—actually, a repertoire of styles—that fit their personality, employees, clients, and firm culture. More importantly, they develop the insight and flexibility to be able to deftly shift their styles to fit the needs of a specific situation or person.

A Fitting Management Style

One way to understand authentic management is to think about it through the metaphor of clothing. Let's say you see a manager you respect and admire wearing a particularly nice jacket. Wanting to emulate that manager's style, you find the same model at a store and try it on. Much to your surprise, it looks horrible on you. You realize it's the wrong size, color, and fit *for you*. What worked for your manager looks unprofessional and awkward on you. If you choose to buy it anyway, you will feel uncomfortable and self-conscious while wearing it.

So it is with management styles. Fit is important, and when the style fits (whether it's clothing or management) you will project an image of competence, authority, and trust. If, however, you decide to slavishly copy someone else's style, you may look bad or, worse yet, feel like you're wearing a straight-jacket that confines you.

SIX LEADERSHIP STYLES

Psychologist and journalist Daniel Goleman (2000) has identified six basic styles that leaders and managers use to get results. Champion managers may use a few of these styles more than others, but they realize that each has its unique value.

- **Authoritative** managers and leaders mobilize people towards a vision. This style has a very positive impact on work climate and works best when a firm needs a clear direction or changes require a new vision. It is expressed in the phrase, "Come with me."

- **Affiliative** managers and leaders build emotional bonds and create harmony. This style has a positive impact on work climate, and it works best to motivate people during stressful circumstances or to heal rifts in a firm or team. It is expressed by the phrase, "People come first."
- **Coaching** managers and leaders develop people for the future. This style also has a positive impact on work climate, and it works best to help firm members improve their performance or develop long-term strengths. It is reflected in the phrase, "Try this."
- **Democratic** managers and leaders forge consensus through participation. This style has a positive impact on work climate, and it works best to get input, buy-in, or consensus from key firm members. It is expressed by the question, "What do you think?"
- **Pacesetting** managers and leaders set high standards for performance. This style has a negative impact on work climate, especially in the long run. It works best to get quick results from firm members who are highly competent and motivated. It is captured in the expression, "Do as I do, now."
- **Coercive** managers and leaders demand immediate compliance. This style has the most negative impact on work climate and works poorly with independent people like attorneys. It is best used only in a crisis or with problem firm members. Coercive managers will say, "Do what I tell you."

Some managers can move easily between these management styles, while others eschew some of them. There are obvious benefits and disadvantages to each style, and appropriate times when a champion manager will use each of them.

- Even though the *coercive* style has the most negative impact when used continually, it may be the best choice in an emergency. In the event of a fire (figurative or literal), a champion manager will be "coercive" and tell you where to go and what to do, rather than being "democratic" and soliciting the views of your fellow firm members in order to build consensus . . . and create harmony . . . before then suggesting an escape plan . . . if it's not too late.
- A constant diet of the *pacesetting* style can elevate individual and collective stress levels and lead to burnout, but it can be very useful when there are tight and rapidly approaching deadlines for specific tasks and projects.
- The *democratic* style works best when relatively few firm members and stakeholders are involved in a making important management decisions or setting key strategies and policies. But when a democratic management style is used for trivial or day-to-day issues, delays are frequent and managers are often perceived as weak.
- While the *coaching* style is great for the long-term development of firm members, it is a poor choice when immediate or short-term results are needed. It works best in combination with other styles.
- Even the *affiliative* style, which builds firms with high degrees of trust and cohesion, can be over-used. Managers who place too much emphasis

on harmony may find it difficult to give negative or critical feedback and hold firm members accountable.

* The *authoritative* style should not be confused with being authoritarian, which is a kinder way of saying coercive. While there is great power in motivating people with an inspiring vision, it must not only be clearly articulated but also well thought out. A flawed direction, strategy, or plan will undercut a manger's effectiveness and the willingness of firm members to follow him or her.

Champion managers are not dissuaded from using any one of these styles from time to time solely on the basis on the impact they have on work climate. They understand that the goal is to develop a repertoire of these styles and the insight to know which to use in a given situation.

CHAPTER SUMMARY

Managers tend to develop their own style of managing that becomes instinctive, comfortable, and hopefully effective. The elements of champion management can be expressed in different styles that fit the manager's personality, employees, clients, and firm culture. Champion managers are able to shift their style to fit the needs of a specific situation or person.

Consider Daniel Goleman's six basic styles that leaders and managers use to get results:

* Authoritative: "Come with me."
* Affiliative: "People come first."

- Coaching: "Try this."
- Democratic: "What do you think?"
- Pacesetting: "Do as I do, now."
- Coercive: "Do what I tell you."

REFERENCES

Goleman, D. (2000, March & April). Leadership that gets results. *Harvard Business Review*. Retrieved from https://hbr.org/2000/03/leadership-that-gets-results

28

Maintaining Authenticity and Integrity

Authenticity is important, and champion managers strive for it. Being highly effective as a manager requires more than honing skills and following the rules of what a good manager says and does to get results. Authenticity is congruence between what a manager believes in and how he or she acts. It's walking one's talk and being honest with others and oneself.

Going through the motions of being an effective manager without actually believing in what you are doing and saying rarely works, especially in the long run. It can be exhausting for a manager to continually try to maintain the pretense of acting like a different person from who they really are. Over time their actions and decisions reveal the differences between what they really think and feel and what they are saying and doing. When employees pick up on these mismatches between their manager's communication (verbal and non-verbal) and conduct, they often grow skeptical and distrustful, wondering what their manager actually wants and means, and whether he or she is being candid or has a hidden agenda. Effective management—let alone championship-level management—is impossible without sufficient trust between employees and managers. Authenticity is one of the keys to building this trust.

Thankfully, very few managers believe authenticity is total freedom for them to say whatever they think, express whatever they feel, and do whatever they want. A few do, however, mistakenly believe unfiltered comments, shooting from the hip, and spontaneously doing their own thing are proof of their authenticity. People may have different opinions regarding whether this kind of conduct is authentic, but it's clearly not management. Authenticity isn't unthinkingly following our every impulse of the moment. It isn't behaving or reacting without considering our options, or how our actions may affect others. It isn't doing the first thing that comes to mind. Authenticity is instead taking the time to:

- Connect with and reflect on what we are genuinely feeling and thinking before we act;
- Figure out the best way to express that thought or feeling (if we choose to express it at all); and
- Then make sure our follow-up is consistent with what we've said.

Authentic managers, like champion managers, have high degrees of emotional intelligence and awareness about what they are feeling at any time. They have a core sense of self and know what their values, priorities, and mindsets are. From this center, they are able to stretch and grow. Trying something new or doing something different isn't a challenge to their authenticity, but rather a possible opportunity for growth and change. For them, being authentic isn't being stuck with the way they are.

LEADING BY EXAMPLE

Being an authentic manager sets an example for the members of your firm. Not only does it build trust, as noted above, it also challenges and encourages firm members to be authentic. No matter how loud and frequently you may preach—whether it's the way you want something done, the way you want clients handled, or a priority you may want to establish—the people in your firm will pay more attention to what you actually do. If you want them to communicate or act in a certain way, you need to model that behavior. If you want them to act with integrity, walk their talk, and be honest, then it's up to you to set the example.

As a manager, you can have great influence on the culture of your firm. Echoing what was written in Chapter 12, your managerial mindset will shape the conversations and interactions you have with other firm members, and consequently the relationships and culture of the entire firm. Every day, you will have the opportunity to demonstrate what good, effective, and championship-level management feels and looks like. Your firm members will be appreciative. You won't need to formally teach them how to manage (although sharing this book or what you've learned from it may be a good idea). By following your example and seeing results, they too will become better managers, leaders, and coaches of others.

CHAPTER SUMMARY

Champion managers strive for authenticity, the congruence between what they believe and how they act. Going through the motions of being an effective manager without believing what you are doing rarely works, especially in the long run. Authenticity builds trust.

Authenticity is taking the time to connect with and reflect on what you are genuinely feeling and thinking before acting, figuring out the best way to express a thought or feeling, and making sure your follow-up is consistent with what you've said. Being an authentic manager sets an example for the members of your firm. It challenges and encourages firm members to be authentic themselves. It enables you to demonstrate what good, effective, and championship-level management feels and looks like to the others in your firm.

29

Continuing Your Learning and Development

After finishing this book, your progress towards becoming a champion manager will not be complete. In many respects, it will have just started. As you can now appreciate, people management skills are complex and nuanced. They take time to learn and master. Both sustained practice and guidance are needed to get to the level where champion management is a habit.

Many of us have had the experience of learning a particular athletic or musical skill and practicing it diligently for several months or years only to later discover that we had been doing it incorrectly all along. The hours we practiced merely reinforced a bad habit or poor technique. We then needed to break old habits and unlearn our old ways of doing things before being ready to learn the right or better way.

The same thing can happen with people management skills. Without periodic guidance, we can slip back into old bad habits or earnestly practice the wrong way of doing something without realizing our error. Having others assess your managerial skills (as described in Chapter 26) is one way you can discover your mistakes and make corrections. The other is to utilize the resources that are now available to help you continue your learning and development as a champion manager.

Law practice management coaches and consultants. Many (though not all) of these professionals specialize in leadership and people management. They can assess your skills and identify areas for your further development. They can act as your thinking partner, be an objective set of eyes, provide new ideas, and give you important feedback that others can't or won't. Working with one is a good way to stay on course and accelerate your learning. (For guidance on how to select and work with them, please see *The Lawyer's Guide to Professional Coaching: Leadership, Mentoring & Effectiveness*, ABA 2012.)

Managing partner groups and roundtables. Small groups of managing lawyers are increasingly coming together to support and share resources with one another. Often a law practice management coach or consultant acts as the organizer and facilitator of these meetings, which usually take place on a monthly or quarterly basis. Face-to-face meetings are far more common than virtual ones, and meetings often focus on a specific management topic, which may or may not be people management or leadership oriented.

Bar association programs and webinars. Relatively few bar association offerings deal with practice management topics, and fewer still focus on the areas of people management and leadership. Although there may not be a lot of programs, there are occasional gems. For the topic of people management and leadership, you will have better luck looking at organizations and websites outside of the legal profession. Before taking a law practice management program or webinar with the hope of receiving Continuing Legal Education (CLE) credits, ascertain whether your state will give you credit for doing so. In some states law practice management topics are not considered substantive or important enough to merit CLE credit, and even in states where they are, there may be inconsistency and confusion as to which specific practice management topics qualify.

Law practice management blogs and websites. A wealth of information and advice (most of it good) on various law practice management topics can be found online. Some of the ones that often cover people management, technology and leadership topics are:

- **Attorney at Work** – *attorneyatwork.com* – advice on creating and managing a law practice from a diverse group of contributors.
- **College of Law Practice Management** – *collegeoflpm.org* – the most important practitioners and thought leaders in the area of law practice management.
- **Jim Calloway's Law Practice Tips Blog** – *jimcalloway.typepad.com* – information on technology, the Internet, and law practice management.
- **Law Sites** – *lawsitesblog.com* – Robert Ambrogi tracks the trends, products, and websites in the legal profession.

- **Legal Talk Network** – *legaltalknetwork.com* –
  podcasts on a wide variety of law practice management and technology topics.
- **The Law21 Blog** – *law21.ca/blog* – Jordan Furlong
  focuses on the direction and evolution of the legal
  profession as technology and markets rapidly
  change.
- **ABA Law Practice Division** – *americanbar.org
  /groups/law_ practice* – the most complete resource
  for law practice management events, publications,
  and CLE.
- **Law Practice Today** – *lawpracticetoday.org* – the
  monthly webzine of the American Bar Association
  Law Practice Division.
- **Adam Smith, Esq**. – *www.adamsmithesq.com* –
  a website with a blog focused on an inquiry into
  the economics of law firms, curated by Bruce
  MacEwen.
- **Edge International Communique** – *www.edge
  -international.com* – a monthly e-newsletter on law
  firm management.
- **The MPF Weekly** – *www.managingpartnerforum
  .org* – a weekly law firm management blog curated
  by John Remsen, Jr.
- **Legaltech News** – *www.lawtechnologynews@
  alm.com* – law technology updates, articles, and
  technology company press releases for the legal
  profession.
- **Technolawyer** – *www.technolawyer.com* – legal
  technology and practice management e-newsletter.

- **Law Office Manager** – *www.lawofficemanager.com* – an e-newsletter and weekly bulletins focused on law office management for administrators.

Law practice management periodicals and books. Several of the excellent books the American Bar Association Law Practice Division publishes each year on management, technology, marketing, and finance have already been mentioned in footnotes. The following is a list of them and other books and periodicals dealing with people management that lawyers will find valuable and interesting.

- *Law Practice* – the ABA Law Practice Division's bimonthly magazine is a great source of articles on practice management and emerging trends in the legal profession.
- *GP Solo Magazine* – from the American Bar Association.
- *Legal Management* – from the Association of Legal Administrators.
- *Attorney at Law Magazine* – a national network of local law magazines.
- *LAW & REORDER: Legal Industry Solutions for Restructure, Retention, Promotion & Work/Life Balance*, Deborah Epstein Henry.
- *Swimming Lessons for Baby Sharks* (2nd ed.), Grover E. Cleveland.
- *Effective Law Firm Management Strategies*, Arthur G. Greene and Sandra Boyer.
- *The Power of Appreciation in Business*, Noelle C. Nelson, Ph.D. (not specific to law firms but worthwhile).

- *The Five Dysfunctions of a Team*, Patrick Lencioni (not specific to law firms but worthwhile).
- *When Professionals Have to Lead*, Thomas J. Delong, John J. Gabarro, & Robert Lees.
- *You Raised Us, Now Work With Us*, Lauren S. Rikleen.
- *Managing the Professional Service Firm*, David H. Maister.
- *The Lawyer's Guide to Professional Coaching: Leadership, Mentoring & Effectiveness*, Andrew Elowitt.
- *Creating the Positive Law Firm*, Anne Brafford.
- *Thanks for the Feedback*, Douglas Stone & Sheila Heen.
- *Difficult Conversations*, Douglas Stone, Bruce Patton, & Sheila Heen.
- *How the Way We Talk Can Change the Way We Work*, Robert Kegan & Lisa Laskow Lahey.
- *First among Equals*, Patrick J. McKenna & David H. Maister.
- *Recruiting Lawyers*, Marcia P. Shannon & Susan G. Manch.
- *Effectively Staffing Your Law Firm*, jennifer j. rose.
- *How to Do More in Less Time*, Allison C. Shields & Daniel J. Siegel.
- *Quiet: The Power of Introverts in a World That Can't Stop Talking*, Susan Cain.
- *Conversational Intelligence: How Great Leaders Build Trust and Get Extraordinary Results*, Judith E. Glaser.
- *Working with Emotional Intelligence*, Daniel Goleman.

- *Leading Leaders: How to Manage Smart, Talented, Rich, and Powerful People*, Jeswald W. Salacuse.
- *Strategy and the Fat Smoker*, David H. Maister.
- *Becoming a Conflict Competent Leader: How You and Your Organization Can Manage Conflict Effectively*, Craig E. Runde & Tim A. Flanagan.
- *Drive: The Surprising Truth about What Motivates Us*, Daniel H. Pink.
- *Lessons in Leadership*, Thomas C. Grella.
- *The Lawyer's Guide to Mentoring*, Ida O. Abbott.
- *Managing People is Like Herding Cats*, Warren Bennis.
- *Smart Collaboration: How Professionals and Their Firms Succeed by Breaking Down Silos*, Heidi K. Gardner.
- *Building Career Equity: How Professionals and Their Firms Achieve Mutual and Meaningful Growth* (2nd ed.), Jan Torrisi-Mokwa.

APPENDIX A

A Quick Diagnostic For Identifying Communications Problems In Your Firm

Check all of the following that apply:

❑ Meetings are too long, frequent, and unproductive.
❑ Disagreements are not resolved.
❑ Decisions are not made in a timely manner.
❑ Teamwork is poor.
❑ Shared understandings and assumptions are lacking.
❑ Requests are unclear.
❑ Promises are not kept.
❑ Feedback is missing, ineffective, or not helpful.

If you checked four or more of the above signs, chances are you and the members of your firm are locked into some very common but seldom useful patterns of communication and action. Take a moment to reflect, and then check any of the following boxes that describe how you and the members of your firm behave from time to time.

❑ We advocate our views.
❑ We minimize others' concerns.

❏ We ask questions to find information that supports
  our point of view.
❏ We ask leading or loaded questions (i.e., we indirectly make statements with our questions or
  we ask questions for which we already know the
  answer).
❏ We defend our point of view.
❏ We use delay tactics.

The greater the number of the above boxes you checked,
the greater are the chances that some or all of the following
are occurring in your firm and hampering its performance.

❏ Firm members don't feel understood or, at times,
  even heard.
❏ Firm members feel either disengaged from or
  coerced by conversations.
❏ Conversations degenerate into ping-pong matches
  (i.e., back-and-forth exchanges).
❏ Agreements aren't reached, conflicts aren't resolved,
  and decisions are delayed or not made at all.
❏ Useful information and new ideas are less likely to
  be discovered and exchanged.
❏ Firm members perpetuate the problems they're trying to solve or create new problems.

And if you're truly curious (and a bit courageous), follow
up by asking the members of your firm to anonymously
answer these same questions. See what they say.

APPENDIX B

Initial Delegation Checklist

❏ **Delegate as early as possible**. Procrastination reduces the amount of time available for the completion of a task and puts unnecessary pressure on both the manager and delegatee.

❏ **Instructions to a delegatee should be clear, concise, and complete**. Written instructions can be useful in tracking a project and providing a delegatee with a record of expectations, timelines, and milestones.

❏ **Be as specific as possible with regard to due dates and timelines**. "Friday at 10:00 am" is a much clearer and more workable deadline than "sometime towards the end of the week."

❏ **If work is lengthy or complicated, then break it down into phases and create a timeline for each phase of the project**. For example, "Your research should be completed by the 20th and an initial draft memo of your recommendations by the 23rd; we'll review it together on the 24th; the final draft should be given to me on or before the 28th; we'll review that on the 30th; and we'll jointly present it at the partners' meeting on the 1st."

❏ **Avoid unnecessary work by being clear about expectations regarding the desired end product**. Should the delegatee prepare an email, a memo, a rough draft, or a finished product? Is a written report necessary or will a conversation suffice? Doing superfluous tasks delays the completion of projects, and often leads to the writing off a portion of the delegatee's billable time.

❏ **If the delegatee's time is billable, provide them with a sense of how many hours it should take them to complete the project**. This not only reinforces deadlines but also motivates them to work more efficiently.

❏ **Provide delegatees with some context: let them know how their contribution fits into the larger picture**. This will focus and expedite their work and is an important teaching tool. It is also an excellent way to motivate and develop firm members.

❏ **Delegatees work more efficiently when they are provided with the resources they will need**. Unless it has developmental value, there's no point in having delegatees reinvent the wheel. Pertinent information, references, and examples of similar work should be shared.

❏ **For complex projects, be clear about what decisions delegatees can make on their own**, which they need to get approval for, and which they can communicate after decisions have been made.

❏ **Help delegatees understand whom they may contact for further information and assistance**. This is particularly important for tasks involving contact with clients and people outside of the law office.

❑ **Check to make sure that delegatees understand instructions and expectations.** Encourage them to ask questions even if everything seems clear. Have them paraphrase and summarize what you've said. Ask them to describe how they will proceed and where they think they may need further guidance.

APPENDIX C

Post-Delegation Checklist

❏ **Establish a written or electronic system for tracking and reviewing tasks and projects that have been delegated.** Indicate to whom the work has been delegated and what the timeline is for its completion. This minimizes the chances of work being late, overlooked, or delegated twice to different people.

❏ **During the initial delegation of a project, set check-in dates to monitor a delegatee's progress—then check in according to that timeline.** Check-ins keep work on schedule and on budget and also give delegatees an opportunity to ask questions.

❏ **Provide delegatees with timely feedback throughout the course of a project.** Feedback early in the process will help delegatees focus their efforts and avoid tangents and false starts. (A detailed discussion of how to give feedback appears in Chapter 6.)

❏ **As part of their feedback, let delegatees see the final work product (or the work due at the end of the phase of a project) so they can see how their efforts contributed to the overall results.** This allows them to see, for example, how their research memorandum contributed to the adoption of a new office technology platform or selection of a new professional liability carrier.

❏ **At the end of a project, thank delegatees and provide them with meaningful feedback**. Let them know what they did well and how they can do even better in the future. Ask them what they have learned from doing the project and what they still have questions about. Be curious about their perspective and find out if anything in the delegation process could be changed to help them do a better or faster job. For larger and more complex projects, it's often useful to conduct a group debrief to discuss lessons learned and best practices discovered or refined.

APPENDIX D

The Flexible and Reduced Hours Checklist

The Flexible and Reduced Hours Checklist governs:

1. What information should be contained in a written flexible and reduced hour policy;
2. What topics should be covered at a "flexible sit-down meeting"; and
3. What issues should be addressed in training lawyers working flexible or reduced hours and those who supervise them.

The Flexible and Reduced Hours Checklist includes:

- Eligibility criteria.
- Description of the range of flexible and reduced hour options.
- Proposal process and what it entails.
- Determination of billable hours, percentage, and/or workload.
- Schedule and location for working.
- Timing and transition to and from flexible and reduced hours.
- Mutual flexibility expectations.

- Communication expectations.
- Non-billable contribution expectations.
- Work/life supervisor, affinity group, and support.
- Assignment process.
- Promotion eligibility and process.
- Compensation, including bonuses.
- Training.
- Travel restrictions, if any.
- Childcare or eldercare coverage, if applicable.
- Strategies to ensure work flow does not negatively impact colleagues and clients.
- Information provided about schedule to clients.
- Technology expectations of responsiveness and accessibility.
- Emergency contact information.
- Applicability to non-equity and equity partners.
- Benefits.
- Vacation.
- Annual review of workload, schedules, and feedback.

From *LAW & REORDER: Legal Industry Solutions for Restructure, Retention, Promotion & Work/Life Balance.* Reprinted by permission of the author.

APPENDIX E

Telework Employees Self-Assessment

A good telecommuting arrangement starts with a good self-assessment. Employees are encouraged to consider the following factors in making an honest determination about their telework capabilities. Record any concerns you may have and how you will address them in order to telecommute.

General
- Do you have sufficient portable work for the amount of telework proposed?
- Are you comfortable working alone for the amount of days you have requested to telework? Will you miss the social interaction of the office?
- Will your teleworking impact your coworkers? Do they need you in the office to complete work? Will they be doing extra work because you are teleworking?
- (In what ways) are you willing to be flexible about the telework arrangement to respond to the needs of (our clients, your) manager, (your) workgroup, and (your) work?

Self-Management

- Do you have the ability to do work with minimal direct supervision?
- Do you have organized work practices?
- Do you have good planning skills?
- Do you have effective time management skills? Are you able to meet schedules and deadlines?

Technology

- Do you feel comfortable with the technologies, if any, that will be needed to telework?
- Are you willing to learn any new technologies required to telework?

Communication

- Do you have the ability to ensure good communication with your manager, co-workers and clients?
- Will you return e-mails, calls and other messages in a timely manner?

Appropriate Space

- Is the telework office space conducive to getting your work done?
- Is the telework office space safe?
- Are dependent care (i.e. child care, elder care, or care of any other dependent adults) arrangements in place?
- Will you be distracted in the telework office space (e.g. by children, friends, television, or other responsibilities)?

Telework Employees Self-Assessment. (2016, October). Retrieved from http://www.telework.gov/

APPENDIX F

Management Self-Assessment Checklist

1. Do I feel that I am more effective now as a manager than I was 6 or 12 months ago? Examples?
2. Do I have a better idea of what to do and how to respond when a problem arises? Examples?
3. Am I anticipating people management issues before they become critical and/or urgent? Examples?
4. When people management problems arise, am I less reactive and more proactive? Examples?
5. When people management problems arise (as they undoubtedly will no matter how good I may be), how quickly and well am I responding to them? Examples?
6. Over the last 6–12 months, have I been proactive in creating policies and procedures for the management and development of firm members? Examples?
7. What have I done in the past 6–12 months to improve or change my firm's culture? Examples?
8. Over the last 6–12 months, has there been a change in how employees are hired and on-boarded? If there has been a change, can it be linked to my management?
9. Over the last 6–12 months, has there been better retention of staff and attorneys? If there has been a change, can it be linked to my management?

10. Over the last 6–12 months, have there been changes in absenteeism and productivity? If there has been a change, can it be linked to my management?

11. Over the last 6–12 months, when and where have I observed good firm morale and engagement? Examples?

12. Over the last 6–12 months, have we implemented new cybersecurity, privacy, and confidentiality policies, procedures, and software? If there has been a change can it be linked to my management?

13. Over the last 6–12 months, have we implemented any new policies or procedures to manage contract attorneys, temps, and interns? Examples?

14. Over the last 6–12 months, have we implemented or updated our anti-harassment and anti-bullying training?

15. Over the last 6–12 months, have we made diversity and inclusion a firm priority? Have we implemented any new policies or programs to support that goal? Examples?

16. Over the last 6-12 months, have we worked to improve communications between employees working remotely and the firm? Examples?

17. Over the last 6–12 months, have we looked at adding flextime or part-time personnel to our attorney, professional, and support staff, or implemented best practices to improve productivity and communication for existing flextime or part-time personnel? Examples?

INDEX

G

H

I